THEORISING WELFARE

THEORISING WELFARE

*Enlightenment
and
Modern Society*

MARTIN O'BRIEN

AND

SUE PENNA

SAGE Publications
London • Thousand Oaks • New Delhi

First published 1998

 SAGE Publications Ltd
6 Bonhill Street
London EC2A 4PU

SAGE Publications Inc
2455 Teller Road
Thousand Oaks, California 91320

SAGE Publications India Pvt Ltd
32, M-Block Market
Greater Kailash - I
New Delhi 110 048

British Library Cataloguing in Publication data

A catalogue record for this book is
available from the British Library

ISBN 0 8039 8906 7
ISBN 0 8039 8907 5 (pbk)

Library of Congresss catalog card number 98-060080

Typeset by Type Study, Scarborough
Printed in Great Britain by Redwood Books, Trowbridge,
Wiltshire

For
Vera and Steve
and
Daniel and John

Contents

Acknowledgements

This book is the product of several years of exposure to, and participation in, debates about the relative merits or otherwise of various strands of social theory. In particular, we would like to thank the participants of the Friday night gatherings in the Moorlands Hotel for their interest, support, humour and general sanity-inducing approach to academic life, and George, a brilliant landlord. Thanks are also due to all the students in the Department of Applied Social Science at Lancaster who have suffered through course 302: *Theories of Welfare States*, and the students in the Department of Sociology at Surrey who survived the course *Social Policy and the Future of Welfare*, for their interest, patience and contributions to thinking through many of the issues addressed in this book. We are grateful to Paul Bagguley, Geoff Cooper, Kate Currie, Hilary Graham, Tom Horlick-Jones, Bob Jessop, Scott Lash, Elizabeth Shove, Chris Smaje, David Smith, Colin Tipton, John Urry and Alan Warde for comments on various iterations of the manuscript. As to the final contents, the usual disclaimers apply. Many thanks to Gillian Stern for Job-like patience and for support for our project and to Jane Evans, Susie Home and all the staff at Sage who helped in the production of the book. Finally, Dan and Debbie have lived through the demands of academia and of this book with great fortitude – we would like to thank them for that and for keeping the domestic sphere ticking over, especially the shopping.

INTRODUCTION

The organisation of welfare in capitalist societies is complex and multi-faceted. People derive their welfare, individually and collectively, from a range of institutions and sites, so that the organisation of welfare involves labour markets, families, friends, voluntary and state agencies, charities, leisure activities and so on. Any exercise in theorising welfare therefore involves attention to a wide range of social processes and practices. This book examines some of the ways in which the complex relations of welfare have been conceptualised: we outline seven important theoretical perspectives through which to make sense of historical and contemporary changes in and struggles around social welfare systems and provision. In particular, we show how conceptions of social welfare are embedded in more extensive theories of society or, in other words, how such conceptions are dependent on wider theoretical perspectives on the institutions, relationships and divisions characteristic of modern societies. At the same time, we contextualise the emergence and major concerns of the different theoretical perspectives in terms of specific historical and contemporary struggles around social inclusion and exclusion, political authority and cultural representation. Our aim is to provide an introduction to the theoretical frameworks within which sociological perspectives on welfare have been formulated and at the same time to highlight some of the social and political contexts within which the concepts, categories and logics of those theories are situated. The book does not produce or champion a theory but is, instead, an exercise in theorising: it is an 'exhibition' of how social theories construct the relationships between state, society, economy, culture, empire, production, consumption and other forms of individual and collective action and experience.

Different theories emphasise different elements from the above list and propose different relationships between them. In our view there is not and cannot be a single theory of welfare that encompasses (and, even less, explains) all of the institutions, relationships, experiences, beliefs and conventions through which welfare resources, opportunities and barriers are produced, administered, contested and changed. Different theories account for different dimensions of social welfare, are involved in different cultural projects and establish different frames of reference for assessing the welfare consequences of the processes of social and political administration. Theories of welfare do not arise in a vacuum: they are tied to social and political struggles around the organisation and distribution of resources, rights and statuses. This connection between theories and the contexts in which they arise and develop is an important feature of our theoretical exhibition. Each section of the book begins with a preface that situates theoretical debates in the context of wider philosophical and political problematics and, in particular, in the context of the debate about Enlightenment philosophy. Each chapter then begins with some brief commentary on important social and political processes and conflicts on which specific theories are focused. The purpose of these commentaries is to provide students with some understanding of the social and historical contexts in which theoretical approaches to social welfare have been formulated and developed: why it is that specific theories emphasise the questions that they do, what conditions and processes are central to different theoretical perspectives.

Theory and the analysis of welfare

Although it is our aim to outline how other people have defined, categorised and classified concepts in the study of welfare, we recognise that any such understanding and, in particular, any understanding of the relationships between social welfare and the wider social and political currents of contemporary societies, demands an exercise in definition and classification. There are very many definitions of 'welfare' and even more definitions of what its 'social' component comprises. It is because of the diversity of definitions that we have devoted the remainder of this introductory chapter to an extended treatment of the relationships between 'theory', 'policy' and 'welfare'. In order to unpack the relationships between the three concepts we first address the question 'what is theory?' As a corollary to this question, 'what is the point of theory in the analysis of policy and welfare?', we then go on to discuss some definitions of 'social welfare', the 'welfare state' and 'the state'.

Social theory and social welfare

What, then, is 'theory' and what is the point of theory in investigating welfare? After all, one might argue that we do not need theory to discover who is poor in society or who gains the most advantage from a benefits system or to measure the impact of the social fund on working class families. In these cases, it might be argued, the facts speak for themselves: measuring poverty or take-up rates of benefits or changes in income as a result of a new social policy appear, initially, to be purely empirical matters. Researchers and policy analysts can simply run computer programs or analyse questionnaires or in some other way seek to measure the objective effects of policies and programmes on given populations. Why, it might be asked, should 'theory', in any sense of the term, be deemed relevant to such an exercise?

This question can be addressed at a number of different levels: at the level of particular policies, at the level of the relationships between policies and their socio-cultural, political and economic contexts or at the level of the historical continuity or discontinuity embedded in broad policy frameworks. Each of these levels is important in understanding why and how social policies develop and change over time and also why specific policies are adopted at particular times – and each requires theoretical explanation and analysis. The reason for this is because *all* social and economic policy and all social and economic research is based on theory at some level. There is no such thing as atheoretical research and no such thing as pure, empirically based policy.

This condition of policy and research is obvious once we understand what 'theory' is. Theory is not simply a word-game, conducted in a complex linguistic system and abstracted from reality by academic professionals. Theory is a dimension of action in so far as it gives direction and meaning to what we do. All people, separately and collectively, hold theories about the way the world works. Some of these theories are little more than vague hypotheses about what will happen if we act in a certain way in certain situations and what we expect from others in those situations. Some of the theories we hold are more complex and express our understandings of the workings of the economy or of how we become ill (or stay healthy) or the distribution of social roles at home, at work and in other contexts. In this sense, theories are generalisations about what exists in the world around us and how the components of that world fit together into patterns. In this sense also our theories are 'abstractions' – they generalise across actual situations our expectations and suppositions about the reasons why certain patterns exist and how we should deal with them.

Most often we are not consciously aware of the details of the different theories we hold about the world; we accept, reject and modify these theories as a matter of routine, without reflection on either how they are put together or which theories are useful in accounting for different situations and experiences. But to understand social policy and social welfare it is necessary to be conscious of theory in two senses simultaneously. First, it is necessary to be aware of the theories and assumptions within which particular policies are formulated and implemented. Second, it is necessary to be aware that different theories bring different dimensions of the effects and consequences of policies into view: they enable us to see elements of the organisation of welfare on which we do not normally focus our attention.

Just as, in our everyday lives, we employ theories as part of the ways we act in the world, so social policies and welfare programmes are also built on theoretical foundations. Theories about the validity of data and research procedures, theories about relationships between the individual and the state, theories about the spread of knowledge and information throughout a population, theories about the role of organisations in social and economic development, all inhere in policies and programmes developed, implemented and managed by different social institutions. In the following chapters we focus, in particular, on the ways that social relations have been theorised through different paradigms – through the paradigms of Marxism, liberalism, neo-liberalism, poststructuralism, political economy, political ecology and postmodernism – and on how these social relations are understood to maintain or undermine differences in rights, entitlements, benefits and opportunities or, in short, how individual and collective welfare is embedded in and determined by the organisation of social relations.

Normative theory and social theory

Our focus on the social relations of welfare is based on the claim that theorising welfare involves simultaneously and necessarily theorising social life: it involves situating the institutional and experiential dimensions of a welfare system in the context of wider social relationships and political struggles. This process of contextualising welfare institutions and experiences is a complex conceptual task. Some of the complexity can be grasped by distinguishing two interconnected components of welfare theory. One component consists of a *theory of social welfare* – a theory about how distributions of resources and opportunities and social patterns of access, participation, inclusion and exclusion support, contribute to or undermine individual and collective welfare. In short, it is a theory of the organisation of social relations and of the impacts of this organisation on individual and collective well-being. A second component comprises a *social theory of welfare* – a theory about how the organisation of social relations (the exclusions, centralisations and marginalisations, liberations and oppressions) comes to express the particular patterns that it does, what social forces and struggles underpin those particular distributions, inclusions and exclusions.

The difference between these two types of welfare theory points to a distinction between 'normative' theory and 'social' theory. The first type of theory is essentially theory that is *for* social policy. That is, theory about human social and economic life that is used in policy and welfare frameworks in order to make them more 'effective', 'rational', 'just' or 'appropriate'. Theories in this sense of the term relate to how people behave, how they learn, how they interact, how their attitudes are formed or changed, how people generate and share resources and so on. Theories of this type are invariably embedded in social policies and the welfare programmes that ensue from them: they comprise the premises and assumptions that guide the formulation of the policy in the first place and its later implementation in social institutions and networks. It is important to be clear that such premises are essentially theoretical: they are, in many ways, 'imaginary' in the sense that the conditions they describe, the logics of action and the structures of provision on which they focus are not existing realities. Rather, they are propositions about how life will be experienced and how welfare will be provided *when the policy is implemented*: they posit a world that does not yet exist but which will be brought into being by the formulation and implementation of specific policy programmes or social practices.

Clear examples of this theory-dependence abound in recent social policies. Policies on community care and the reduction in institutionalised populations with which they are connected, display several theoretical logics which, judging by the ferocity of the debate over the policies, are in themselves highly contentious. The theoretical foundations of community care policies can be described at a number of different levels. First, the very *concepts* of 'community' and 'care' are the subject of theoretical and philosophical dispute (Hampton, 1970; Bell and Newby, 1974; Finch and Groves, 1983; Waerness, 1984, 1987): disagreements over the boundaries of terms like 'community' and 'care' and how they relate to social action in diverse situations are interminable. Second, community care policies embody theories about how people maintain or improve their welfare through their ordinary, everyday activities, about how institutions affect people, about the role of information management in ensuring effective service delivery, and much more (Willmott, 1985; Bulmer, 1987). Third, like all social policies, community care exists within broader packages of welfare programmes and is implemented in the context of wider economic, social, political and cultural conditions (Sullivan, 1987; Ungerson, 1987; and the collection edited by Showstack Sassoon, 1987) which themselves are the subject of theoretical and conceptual dispute.

The more exact details of community care policies and the intricacies of the debates surrounding them do not concern us at this point. The example is offered to illustrate some of the ways that social policies and welfare programmes are underpinned by theory: in this case, theory as applied in order to achieve more 'effective', 'appropriate' or 'humanitarian' welfare arrangements.

It is because this type of theory is about making programmes more effective and appropriate, because it is about how people *should* act, how organisations *should* relate to the populations they serve, that it can be called normative theory: at its simplest, theory that is directed towards changing norms – of behaviour, attitude and belief, personal and organisational responsibility for care, as well as the 'normal' operations of social institutions and political or economic organisations, and so on. Normative theory should not be taken only in a negative sense – as referring only to the manipulation or direction of people's behaviour and belief patterns. Some of the most critical, radical theories in social science express normative logics. In liberalism, Marxism and political ecology there is a concern with changing people's behaviour as well as social institutions in order to create more egalitarian or more accessible democratic structures and social relations. In this book, we encounter many of these normative concerns as we investigate the different social theories of welfare.

The second type of theory we wish to distinguish is what we might properly call 'social' theory. That is, it comprises theories about *how* social policies and welfare programmes emerged, *how* they come to take the forms that they do and *what* are the relationships between policies and programmes and the societies in which they are situated. A good example of this type of theory is perspectives that surround the concepts of 'Fordism' and 'post-Fordism' (see Chapter 5). Basically, these theories propose that the forms taken by social policies can be understood through comparisons with developments in systems of production and industrial organisation. In the period between (approximately) the 1920s and the 1960s, it is proposed, the dominant system of industrial production was characterised by the implementation of 'Fordist' principles. These principles of production comprised the mass manufacture of goods – the assembly-line being the dominant image of production work – in which large numbers of workers were gathered to perform standardised and ritualised tasks. This mass manufacture not only gathered large numbers of workers together, it also generated vast numbers of standardised products – millions of black Ford Populars, all exactly alike, millions of steam irons, washing machines, tables and other household goods with little or no variation between them. The standardisation of mass manufacture was achieved through centralisation of control over the production process in everything from the purchase of machinery to catering arrangements and wage structures. Similarly, welfare provision also operated according to 'massification': welfare benefits were targeted at mass needs, they were standardised for the entire population with little flexibility to address different social and cultural contexts and were managed and controlled centrally, in the institutions of the welfare state.

From the 1960s onwards industrial Fordism in Europe and America began to break down – under the impact of globalisation, increased competition from Pacific production centres, increasing prices of raw materials (especially oil) and the growth of political opposition movements demanding flexibility, local control and choice in the use of goods and services. The production of standardised goods was replaced by the production of specialised goods intended not for mass consumption but for specialised niche markets – one has only to think of the almost limitless differentiation in styles of motor car to see the growth of this type of production logic: it is possible to purchase a BMW or a Ford motor car, for example, in thousands of varieties of colour combination, engine sizes, interior and exterior design features, wheel-type and so on, combined with the various finance, insurance and licensing deals. The days when millions of cars would roll off a production line with no distinction between them are passing – if they have not already done so. This flexible production system is paralleled by the devolution of a number of key operational decisions to the level of the individual plant or plant-group: decisions about best purchasing policy, about catering, shift and work arrangements, about the structure of the market supplied by the plant's activity are, within the framework of a parent company's executive goals, left to local or regional managers who are more aware of local conditions and can react faster to market changes than a head office located, perhaps, on the other side of an ocean.

This period in industrial history has been called 'post-Fordist' simply in recognition of its emergence out of and its apparent break with Fordist principles of production and manufacture. Some writers argue that we can analyse contemporary developments in welfare provision in terms similar to those employed when investigating industrial production. Hence, recent changes in social policy – increasing emphasis on service flexibility, the break-up of centralised welfare authorities into purchaser and provider units and the increasing reliance on voluntary, informal and private provision of services in contemporary policy – are all taken as indicators of a shift in welfare provision from Fordist to post-Fordist principles.

Again, the precise details of this perspective are not our concern here; the ins and outs of Fordism and post-Fordism are dealt with in Chapter 5. The discussion is included here as an example of theory applied to the broad sweep of developments in social policy and welfare programmes. These theoretical perspectives relate features of contemporary welfare programmes to patterns of social and economic change. It is because this second type of theory does this – that is, it points to interconnections between policy, welfare, economic and social change – that we can call it 'social theory' as distinct from 'normative theory'. It is this second type of theory with which we will be most concerned in the remainder of the book.

Social welfare

Social welfare is theorised in several distinct senses. One way is to construe social welfare in terms of 'well-being', that is, in terms of the levels of health, security, material prosperity and participation and so on, experienced by members of a population – individually or collectively. In principle, it is possible to assess the 'levels' of welfare enjoyed by individuals and groups by devising scales in which 'wealth', 'security' or 'participation', for example, can be measured. Through a combination of statistical data on income distribution, mortality or morbidity rates together with self-expressed measures of satisfaction, personal security or community action, researchers have studied the impact of specific policy programmes on particular populations. Over time, evaluation research of this kind has become more sophisticated, incorporating dimensions of feelings and opinions as well as officially published data on income, morbidity or take-up of services.

In a second sense social welfare comprises a *system* of social and institutional relationships through which people secure or maintain their individual or collective welfare. That is, it refers to the means and conditions in and through which a more or less healthy, wealthy and secure population is *reproduced* over time (or not). In practice, the system can be described in many different ways. The public/private, official/unofficial institutions and networks that supply or accrue different kinds and levels of resources and services may be the focus of attention. Alternatively, the emphasis may be on the connections between layers of social structure – such as politics, economics and culture – and patterns of social practice – patterns of coercion, exchange or symbolisation, for example.

In a third sense, social welfare can be conceptualised as a discourse – which latter is also described in a number of different ways. For the sake of simplicity, and clarity, here, a 'discourse of social welfare' comprises an organisation or matrix of knowledges – a culturally constructed and politically sanctioned framework for defining experience and for realising definitions in practice. A discourse of social welfare gives definition to the world in both the conceptual and material senses of this term.

The social theories of welfare that we outline in this book are structured by their relationships to these conceptual frameworks – the experiential, the systemic and the discursive. They outline and provide ways of understanding the connection between practices, institutions and knowledges in policies and programmes of social welfare.

The welfare state

As with all the terms we have discussed so far, different social theories construct the place and function of the welfare state in society through different conceptual lenses. One construction proposes that the welfare state is a form of state in its own right. Thus, the welfare state is not an absolutist state, a federalist state, a capitalist state or a totalitarian state, for example, but is a distinct political form, representing a distinct organisation of political powers. This thesis is represented strongly in comparative studies of social welfare systems that treat Britain, Germany or Sweden, and so on, as 'welfare states' (Wilenski and Lebeaux, 1958; Esping-Andersen, 1990). A second construction proposes that the welfare state comprises a collection of organisations of policy formation and implementation, as in the social administration literatures examining the workings of parliament, the civil service or local authorities, for example (Titmuss, 1968; Johnson, 1990). A third construction proposes that the welfare state comprises a distinctive pattern of 'functional differentiation', that is, a distinctive form of specialisation and control over the roles and resources that provide for welfare (Luhman, 1990). A fourth construction proposes that the welfare state is a vehicle of specific forms of power (such as gendered and/or racialised power, for example). Here the welfare state is a site of political conflict around specific (patriarchal or racialised) structures of control and oppression (Wilson, 1977; Pascall, 1986; Walby, 1990).

Some social theories of welfare reject the focus on the welfare state altogether, emphasising the patterns of cultural and social division that maintain inequality and disadvantage both within and outside the formal institutions of welfare state services. Here, the focus is on the everyday struggles and conflicts that sustain broader hierarchical relations within and between social groups. The organisation and distribution of welfare services and resources is understood as a dimension of these struggles, not as a response to the disadvantages that seemingly underpin them.

Theory and enlightenment

The different concepts of 'social welfare' and 'the welfare state' that we have outlined above neither cross easily from one theoretical perspective to another nor direct attention to the same social and political concerns. They are part of more extensive analytical and philosophical systems which, in turn, uphold different logics of assessment and evaluation, argumentation and interpretation. In fact, interpreting and reinterpreting – giving meaning and significance to observations on the institutions, relations and operations of welfare, seeing connections between social, political, economic and cultural forces – is what a social theory of welfare is for. The theoretical frameworks that we outline in this book each provide ways of seeing and interpreting these connections. Liberalism, Marxism, neo-liberalism, poststructuralism, political economy, political ecology and postmodernism are shorthand labels for particular ways of arranging and rearranging concepts in order to make sense of the patterning and control of social relations and their implications for social welfare.

Each of the perspectives outlined in the book represents a relationship to the European Enlightenment of the eighteenth century. Each expresses elements of a theory of knowledge that supports, contests or subverts the central assumptions and rationalities established in the social, cultural and political systems that carried forward (and continue to struggle over) this epistemological transformation. Indeed, it is difficult to understand the significance or development of contemporary (natural and social) sciences without an appreciation of the place of the Enlightenment in their formation and organisation. This is why we have begun each of the book's sections with a preface outlining the central philosophical and epistemological commitments represented by the different social theories of welfare that we have included.

The term 'Enlightenment' is a shorthand for an array of intellectual, cultural and political forces. In historical terms, the word 'Enlightenment' is used to refer to the period spanning most of the eighteenth century which promoted new philosophical systems for understanding both the natural and human worlds (Hamilton, 1992: 24). The Enlightenment represented a major shift towards secular explanations of the natural and social world, an important characteristic of which was the separation of 'Man' and human 'Reason' from the natural order. The eighteenth century Enlightenment is confined to a particular geographical region -- (largely) Western Europe – dominated by specific intellectual centres in England,

Scotland, France, Austria and Holland. The communication and dissemination of the new philosophies was itself dependent on certain technological and social developments, of which the printing press and the new
secular publishing industry are of particular importance. Thus, although
the Enlightenment is commonly understood as a specific historical period,
it also refers to a number of intellectual, cultural, social and political
developments. In order to capture the relationships between the historical
reference, on the one hand, and the intellectual, cultural, etc., references,
on the other, it useful to make a distinction between *the* Enlightenment –
the period of the eighteenth century – and 'Enlightenment' – the transformed worldview which emerged. The distinction was proposed by Kant
(in 1784) to question whether eighteenth century European societies had
achieved the status of Enlightened, 'mature' civilisations. Kant asked the
question: 'What is Enlightenment?' He responded:

> Enlightenment is man's leaving behind its self-imposed immaturity. Immaturity
> is the inability to employ one's own intelligence without being directed by
> someone else. This immaturity is self-imposed if it results not from a lack of
> intellect but from a lack of willingness and courage to use it without another's
> guidance. Supere Aude! – 'Have the courage to use your own mind!' – that is
> the motto of the Enlightenment. (Ball and Dagger, 1991: 107)

The 'courage to use your own mind' meant questioning accepted wisdoms
and applying one's intellectual powers to moral, political and social questions, refusing, as Kant remarks, to be 'guided' by established opinions
and beliefs. In this very basic sense, Enlightenment meant the freedom to
think, to philosophise about the world outside of the inherited traditions
and creeds of the past. Enlightenment opened up the world to the rational,
independent and autonomous thought of human beings and, in turn,
subjected all of the institutions of church, state and law to the power of
that rational thought.

Thus, the historical period of the eighteenth century is not *arbitrarily*
called the Enlightenment: it represents an era in which philosophy understood itself as entering the light of reason from the darkness of myth and
superstition; as casting off the dead weight of tradition and habit – in
thought and in deed – in favour of rational, logical, mature, worldly
exploration. The rise of scientific and secular-philosophical interpretations
of nature and society undermined the legitimacy and dominance of established theological worldviews and opened up a space in which social,
ethical and political relationships could be understood as a result of
human action and organised through such action. Once theological worldviews ceased to legitimate both social relationships and political power,
for example, the idea that the monarch ruled by divine right, a series of
renewed debates about how to understand human action, social organisation, political authority and the proper relationship between individuals
and their socio-political environment emerged. In Touraine's words,
'*Society* replaces God as the principle behind moral judgement' (1995: 16),
meaning that the criteria which inform evaluations of social life and

political institutions cease to be religious. The Civil War in England culminating in the English Bill of Rights of 1689, the American Revolution of 1775–81, the French Revolution of 1789 and the Declaration of the Rights of Man and Citizen, adopted by the Assemblée Nationale in 1789, were representative of the way in which Christian thought had become increasingly secularised and the power of the Church, as the embodiment of the divine power legitimising monarchial rule and the privileges it guaranteed, subject to widespread challenge (Hobsbawm, 1995a).

Whereas the social and political systems of the feudal past were seen as sluggish, unjust and arbitrary, the new philosophies and sciences associated with Newton, Locke, Montesquieu and their historical contemporaries offered a new world of growth, liberty and rational political organisation. Rejecting the authority of tradition and religious thought, the period of the Enlightenment saw the rise of faith in Reason as the means through which order and progress can be achieved. The Enlightenment seemed to promise freedom from dependence on nature through the application of scientific knowledge; freedom from the political tyranny of inherited monarchial authority through the development of rational government; and intellectual freedom to challenge the fixed precepts of established wisdom through the newly developed, human-centred philosophies of Descartes and Pascal, for example. No longer simply subjects of God, Enlightenment philosophies proposed that legal and moral entitlements, duties and rights are intrinsic to membership in a political community whose function was the guarantee of religious and economic freedom.

These freedoms themselves appeared to hold the key to progress: on the basis of the new philosophies, sciences and political institutions would emerge an ever-expanding body of knowledge, an ever-increasing technological sophistication and an ever more securely ordered social world. Enlightenment philosophers and, later, social scientists were divided over the extent to which the progress promised by Enlightenment was being realised in the turbulent world of eighteenth and then nineteenth century Europe. Some saw European civilisation itself as a summit of all human history, others predicted the collapse of the existing order and the emergence of a brand new world in which the gains and advances of Enlightenment would be shared by all humankind. The impact of the Enlightenment was felt across Europe and into the colonies that European nations had acquired by ('Enlightened') military force and continued to resonate across the war-ravaged nineteenth century. But, in large measure, Enlightenment thinkers were secure in their belief that reason, logic and science could be applied universally – to history, to nature, to the human body and mind, to society – and that a single philosophical system could be developed within which the mysteries of the inner and outer universes would reveal themselves to human understanding. In particular, the Enlightenment inaugurated a faith in science as a progressive force which could understand, and hence solve, problems in the natural and social worlds. In contemporary social theory the Enlightenment represents the transformation from the premodern to the modern world.

Each of the theories we outline in this book represents a relationship to the Enlightenment and the associated question of modernity or modernisation. In fact, they can be grouped according to the nature of this relationship. Marxism and liberalism (Part One) view modernisation as an inevitable historical trajectory which, over time, will lead to the realisation of Enlightenment across the globe: modernisation, on this account, is inaugurated by, and consequential on, Enlightenment. Thus, Marxism and liberalism are theories of universal modernisation: modernisation is built into the rational operation of Enlightened institutions. Each views the failures of such institutions to bring about the desired ('Enlightened') outcomes as results of the political or social machinations of vested interest groups – classes or parties, for example – which, ultimately, will be swept away in a progressive unfolding of human history.

Neo-liberalism and poststructuralism (Part Two) represent a challenge to this faith in universal Enlightened modernisation. In each case, the modernisation of social institutions is viewed as an excessive rationalization of knowledge and practice: modernisation, on this account, produces the political subversion (neo-liberalism) or the political diffusion (poststructuralism) of the forms of power and authority over social life defined in and through Enlightenment philosophy. Both perspectives represent a 'counter-Enlightenment' philosophy although, of the two, poststructuralism is by far the more radical, suggesting that Enlightened modernisation represents the emergence and imposition of a system of power rather than the cleansing light of rational knowledge.

The theories in Part Three, focused on contemporary political economy, political ecology and postmodernism respectively, represent a much more ambivalent relationship to both Enlightenment and processes of modernisation. Whilst each is dependent on specific categories of Enlightenment thought, and whilst each theorises processes of political and economic modernisation, each also raises important questions about the assumptions and analytical logics embedded in classical conceptions of progress, emancipation and freedom. In particular, they raise questions about the consequences of modernisation for different groups of people, about the conception of linear progress proposed in both Marxism and liberalism and about the notion of an 'end-state' of history where either the free and prosperous liberal society or the emancipated and equal socialist society are realised. In short, they reject the universality of Enlightened modernisation and focus, instead, on the latter's irregularities and unevenness. Such irregularities are understood not as by-products of the modernisation process but as central features of what modern society necessarily represents. It is in this basic (and, here, simplified) sense that the chapters in Part Three represent 'post-Enlightenment' philosophy. In the concluding chapter we offer a critical appraisal of the different perspectives outlined in our theoretical 'exhibition'.

PART ONE
ENLIGHTENMENT AND PROGRESS

Preface

The possibilities of Enlightenment were understood in different ways by different thinkers. A preoccupation with power and its foundations, what rights individuals could properly lay claim to, and what form of political organisation could guarantee individual rights forms the substance of intense philosophical disputes across the eighteenth and nineteenth centuries. A major division existed between philosophers associated with the Scottish Enlightenment, such as Locke, whose works provide an important inspiration for liberalism, and those of the French Enlightenment, such as Rousseau, who provide many of the foundations of socialist and Marxist theory. Against Locke's view that free will characterises human activity – that the primary purpose of this activity is labour, and that its protection through laws enabling individual freedom to act, trade and own property is the proper role of political authority – was counterposed an alternative understanding of social order based on individual submission to a general will expressed in a social contract between individuals and the state. Based on the idea that there exists a natural order in the world, the social contract represents the insertion of individuals into that order, one which can be orchestrated by the application of reason to political life (Touraine, 1995: 24–56). Here, the 'natural order' substitutes for the 'cosmic order' of religious worldviews. Whilst there is no longer a transcendental order of humanity, Enlightenment thinkers nevertheless have a conception of some overall order in human organisation. For Rousseau in *The Social Contract* (1762) the natural order represents a harmony which is lacking in forms of social organisation based upon the principle of the private ownership of property. Rousseau's critique of the inequalities of his time was based on the assumption that individual and collective interests could be reconciled through a political order which embodies the application of reason to social life, for it is through reason that the natural order is discovered. Political sovereignty can encompass the general will and, by the submission of individuals to it, inequality and injustice can be eradicated (see Tourraine, 1995).

The idea that the human world is governed by natural laws, that reason can uncover these laws, and the social body can function in accordance with them is an important theme of Enlightenment philosophy. For Locke, political society is founded on the right to own property, the right to freedom and the right to resist oppression. The inequalities stemming from economic processes are not the business of political authority, whose purpose is to ensure a system of natural law which protects individuals' rights and, in so doing, reconciles the interests of the individual with those of society. For Rousseau, freedom and justice are achieved by the subordination of individual interests to the general, or common, good, which is defined by equality rather than inequality. These debates between the natural law tradition and the communitarian tradition formed the background to the development of social thought in the nineteenth century. The possibilities for social harmony, social order, individual and collective freedom, became increasingly focused around the questions of equality and inequality as the industrial revolution gained momentum and its effects became increasingly obvious. It is during this period that early socialist – both utopian and non-utopian – and communist ideas were being developed in France, following the left wing of the Revolution and strongly influenced by Rousseau's egalitarian arguments (Hobsbawm, 1982: 5). For others, such as the eighteenth century moral philosopher Adam Smith, the practical application of reason by individuals in law, science and, especially, commerce would itself result in the improvement of the human condition: progress would arise by the mechanical workings of the invisible hand of capitalism; each individual, acting only in their own, rational interest would contribute to the general increase in national wealth and thereby, unintentionally, improve the lot of humankind. Others, such as the nineteenth century revolutionary theorist Karl Marx, considered the 'invisible hand' as no more than an ideology which masked the fact that, within the capitalist system, wealth became concentrated in ever greater quantities in ever fewer hands. In contrast to Smith's optimism, Marx proposed that the capitalist system was doomed from the outset: it would create the conditions for its own overthrow by nurturing a common class consciousness among the proletariat. Armed with this consciousness and with the technologies and sciences of capitalism, the proletariat would become an unstoppable historical force for change, leading to the final revolution and the birth of communism. In spite of these differences in the assessment of the inner workings of capitalism, Smith and Marx share a belief in historical progress: whether the present is understood positively or negatively, historical progress is inevitable.

Enlightenment, then, represents a relationship to the development, application and circulation of knowledge about the world: contemporary debates about social policy and welfare are structured through frameworks and traditions inherited from the eighteenth century European Enlightenment and have developed either through a defence of Enlightenment principles and assumptions (such as progress, justice and reason) or through a critical engagement with the epistemological premises and empirical categories bequeathed by that intellectual revolution. In this section we examine two theoretical frameworks that emerged and consolidated in the period following the Enlightenment and outline their contributions to contemporary analyses of social welfare: liberalism and Marxism. In respect of each of these theoretical paradigms we go to some lengths to explain the nature and origins of the questions that they pose to the relationships between social welfare and social change. In particular, we explore why these approaches developed as they did and how their conceptions of social welfare are rooted in different assessments of the nature of social institutions, social participation and social change.

1

Liberalism

A good deal of confusion surrounds the word 'liberalism', a confusion which is only exacerbated when it is prefixed by 'neo' or when the word is preceded with a capital 'L' – as in the Liberal Democrats. The confusion stems partly from misreadings of what liberals have had to say on human welfare and partly from deeply entrenched views about the existence of a unifying liberal ideology – often seen as entirely individualistic, inegalitarian and reactionary. Such understandings betray only a very limited appreciation of the wealth of political, philosophical and theoretical contributions that liberalism has bequeathed to contemporary social thought and political action. Even the term 'liberalism' itself can confuse the series of analyses and political programmes that liberal thinkers have advocated and implemented since the eighteenth century Enlightenment. As John Gray (1989) points out, it is more realistic to think in terms of *liberalisms*, in the plural, as a collection of related philosophies about the roles and functions of individuals, groups and institutions in managing, directing and controlling the character and progress of human social life. Some liberal thinkers are individualistic in the extreme, stressing personal autonomy and freedom as the only goal of social organisation; others, whilst maintaining a commitment to individual freedom, are more open to the promotion of collective strategies for social and political development. Some view state interference into social life as inherently evil or dangerous; others view such interference as justifiable in order to bring about progress and enlightened reform. The history of liberalism is a history of change and reorientation as well as a history of intellectual division and political dispute. There is not a single, unified, liberal ideology which can be used to explain the formulation and implementation of social policies. Certainly ideology is important but, as we will try to show, liberal theories of welfare are complex amalgams of radical and reactionary, progressive and regressive elements, referring back to the past and forwards to the future, at some times stressing freedom, at others emphasising constraint.

In this chapter we explore the webs of liberal theory and philosophy at a number of different levels. Historically, we show some of the major lines of transformation in liberal political philosophy and in the social contexts to which they refer. Theoretically, we examine liberalism's relationship to the whole or the totality, a relationship that underpins liberal concepts of political action. Analytically, we show how concepts of individual and social welfare derive from underlying ideas about the proper organisation and regulation of human life. In order to address these levels of liberal political philosophy we deal first with liberalism's relationship to the Enlightenment before exploring historical developments in liberal theory.

Liberalism and Enlightenment

In the preface to this section it was noted that contemporary debates around welfare, the state and society were forged on the anvil of eighteenth century Enlightenment. In terms of the ways that theories and explanations are constructed, the development of moral outlooks on political and economic processes, the rights of individuals and the techniques for understanding and regulating social life, contemporary academic and policy frameworks continually reaffirm and reassess principles and beliefs embedded in Enlightenment philosophy. In many ways, liberalism can be viewed as one of the first and most fundamental political consequences of the struggles, gains and losses that define this period of Western history. The origins of modern liberal ideas are bound together with a number of social and political changes occurring in the period. These include the demise of the monarchy and the rise of parliament as the central organ of government; the decline of the secular authority of the church and the rise of religious individualism; the growth of capitalism and the associated shift from an agricultural, feudal, economy to an industrial economy founded largely on wage labour; and the rise of science and rational calculation as the litmus test of progress and development in almost all spheres of human life. The point is that classical liberalism emerged as much out of political and economic developments, disputes and conflicts in society as it did out of mere speculation on the part of its leading philosophers. This connection is embedded in the very bases of liberal philosophy, namely, the relationship between reason, freedom and the state, to which we turn next.

Liberty, property and morality

> Liberty is not a placard to be read at the corner of the street. It is a living force to be felt within and around us, the protecting genius of the domestic hearth, the guarantee of social rights, and the first of those rights. (Felicité de Lamennais, *Paroles d'un Croyant*, Paris, 1858; cited in Bramstead and Melhuish, 1978: 473)

Liberty, in Enlightenment philosophy, comprises a moral injunction to the effect that no individual human is or morally can be subject to another's power or 'will' without that individual's consent. Thus, John Locke, writing in 1690 in the 'Second Treatise of Government', proposed that:

> Men being . . . by nature all free, equal, and independent, no one can be put out of this estate and subjected to the political power of another without his own consent, which is done by agreeing with other men, to join and unite into a community for their comfortable, safe, and peaceable living, one amongst

another, in a secure enjoyment of their properties, and a greater security against any that are not of it. (Locke, 1690; cited in Bramstead and Melhuish, 1978: 240)

By 'estate' Locke means a type of social organisation that is made up *only* of free individuals giving their consent to a form of authority governing according to the doctrine of natural rights. The latter proposes that human beings hold rights simply by virtue of their being human, outside of any social process or structure. Any social power which infringes upon these timeless, asocial rights is morally unjustifiable. For Locke, these rights refer to 'men's lives, liberties and estates' and amount to a series of injunctions against a political state or other powerful body to refrain from causing harm to any human, preventing a person from doing as they please (so long as this causes no harm to another) and to dispose of goods and other property as they see fit. These rights – to live as you wish, to act as you will and to amass what you can – are not conferred upon people by the society in which they live, but are fundamental conditions of being a human. Since, for Locke, these rights precede the organisation of society, then it follows that no social body can legitimately interfere with them. Thomas Paine's *Rights of Man* (published in 1791) and Mary Wollstonecraft's response, *Vindication of the Rights of Women* (published in 1795) are important manifestos of individualism, appealing to Locke's idea of natural rights as the basis for a social compact between individuals and the state. All are, or should be, equal before the state: the law is, or should be, rational rather than personal or spiritual.

The doctrine of natural rights, as applied to individuals, is paralleled by a commitment to a moral interpretation, a moral 'theory' of the state in society. Enlightenment philosophy counterposed society to nature as order to chaos: in a state of nature no laws regulated conduct; each person acted only in their own interests without regard for the consequences for others, without any codes or rules to guide their actions; they were 'free' to do as they pleased. The key political issue revolved around the question: when human beings leave the state of nature and organise into communities and societies, by what right are the actions of individual people governed and regulated? That is to say, what is the moral basis of government? The response was to assert that government may act only in the interests of the freedom of the individual; that government had no wider role in the organisation and regulation of civil life; that the only legitimate basis of government was to maintain a legal framework in which the greater majority of people could pursue their life's goals without undue interference from others. Freedom, in liberalism, is the 'political guarantee' of government.

This 'minimal' conception of the state implies a concept of 'legitimate power'. Legitimate power consists in rule by law and not rule by persons: the power and authority of a state derives not from the greatness, capacity or Divine right of its functionaries, but from the state's universal application of procedural (primarily legal) rules. So long as these rules are applied impartially to all, taking no account of status or creed, then the state is 'moral' and has the right to draw upon the support of the people. Again, this politics of state is strongly tied to the rebellion against established authority. Many early liberals were made up of religious minorities and other groups who enjoyed few rights with respect to the monarchy and the established church traditions. In their view, state power was vested in persons – whether a monarch, a dictator, or self-appointed parliamentarians – whose interests dominated the frameworks of economic exchange and social behaviour.

The minimal state was not only a moral issue in the sense that we might understand morality in a commonsense way. The morality of the minimal state was bound together with a philosophy of social evolution that was formulated most clearly by Adam Smith. Smith's *An Inquiry into the Nature and Causes of the Wealth of Nations* (1776) pulled together into a single evolutionary doctrine many of the political, philosophical and economic theories of the later eighteenth century. It deals with how a society that is neither planned nor operating under the guidance of a great tradition can lead to the rational production and distribution of goods and wealth. Specifically, it seeks to demonstrate how the private, selfish actions of individuals, pursuing nothing but their own personal advantage, will lead to competition for the supply of goods. In turn, such competition will lead to the production of requisite quantities of goods at the sorts of prices that will ensure their distribution throughout the society. It is, in part, a treatise on how self-interest leads to social harmony, and competitive struggle to efficient benevolence, all of which is achieved through the mechanism of market demand. By demanding coffee instead of tea, cotton instead of wool, copper instead of tin, and so on, consumers encourage increases or decreases in the prices of goods and, in turn, changes in the quantities of their production. By exerting their individual and personal demands through the market, consumers exert their influence on the total production, availability and price of goods in society.

Thus, the market is self-regulating: consumers do not plan to increase or decrease the total quantity of coffee or copper in circulation, nor do they plan the prices at which the numbers of these objects will be available. The availability and price of these goods is a consequence of each consumer's private wants and desires: it represents an 'invisible hand' that leads to competition to supply goods and adjustments in their prices. At the same time, the 'invisible hand' applies not only to goods but also to capital and labour. In Smith's view, the accumulation of capital did not mean simply the accumulation of individual wealth, although this was certainly an important component. It also involved the accumulation and expansion of the means to produce wealth, specifically, the machinery of production. As the machinery of production expanded the demand for labour also expanded. Since labour now became a commodity in demand then, like any other commodity, its price – that is, wages – increased, leading to a reduction in profits. However, with higher wages the living standards of labourers also rose, and so more labourers survived to produce more children who would become labourers. As their numbers increased, they increased the competition for wages and thus depressed their levels, leading to a stabilisation, and potential reduction, in the number of labourers. Once more the accumulation of capital could begin in a context of low wages and high profits, leading to an increased demand for labour, and so on, *ad infinitum*.

The dynamism of the market thereby resulted in continuous increases in the absolute wealth of the whole population. Whilst society would always remain stratified, the level of riches enjoyed by all of its members would inexorably rise through the accumulation of capital. So long as the market was left alone, free of the distorting interference of organised monopolies or politically motivated social bodies, the wealth of nations was assured. Note that Smith's book is about the *dynamism* of capital accumulation: it projects, into a (far-away) future, not an equalisation of individual wealth but a stable, well-ordered and contented society where all persons enjoy sufficient wealth to leave behind the brutish existence of the feudal and early industrial world. *Laissez faire*, and the world will be a bounteous place. Since the market mechanism in itself is what ensured the production of the requisite quantities of goods at the requisite prices, and since this production is *dynamic*, then any interference into that mechanism inevitably inhibits the growth of human welfare. Thus, observes Heilbroner (1986: 74), the accumulation of capital and the self-interested pursuit of individual gain represents nothing less than a moral law in which 'all the grubby scrabbling for wealth and glory has its ultimate justification in the welfare of the common man'.

In these ways, *The Wealth of Nations* discovers in the ordinary and apparently disorganised scheme of human life a grand rationality that ensures the prosperity and welfare of the social whole. It is a classic (perhaps *the* classic) example of the way that Enlightenment philosophy produces a theory of society and social welfare.

Each of these Enlightenment themes is central to the development of philosophical liberalism: the political guarantee of freedom, government according to abstract laws and rules, and moral and economic individualism, are the foundations of liberalism's political-philosophical system. When examining the shifts and reorientations of liberal thought across the nineteenth and twentieth centuries, it is necessary to keep in mind these building blocks of the liberal approach to political life. We turn to these shifts in emphasis next, proposing that three forms of liberal political philosophy can be extrapolated through liberalism's historical relationship to power. We organise the discussion in relation to three periods, or three waves, of liberalism: from the 1830s until the 1850s; the period from the 1860s until the turn of the twentieth century; and from the First World War until the present. The periodisations are not intended to form a strict evolutionary narrative of liberal thought. Rather, they indicate how specific features of liberalism's relation to Enlightenment come to predominate in its theories of welfare.

First wave liberalism

In 1832 the Reform of Local Government Act gave to an aspiring class of industrialists, manufacturers and merchants – liberals almost to a man – a larger say in government than they had ever experienced. The male capital-owning classes became established as political leaders in the new era of industrial development, economic growth and imperial exploitation. The Act represented the culmination of a hundred years of struggle to gain political influence and appeared to vindicate the principles of individualism, rational economics and moral freedom that had solidified in Enlightenment philosophy. At a stroke, liberal men immediately consolidated two interconnected spheres of their social power: the gendered division between public and private and the dissociation of their government from collective responsibility. The first two major pieces of legislation enacted by the first liberal parliament were the disenfranchisement of women following the 1832 Reform Act and the replacement of the 1601 Poor Law with the market-oriented provisions of the 1834 Poor Law Act. The first case represents the emergence of a crude social theory in liberalism that defined who is included in and excluded from public power, the second indicates the practical application of early liberal political economy.

Liberal social economy

One of the major effects of legislation during the first liberal parliament was to detach political economy from domestic authority; to circumscribe divergent realms of social development – the political, the public and the institutional, counterbalanced by the familial, the private and the everyday. Whilst the former would be the subject of rational progress, the latter would be the subject of normative retrenchment; the 'public' was to facilitate the realisation by 'man' of his abstract destiny, the private was to reproduce men to encounter that destiny. The gendered division of public and private, enshrined in the 1832 disenfranchisement of women (further entrenched by the 1835 Municipal Corporation Act), was a manoeuvre on the part of liberal men to secure a system of rule in which 'state' and 'household' would be formally distinct. Prior to the 1832 reform, the franchise had depended on possession of property and the political exclusion of women had been an economic *fait accompli*: very few women acceded to property through inheritance with the consequence that women, with some exceptions, were largely excluded on 'technical' grounds from casting a vote. The expansion of capitalism – and particularly its planned expansion by eager liberals – brought with it an assured overall expansion of property which, importantly, could be acquired by economic activity – in the 'free' market – rather than by inheritance. Under such a system, it was theoretically possible for women to amass property and thereby attain voting rights in their own name. The move to disenfranchise women is of particular note because many women, founding their politics in Enlightenment principles of reason and justice, were active public figures at the time. In the 1820s and 1830s the political philosopher Anna Wheeler and the political economist Harriet Martineau, for example, condemned the partiality of dominant political discourses and their manipulation of Enlightenment philosophy to establish male public and private domination. After 1832, the welfare of British society was to be maintained and progress achieved by pairing off distinct realms of activity – the public and private, the political and the personal, the legal and the moral, the civic and the domestic. First wave liberal theories of welfare are confused attempts to stipulate where the intersection of these domains lies and how their separate organisation is to be maintained.

The philosophical principles enshrined in liberalism's political ideology were paralleled by a burgeoning civil orthodoxy, equally contradictory in its analysis of the relationship between rights and property. On the one hand, the foundation of this ideology stressed the natural operations of markets and the 'utility-maximising' principle of ordinary human conduct. On the other hand, the free marketeers also drew on controversial concepts of social inequality – for example, that the poor and uneducated did not know how to behave politically in a free way – which had distinguished Enlightenment origins. Condorcet (1955 [1795]), for example, points to three types of inequality that exist in the 'enlightened nations of Europe': inequality of wealth, of status and of education. He argues that the first two can be reduced (but not eradicated) by reforms in the civil law and by the provision of charitable and public funds to ameliorate poverty in old age. The third of these inequalities was to be tackled through an education ('by a suitable choice of syllabus and of methods') which 'can teach the citizen everything he needs to know in order to be able to manage his household, administer his affairs and employ his labour and his faculties in freedom; and to know his rights and to be able to exercise them; to be acquainted with his duties and fulfil them satisfactorily' (Condorcet, 1955: 174). Condorcet then proceeds to construct this process as a progressive, enlightening 'perfection' in which, eventually, all humans could share in the fruits of a free association of wealth-producing individuals: 'The real advantages that should result from this progress, of which we can entertain a hope that is almost a certainty, can have no other term than that of the absolute perfection of the human race' (1955: 174).

Condorcet's liberalism was strongly democratic and he advocated universal equality of rights. Yet, one of the ideological consequences of this incomplete faith in enlightened progress was to entrench a politics of exclusion into the foundations of the liberal project: those not educated in the 'correct' way to manage their household, employ their labour and otherwise perform their duties could not be expected to participate in the public regulation of collective life. The terrain of this exclusion became vast indeed – women were to be excluded because their education fitted them (as Condorcet had acknowledged) to a domestic role; the labouring, impoverished masses were to be excluded because they were ignorant of enlightened action; and, later, the colonised were to be excluded because they were not sufficiently evolved to handle the reins of political power with wisdom and commitment. The 'progress' that Condorcet prophesied – and the exclusions to which it gives rise – comprises a social economy: a system of rights, statuses and entitlements whose organisation and control is the enlightened business of liberal government. The politics of this social economy has re-emerged in many liberalisms ever since Condorcet's original formulation.

Liberal political economy

The second area of legislation – the reform of the Poor Law – indicates the consequences of early liberal political economy. Its effect was to remove from the state any responsibility for provision against poverty and sickness except in the most extreme cases of destitution. In summary, the Act devolved responsibility for maintaining the poor to parish level, enjoining parishes to make provision as necessary for the poor and also to act vigorously against unscrupulous or fraudulent use of the relief scheme. It instituted the infamous system of workhouses in which anyone who could not support themself was to be incarcerated. The Act and its provisions amounted to one of the most hated pieces of legislation in the history of British social policy and was in every respect the most useless bulwark against poverty and misery that could be imagined. The poor lived in fear of destitution because no matter how hard the trials of 'ordinary' poverty, incarceration in the workhouse was infinitely worse: not only because of the stigma and shame that was associated with the system but also because the 'relief' obtained therein amounted, often, to a form of slavery involving long hours of arduous work for little or no reward, the separation of families, a starvation diet and atrocious living conditions. Yet, the Act was a piece of legislation inspired by the visions and goals of eighteenth century Enlightenment, steeped in notions of moral conduct, knitted together with rational philosophies and designed to promote wealth, harmony and well-being. How had this come about? After all, we have seen that the foundations of liberal philosophy stress freedom and autonomy, social progress, the universal spread of reason and the limitless potential of the individual human being.

When, in 1832, a share in governmental power was won by the most vigorous supporters of liberal doctrines, these visions and goals were carried into the political arena and with great fervour liberals sought to realise them immediately through the machinery of public administration – hence the contradictory nature of the Poor Law Reform Act. Liberal political economists and their parliamentary activists believed that economic processes would themselves result in increases in the standards of living of the whole society. Hence, their legislation is determined by this overriding factor. The new Poor Law of 1834 'had as its purpose the

reinforcement of market principles. Old forms of local or national
provision for the relief of distress were believed to undermine the incentive to work. They were therefore to be swept away, and a system imposed
which would conform to the recently discovered 'laws' of economics
(Arblaster, 1984: 251).

Anthony Arblaster sums up the dogma of liberal economics in this
period by quoting from Macaulay:

> Our rulers will best promote the improvement of the nation by strictly confin-
> ing themselves to their own legitimate duties, by leaving capital to find its own
> most lucrative course, commodities their fair price, industry and intelligence
> their natural reward, idleness and folly their natural punishment, by maintain-
> ing peace, by defending property, and by observing strict economy in every
> department of the state. Let the government do this: the people will assuredly
> do the rest. (1984: 252)

Arblaster describes vividly the consequences of this dogmatic approach to
social and economic management for the poor in the era of the workhouses, an approach which accepted poverty as the source of labour and
labour as the source of wealth: if no one is poor, liberals argued, no one
will work; if no one will work no one else will get rich. Poverty must be
accepted: interfering in the market by relieving or ameliorating the
conditions of the poor was viewed as a distortion of the laws of progress,
freedom, civilisation and economic stability.

The poor must suffer for the greater harmony and happiness of the
political whole – and suffer they did. When, between 1845 and 1848, the
potato crop failed in Ireland for three years out of four, the mass of the
Irish population was reduced first to penury and then swiftly to famine.
The Whig government stood aside and watched, convinced in the long
term accuracy of its *laissez-faire* doctrines, as thousands died of malnutrition, as thousands more were struck by disease and infirmity and as yet
more thousands fled to swell the slums of Liverpool, Manchester and
London. Liberals pinned their theory of society on the health, welfare and
functioning of the whole, on the inevitable progress towards a harmoni-
ous, wealth-producing social order which must ensue from free economic
activity. So focused were they on this vision of progress, of the greater
good of rational, enlightened development, that the actual conditions of
the poor (who, by their own admission, created the wealth that liberals
desired to expand) became of secondary significance, a mere detail in a
grand socio-economic design for universal liberty and prosperity. Liberals had their eyes on the prize of harmony and enlightened well-being *in
the future* when the benefits of following natural economic laws, a rational
approach to minimal government and the application of science in the
organisation of industry and manufacture would finally secure freedom
from the stranglehold of tradition and arbitrary power. Early nineteenth
century liberals enacted the contradictory philosophies of the Enlightenment: on the one hand, they sought to realise principles of universal justice
and argued passionately for freedom, progress and improvement; on the

other, they accepted the status quo – including the poverty of the masses – and could find no means by which to bring about the changes which, philosophically, they had proposed. Liberal political economy, as it solidified in the period following the 1832 accession to power, adopted a rigid and minimalist concept of society, focusing on the progress of an abstract 'whole'. It represented a politicised movement whose social theory revolved around the control and organisation of property and its division into separate structures of control.

Second wave liberalism

In the second half of the nineteenth century new emphases in liberal philosophy emerged. These new outlooks consisted in a belief that state action in social and civil life is a necessary evil; an idea that the increasingly complex societies of Europe could no longer be left unregulated; and the philosophical incorporation of new scientific ideas, especially of evolutionism, and an organic understanding of social structure.

Second wave liberalism of the late nineteenth century expressed an inbuilt mistrust of interference into, especially, economic behaviour combined with new perspectives on the functioning and evolution of society which suggested the necessity of such interference. These tensions gave rise to two further theoretical frameworks in liberalism, one of them focused 'internally' on the administration and organisation of the 'home' society; the second focused 'externally', on the relationships between politics and empire.

Charity, morality and social administration

The rise of organised charity deserves comment, since, to all intents and purposes, it appeared to contradict one of the building blocks of early liberal political economy: that a centrally administered, politically motivated system of social intervention necessarily undermined the self-interested pursuit of wealth and profit by undermining individual self-reliance and effort. Beginning initially on a city-by-city basis from the late 1840s (notably in Liverpool, Manchester and London) many voluntary relief schemes effectively merged into a national organised effort at the end of the 1860s. The meteoric rise of organised charity in the nineteenth century was one of the key reasons why, in spite of the harsh strictures of the Poor Law Act and its emphasis on the workhouse, more than four times as many people received relief outside of the workhouses as inside them for the 66 years from the Act's introduction to the turn of the century (see Bosanquet, 1968 [1895]). The philanthropic movement held classical liberal doctrines dear to its heart. It was concerned as much with repressing fraudulent use of charity as it was with relieving the distresses of poverty, as concerned to distinguish 'genuine' need from wilful misuse of funds as it was to redistribute the vast wealth pouring into the coffers of the bourgeois class. The Charity Organisation Society (COS) as it later styled itself, was founded in 1869 as the Society for the Organisation of Charitable Relief and Repressing Mendicity. Imbued with a vision of 'scientific' charity and extolling the moral virtues of self-help and necessary personal sacrifice on the part of the poor, the philanthropic movement comprised a counterpart in the voluntary sphere of charity to the rational individualism embedded in liberal political theory. Yet the movement was symptomatic of a profound change in that rationality and helped to construct the political channel for a reorientation of liberal theory in the second half of the nineteenth century. The change revolved primarily around the apparent benefits of a combined approach to moral surveillance and social administration which liberals of the period attempted to graft on to firmly established commitments to ideals of representative government, an unregulated economy and freedom of labour. It is in this period, albeit unintentionally, that liberal philosophy first began to grapple with concrete and complex issues of social welfare – as opposed to abstract issues of holistic progress. Liberal philosophy was 'socialised' out of its raw, politically circumscribed representation of bourgeois interests.

The philanthropic movement headed by the COS had shown that an organised, centrally administered approach to poor relief did not necessarily contradict the central tenets of classical liberalism. Its development of the casework method of tendering assistance – focused on the *circumstances* of each individual, rather than on the individual as such – indicated that it was possible for a well-regulated authority to manage and administer social problems without undermining ideals of individual responsibility for poverty and personal accountability for collective assistance. It promised a form of *social administration* which supported the principles of *economic individualism* and thus appeared to reconcile in practice a dilemma that liberalism had been unable to resolve in its own collection of theories of progress and development.

The social activism of the COS and its supporters was inspired as much by a desire to bring about moral and spiritual betterment and to generate a sense of solidarity between the middle and working classes as it was to improve the material conditions of the poor. This paternalistic attempt at solidarity issued several challenges to liberal conceptions of democracy and inclusion in the political governance of the modern state. The philosopher T.H. Green, for example, who also laid many of the foundations for imperial liberal philosophy, was an ardent supporter of the Reform League, which pressed for the extension of the franchise in the 1860s and, along with William Gladstone and many of the League's colleagues working in the charity organisations, was also active in the temperance movement. Other liberals argued that a disciplined working class, educated in civilised morals and the principles of rational self-control and showing proper respect for their superiors, had every right to take part in the political system and thereby share in the collective self-determination of British social life (see Arblaster, 1984: 273). At this time, a similar argument was applied to the demands for women's suffrage – which was radicalised by the failure of the 1867 Reform Act to provide votes for women. In one sense, the paternalistic view was a child of liberalism's changing reaction to democratic politics but it was also stimulated by a growing consciousness of 'Empire', to which we return below.

Liberal democracy

Liberal political economy, defining a form of rule which relied on the facilitation of property and capital, had not engaged practically with the problem of democracy and the parallel problem of national citizenship. Liberals promoted *formal* equality before the law for all (tax-paying men) but did not promote equality in a *substantive* sense. The notion of a political citizenry, deriving rights from the mere fact of membership in a society, achieved little support in liberal political philosophy. The reasons for this centred on the belief that political rights were not automatic but accompanied personal and social enlightenment. Agitation on the part of the working classes, popular uprisings in Britain and France, industrial disruption and the growing number of crimes against property generated both fear and mistrust among liberals and reinforced the view that only certain sections of society were fit to take part in the political process. Such views were embedded in mid-nineteenth century liberal political theories, even where these were broadly sympathetic to democratic claims.

At the beginning of the nineteenth century Alexis de Tocqueville (1946 [1804]), for example, held out the American system as a vision of the future, a future in which democracy was inevitable, even fated, although he warned of its dangers, including anarchy and social standardisation. The theme was later taken up by John Stuart Mill who developed his father's vision of an ideal type of representative government, contradictorily promoting universal male and female suffrage at the same time as warning against the potential dangers of a wider democratic franchise. He argued that the middle and aristocratic classes had the interests of the impoverished and working people at heart – that the political interests of working classes could be represented satisfactorily by those who were educated and intellectually superior – and represented the emergent bourgeois political class as a class of magnanimous benefactors who, through their wisdom and humanity, were able to take forward the ideals of Enlightenment, occasionally even scolding them for their zeal. J.S. Mill (1948 [1861]), like de Tocqueville, was always fearful of the tyranny of the majority – of the suppression of minority interests and the creative individualities which these could potentially bring forth. As a safeguard against this suppression Mill strongly emphasised the need for *local government* – as a safeguard against the tyranny of a centralised political power.

Many second wave liberals expressed deep concern about the creation of democratic political structures, arguing that the great mass of Europe's poor were incapable of participating in their own government through lack of learning. This moral superiority was carried over into the development of liberal philosophy in the later part of the nineteenth century. The Italian Nationalist Giuseppe Mazzini justified the political dominance of the bourgeois class by arguing that:

> Humanity is only now beginning to comprehend that progress is the law. It is beginning vaguely to comprehend somewhat of the universe by which it is surrounded; but the majority of the individuals that compose it are still incapable, through barbarism, slavery or the absolute absence of all education, of studying that law and obtaining a knowledge of that universe; both of which it is necessary to comprehend before we can know ourselves.
>
> Only a minority of the men who people our little Europe is as yet capable of developing itself towards the right use and understanding of its own intellectual faculties. (Mazzini, 1867 [1858]: 309)

Second wave liberalism encapsulates a contradictory moral paternalism – inspired, in part, by the experience of charitable work and a mistrust of democracy, and in part by shifts in liberalism's philosophical system. In contrast to liberals in the earlier part of the century, for whom enlightened government consisted in the division of the social economy from the political economy and the subsumption of the former to the latter, second wave liberalism promoted a more social interventionist political role. None the less, the right of 'men' to rule over the division was firmly upheld, even whilst they recognised that if society were to remain ordered it would be necessary to widen the bases of their power. By the 1860s women were still excluded from voting through the stipulations of the 1832 Act. Although unmarried, qualified women (that is, women of independent means) were technically included in the municipal franchise as a result of Brougham's Act of 1850 (which stated that in all Acts the word 'male' should be taken to include 'female' unless otherwise indicated), married women were excluded under the law of 'coverture'. This law affirmed that a woman's property was represented by her husband and when this was modified in 1870 a separate Act specifically debarring married women from voting was placed on statute (Morgan, 1975: 10–13). When the franchise was extended in 1867 to include urban (but not rural) working class males who paid taxes the injustice of the Act's direct sex discrimination galvanised women's fight for inclusion in public decision-making.

These manoeuvres and struggles represent the persistent tension in nineteenth century liberalism around the issue of social stratification. In liberal theory, society is, and should be, stratified: some people are more 'fit' to govern than others, some are more qualified to make public decisions, some are more suited to manual labour, some are more proficient in the domestic arts, and so on. A central problem for liberal theory in the second half of the nineteenth century was how to sustain this philosophy of social stratification – a stratification viewed as natural and inevitable –

and at the same time engage in a more interventionist political practice. One of the most important theoretical perspectives through which the tension was addressed was evolutionism.

A major source for these transformed views was Charles Darwin's *The Origin of Species* (published in 1859), which provided an important lever for change in liberal political theory. As we have noted, the Enlightenment bequeathed to liberalism a notion of 'progress' which, essentially, represented a crude form of evolutionism. Mid-nineteenth century Europe was captivated by versions of evolutionary theory – Saint-Simon and Comte in the 1820s and 1830s had focused on evolutionary mechanisms in their attempts to formulate a sociology which could explain the distinctive characteristics of European civilisation, and similar ideas were circulating among European intellectuals throughout the period. Such evolutionary theories comprised versions of 'historicist' philosophy, to which we return in Chapter 2. They were based on the idea that human societies as a whole – guided by various invisible forces – were moving purposefully through history towards increased prosperity and power. Only Malthus' work on the struggle and conflict for resources which, he had claimed, accompanies a growing population in a static environment, had cast much of a shadow on the optimism of the evolutionary doctrine. According to Malthus, a society's capacity to produce food increases only mathematically – that is, in equal gradations: 1–2–3–4–5, etc. The population, on the other hand, increases geometrically with every graded increase in productive power – that is, it doubles: 1–2–4–8–16, etc. The consequence would be eternal misery for the mass of mankind, the everlasting presence of enormous disparities in wealth between the fortunate few and the unfortunate many and, ultimately, an unavoidable war of survival pitting all against all.

Darwin transformed Malthus' ideas on conflict and competition into a descriptive scheme outlining the process of the whole of biological evolution, simultaneously extracting much of the extreme pessimism of Malthus' original formulation. In *The Origin of Species*, Darwin argued that competition for resources in the environment did not consist in an eternal war for survival, as Malthus had claimed. Rather, the competition resulted in the adaptation of species which, in turn, resulted in their specialised exploitation of particular parts of nature. Species mutated over time as the resources in their environments changed in order to optimise their capacity to survive. The different species may not be linked biologically but they were interconnected in nature: each depended on others in its environment. Whilst Darwin's theories referred to *biological* evolution, they were themselves quickly 'adapted' to apply to *social* evolution. Of particular import was Darwin's observation that the transformation or mutation of a whole species would be visible in the individual members of that species. In other words, the direction of mutation would be visible in the physical structure of a single species member. Thus, the 'level' or 'type' of development of individuals would act as signals of the development of the whole.

The application of this theory to the social, as opposed to the natural, world took a number of different forms. Some, such as Spencer (1940 [1884]), focused on the implications of Darwin's observations for the 'fitness' of different strata to be full members of the social organism as a whole. In Spencer's view, the 'fitness' (that is, the capacity to adapt and survive) of the human species would be guaranteed through the evolution of its highest members. The more developed members of the species would naturally survive, adapt and progressively mutate. The less developed members, on the other hand, would naturally become extinct. In consequence, Spencer argued, any artificial support for the lower orders of the species would undermine the fitness of the species as a whole: their stock would be transmitted through the generations, weakening the overall stock of the species. Ameliorative action by the state or other organised bodies to maintain such groups artificially would interfere with the process of 'natural selection' and upset the entire natural order. The rest of the society would have to carry what was effectively dead weight, resulting in a diminution in the powers and capacities of the society. The welfare of the whole would best be served by allowing the weak and underdeveloped sections to die out, leaving behind the more advanced and fittest members to transmit the highest achievements and powers to succeeding generations. Spencer's and other versions of social Darwinism quickly became tied to the theoretical and empirical programme of the eugenics movement which sought to distinguish – on rational, empirical grounds – between 'fit' and 'defective' members of the human race (cf. Galton, 1889, 1907; see also Williams, 1989).

Others, such as Kidd (1894) and Pearson (1905), in England, and Durkheim (1893) in France, proposed that the organised bodies of state, family, community, church, and so on, comprised social institutions that functioned like the organs of a living creature. Individual interests, desires and needs should be subordinated to group interests and needs in order to promote the welfare of the whole. In contrast to Spencer's concern with the individual members of the species and their evolutionary level, the structure and functioning of the group, its institutions and cultures, became the focus of attention. Durkheim's (1984 [1893]) description of the functions of social institutions represented the most developed nineteenth century version of this theory. 'Higher order' social functions – of social cohesion, regulation and maintenance, for example – were carried out by complex institutions – such as the political state or the church. 'Lower order' social functions – of reproduction, interpersonal bonding or language acquisition, for example – were carried out by simpler, yet more flexible institutions – such as the family or community. In liberal political theory, this second version of social Darwinism came to focus on differences between races in the imperial struggle for world domination.

The followers of the first school of Darwinian theory are characterised by Semmel (1960) as 'internal social Darwinists' because their attention was drawn towards the structures and functions of species' members and their evolutionary level compared with other members of the same species. The followers of the second school comprise 'external social Darwinists' because they focused on the relationships between 'races' within the same species. Both 'internal' and 'external' social Darwinisms were structured by the encounter with imperialism.

Imperial liberalism

The problem of liberal democracy in late nineteenth century Britain was framed between two currents of social change. The first current, as we have seen, resonated in contests over political rule at 'home' – over the franchise and the benefits of state intervention, for example. The contests persistently challenged liberals to respond to fundamental ambiguities in their philosophical system: who should and should not be included in the franchise? Which social strata should and should not receive what kind of state support? Who should and should not wield political power? How should the will of the people be expressed? In short, they posed the wider question of inclusion and exclusion in the socio-political institutions of Britain. The second current situated Britain in the context of competing imperial powers – including Japan, Germany, France and the United States of America – and increasingly powerful colonies – especially following the Boer War (1899–1902). Germany, in particular, was seen as a threat to British interests: the growth of its core industrial strength in minerals, steel, shipbuilding and manufactures was accompanied by a more expansionist international posture – in terms of both an overall enlargement of Germany's economic markets and an extension in its political influence. Whilst Germany was often cited as the major competitor, other European nation-states were also pushing at the limits of British Imperial dominion. Britain's empire was being reconfigured both by insurrection and armed conflict in the colonies and by the rise of counter-empires in Europe and beyond.

Yet, liberal theory faced both the stimulus to social reform and the stimulus to imperial power simultaneously, not simply as contingent events to which responses had to be made, but as theoretical logics embedded in its contradictory political philosophy. The empire, in its very existence, represented a philosophical problem for liberals: how to reconcile the principles of liberty with the practice of colonisation; how to advocate one system of moral and procedural rule in one country (at 'home') and a different system elsewhere ('abroad'). This bipolar dilemma – *government* at 'home' and *governance* 'abroad' – plagued liberal theory during the last decades of the nineteenth century. The polarity is revealed most clearly, however, in the 1906 Liberal administration in which liberal 'Radicals' (domestic social reformers and free-trade supporters) dominated in domestic policy-making whilst Liberal-Imperialists (tariff reformers and Imperial League supporters) dominated in military and foreign policy-making. Lloyd George's budget of 1909 – often hailed as the precursor to much wider social reforming zeal – was actually targeted at both horns of the dilemma, motivated by the two ideological vectors of turn-of-the-century liberal philosophy. The budget raised revenue for interventionist social programmes and for increased military expenditures at the same time. Liberalism's polarised political focus (exemplified in the 1906 administration) presaged the collapse of its organised political influence. Lord Rosebery warned of the political dangers of the division in 1901 – proposing that the collapse of liberal political power would undoubtedly occur unless it could be resolved (Semmel, 1960: 60) – and its accuracy has echoed across the twentieth century ever since.

The theoretical dilemma posed by imperialism was not simply a question of ethics: British liberals both defended and condemned the empire (although not in equal measure) on moral as well as rational grounds. The problem centred more importantly on a political gap opened up by liberal humanism and its conception of 'inclusion' in, or belonging to, an enlightened public sphere. At the turn of the twentieth century, British liberalism grappled with the desire to universalise its philosophical principles in a new world order and yet at the same time confront challenges to the British empire in an increasingly competitive international political economy. Under these conditions, liberal philosophers – including Green (1941 [1882]) and Bosanquet (1968 [1895]) – opted for an 'external social Darwinism', supplementing Macaulay's desire for national improvement with a racial inflection and defining their political enterprise in terms of the nation and the race, rather than the society as such, as the common entities through which liberal goals were to be achieved. The strength and potency of the nation-state emerged as the basis for social progress and social reform: poverty, sickness, lack of education were construed not as individual problems but as national problems. The capacity of the nation-state to compete in an aggressively imperialist world was seen to depend on the 'fitness' and 'development' of its human and technical resources. Indeed, within this frame of reference society was defined *as* nation. Benjamin Kidd (1894) proposed that the evolution of races and their struggles for domination were dependent on the 'social efficiency' of the nation: society must be efficient in order that the nation may serve the interests of the race. Kidd contrasted Anglo-Saxons with 'Teutonic' and 'Celtic' [French] races, arguing that each strove for optimum 'social efficiency' because it was through this quality 'that nations and peoples are being continually, and for the most part unconsciously, pitted against each other in the complex rivalry of life' (Kidd, 1894: 241).

Such a theory implied that the individual would thrive when society as a whole was functioning correctly: that individual welfare was tied to national and racial order. When the nation and the race were 'fit' so were the individuals who comprised them. Samuel (1902: 37) states the case:

> The purpose of Society is to create, not merely capable electors, useful servants, law-abiding subjects and skilful workers; its purpose is to create a high type of men.

The idea that society has a purpose, that it is active in moulding, fabricating (or 'creating') individuals, was tied to a much older liberal politics of government. The issue for liberals was the extent to which a people were fit to take part in their own ruling; whether they had reached a maturity and awareness compatible with the exercise of political judgement. Only under particular conditions, and only after a certain level of education and training, would it be reasonable for political inclusion to be granted. In relation to Britain's empire, Samuel sums up the argument neatly:

> Because we think freedom better than control, we do not count it a kindness to let a child do whatever he likes, or a sick man eat whatever he fancies; and because we hold that democracy is good for the Englishman or the Frenchman, we need not pedantically pretend that it must always be good for the Indian or the African as well. (Samuel, 1902: 330)

The question, however, did not merely apply to 'foreign' peoples: continuing struggles for the extension of the political franchise exercised liberals at home, also, raising the issue of citizenship in 'modern' – as well as 'primitive' – society. Turn-of-the-century liberalism is characterised both by suspicion of the politically organised working class and its expression in the Independent Labour Party and by the desire to retain the separation of domestic and public life by the continued exclusion of women from the franchise. In relation to working class agitation, even limited social reforms were often viewed as potentially disastrous. In the second case, the pace of change was considered too fast: women were not yet 'fit' to take on the burden of the franchise and share 'in the government of the British Empire' (Samuel, 1902: 252).

Second wave liberalism thus encounters the political problem of incorporation in a new way. Whereas liberal political economy theorises citizenship as a function of property, its control, division and organisation, liberal imperialism theorises citizenship as a function of social character: a capacity and a duty as well as a right. The second wave liberal project theorised the coordination of public–private, political–civil relationships as requirements of the Imperial Nation. The shifting emphases of liberal political theory during the period were aimed at theorising the nation and its human and industrial resources in order to underpin a strong position for the 'race' in competitive world markets. The welfare of the 'nation' and the 'race' became liberalism's justification for imperial exploitation and for overhauling the Poor Law at the same time. The British nation and race must be brought to their peak in order to compete 'efficiently' in the struggle for world domination, the achievement of which, in turn, would ensure the welfare of the nation and the race.

Third wave liberalism

> I do not wish to live under a Conservative Government for the next twenty years. I believe that the progressive forces of this country are

hopelessly divided between the Liberal Party and the Labour Party. I do
not believe that the Liberal Party will win *one third* of the seats in the
House of Commons in any probable or foreseeable circumstances. . . . As
things are now, we have nothing to look forward to except a continuance
of Conservative Governments, not merely until they have made mistakes
in the tolerable degree which would have caused a swing of the pendu-
lum in former days, but until their mistakes have mounted up to the
height of a disaster. I do not like this choice of alternatives. (John Maynard
Keynes, 1926, *Liberalism and Labour*; cited in Bramstead and Melhuish,
1978: 709)

Keynes' epitaph to liberal government signals an important feature of
third wave liberal philosophy, namely its dissociation from executive
power. A Liberal government has not been elected to office since the Great
War, although the Liberal Party has shared power in coalition governments. After the First World War, liberalism retains the emphasis on
national and social progress but these are subsumed under new theoretical imperatives. Of particular note is the intersection between *managerialism* and *radicalism* in liberal political theory. Liberal managerialism views
the state as a 'directive intelligence' in a risky and uncertain world,
supports an enlargement of the public sphere and forms of technocratic
government, and promotes the goals of opportunity and efficiency
(Keynes 1927, 1940; Beveridge, 1936; Watson, 1957). Liberal radicalism
focuses on the social pluralism of the modern world, supports an enlarged
culture and forms of contractarian government, and promotes the goals of
community and tradition (Berlin, 1968, 1990; Rawls, 1971; Walzer, 1983;
Taylor, 1989).

Liberal managerialism

Liberalism, in the period following the First World War, is characterised
by the growth and consolidation of a technocratic theory of social administration. This theoretical framework distinguishes the approach of Keynes
and Beveridge, in particular, and derives from the combination of liberal
exclusion from political power and the failure of free market economics to
deliver either economic growth or social stability. In particular, liberal
managerialism responds to the growing influence of socialist theories and
focuses its attention more explicitly on the nature of the *capitalist* economic
system rather than on the 'invisible hand' guiding all of economic life.

The managerialist thesis, especially as put forward by Keynes, contends
that, left to itself, there is no reason why a capitalist economy should
deliver sustained growth in total social wealth. The behaviours of economic actors in investing, saving or expending their resources are not
entirely predictable 'facts' that can be fed into an economist's statistical
tables. The behaviours of producers, investors and consumers are subject
to intuitions, desires and whims as much as 'rational' calculations of
maximum profit. Thus, the behaviour of an entire economy is itself subject
to important uncertainties and risks. Indeed, for Keynes, the uncertainties

were a central feature of what capitalism represented as an economic system. In contrast to the 'planned' economy of Soviet Russia, capitalism possessed no automatic political mechanism by which to regulate the cycles of investment, production and consumption. These cycles were as likely to result in recession and depression as in growth and accumulation. Paradoxically, for Keynes, this was one of capitalism's major strengths as a social system, for it enabled the unfettered pursuit of individual innovation, creativity and profit in a framework that did not predetermine what choices could and could not be made. The problem was how to ensure that the uncertainties of the economic system neither condemned capitalism to prolonged stagnation and weakness nor led to such rampant social divisions that the very fabric of the system was ripped apart by social and political dissent, insurrection and, ultimately, revolution. Keynes viewed capitalist societies as great machines or engines of wealth production to which human intelligence could be applied in order to resolve the inefficiencies and wastes that their uncoordinated operations generated. In particular, uncoordinated capitalist economies were likely to produce long-term underemployment and a consequential economic polarisation between rich and poor. In this regard, Keynes was restating Disraeli's 'two nations' problem: that without some form of positive and organised intervention, a society fixated on the 'rational' pursuit of profit would inevitably lead to such extreme divisions between the haves and the have-nots that there would emerge not one but two societies across whose boundaries no commerce or contact would take place. In order for capitalism to run smoothly, therefore, it was necessary for a 'directive intelligence' (in practical terms, the state) to take action on society's behalf. Such action would include currency and credit controls, the dissemination of reliable data and information on the state of the economy, and investment in public works, both as means of sustaining business confidence in the system and as means of 'pump-priming' economic investment and development (Keynes, 1926, 1940).

When they were formulated, Keynes' ideas were regarded as heresies by orthodox economists and political scientists (Heilbroner, 1986), including, for a time, Beveridge (Harris, 1977: 323 *et passim*), although he later adopted them in the (1942) report on *Social Insurance and Allied Services*. Like Keynes, Beveridge viewed capitalist society as a great machine or organism that functions according to its own logics. More than Keynes, however, Beveridge believed that the machine's laws could be understood in their entirety by the application of positivist social science to the explanation and prediction of institutional and social life. This 'science' was a professional, highly technical activity that required much training and should not be confused with the mere application of 'intelligence' to human problems. Beveridge viewed capitalism as a complex society whose foundations and operations were obscure and mysterious to the untrained, lay public (including politicians). Thus, the role of science was to provide accurate and reliable expert guidance and supervision to government to enable it to maintain social and economic equilibrium in the system. Although the basic ideas of government by technocracy were contained in Keynes' work, Beveridge promoted them with the most vigour. In 'My Utopia', a lecture delivered at the London School of Economics in 1934, Beveridge argued that the ideal society would be run neither by elected representatives nor by dictators but by 'social doctors' – professional administrators acting on the advice of experts – who would form a bureaucratic and public-spirited élite (much as J.S. Mill's munificent bourgeois class) acting in the best interests of society-as-a-whole (see Harris, 1977: 328, 472).

Beveridge's technocratic philosophy represented a response to liberalism's abiding political problem: the reconciliation of individual interests with collective government. Beveridge's own social theory of capitalism was never stable – he supported free-market theories in the 1920s and early 1930s, then became an adherent of Keynesian economic planning and state management in the late 1930s and early 1940s and finally took up elements of communitarian philosophy (see below) after the Second World War, supporting a proactive governmental role for autonomous and semi-autonomous bodies (charities, friendly societies, restricted trades associations) within an enlarged public sphere. Thus, although Beveridge was the visible architect of the postwar social welfare system, it was Keynes' theories on capitalism and the role of the state that provided Beveridge with the framework in which to develop his plans. The plans were fundamentally 'Keynesian' in all respects: they accepted the principle of 'uncertainty' in the workings of capitalist economies, they situated the state as the 'directive intelligence' smoothing capitalism's booms and slumps, they attempted to re-integrate the 'two nations' that Keynes had recalled, and they emphasised the centrality of employment as a means of tying individuals into both the capitalist economic structure and its social benefits. Employment was both the individual's contribution to the society and the vehicle through which individuals would be insured by society. By promoting a 'social compact' between labour, the state and capital, promising both sustained growth and sustained welfare, the employment–insurance relationship has been the centrepiece of liberalism's contribution to the theory of welfare during its third wave. So long as bureaucracies are guided and supervised by sufficient 'expert' knowledge, and so long as the organisation of credit, currency and information is well managed, there is, in theory, no reason why the stagnant and socially divisive societies of the 1920s and 1930s should recur. The proper balance between individual freedom and collective government, it seemed, had been struck.

Liberal radicalism

That the 'equilibrium' sought by Keynes and Beveridge was never realised is not merely a consequence of unfortunate circumstances undermining a basically sound position. Neither Keynes nor Beveridge was able to specify why – even if every part of their theoretical and practical endeavours had been realised to the full – the social compact should reconcile the tension between freedom and government or between the individual and the collective. Both Keynes and Beveridge held very limited (technocratic, in fact) concepts of society and of justice that are not shared by other liberal theories and philosophies. Although the arguments and theories we outline below do not belong to a single 'school' of liberal philosophy (Rawls is a contractarian liberal, Berlin has been called an 'agonistic' liberal; see Gray, 1996), none the less each theorises liberal values and principles as rooted in communal forms of life. A liberal theory of welfare and a liberal politics of the good society can be derived from the ethical foundations of communal life.

To the extent that liberal society, in theory at least, comprises much more than economic behaviour *per se* – involving cultures, politics, sentiments and traditions – the grounds on which individuals may decide to pursue (or not) a course of action, or support or resist a political programme, will extend beyond calculations of profit and loss and will have consequences whose resolution will similarly lie outside the scope of technocratic, economic planning. Liberal radicalism, as we present it here, contends that conflicts and tensions are endemic to the liberal social order and are not merely 'by-products' of the iniquities of capitalism: they arise in the very nature of the relationships between beliefs, actions and institutions in a liberal society.

The most significant liberal political theory to emerge in the postwar era is Rawls' (1971) *A Theory of Justice*. Here, Rawls contends that there is a theory of justice embedded in liberalism which supports the reduction and, ultimately, elimination of inequality. He suggests that a person guided by liberal principles will accept that any decision about resource distribution which is just entails an improvement in the circumstances of the least well-off in society. In a liberal society it is unjust that social arrangements should operate to the exclusion, marginalisation or disadvantage of one group of persons to the benefit of another group of persons. Rawls infers that, on this basis, the principle of 'liberty' in liberal political theory should apply to *each* as well as to *all*, meaning that a true liberal community is one where procedural social and economic inequalities are so arranged as to maximise the chances of the least well-off to become as free as the most well-off. That is, unequal distribution of goods, opportunities and satisfactions is compatible with liberal principles only so long as the unequal distribution acts to equalise substantive inequalities between people. Rawls' theory of justice is based on a 'morality of principles' which is associated with a 'critically reflective posture of citizens'. This position construes the liberal society as one where the achievement of justice, fairness and cooperation is built into the conduct of persons and institutions. On this account, liberalism is the *pursuit* of such a society, even where it is manifestly absent (DeLue, 1989: 106–7).

The idea of liberalism as a project – that is, as embodying ideals towards which people should strive, regardless of whether or not the desired outcomes are achieved – is a characteristic of Berlin's 'agonistic' liberalism. In contrast to Rawls, Berlin's (1968, 1990) liberalism implies that liberal values cannot be devised in advance of the forms of life in which they are organised as traditions and cultures and then applied to any and all social and economic arrangements as if they represented political tools for social reform. Principles of the 'good' and the 'just', what 'cooperation' or 'fairness' means, are not commensurable across traditions. Berlin does not deny that there are universal principles or values, nor that these can guide how persons or institutions should act in the world. His point is that the enactment and realisation of those values in specific cultures and traditions will render them 'incommensurate'. That is, there are many true and objective values, only some of which will be embodied in conduct, institutions and societies at any one time. In consequence, there is as much likelihood of conflict over universal values as there is of agreement. The task of the liberal is to support the pluralism of values, not to undermine it, and the liberal must, therefore, accept that conflict will persist over which values should and should not be upheld in any particular arrangement of society. Berlin's 'agonism' consists in the fact that he both upholds the liberal project – of supporting liberty at all costs – whilst at the same time undermining the bases on which the ideal of liberty has been constructed – the substantive universality of liberal values.

In common with Berlin, Bernstein (1983), Walzer (1983) and Taylor (1989) accept that values cannot be derived in advance of the cultures and traditions in which they are situated. They go further than Berlin, however, in proposing that any particular values cannot be considered apart from the social and historical contexts in which they are formed, supported and transmitted and that upholding certain values over others is inextricably bound to upholding certain forms of community – or ways of life – over others. Thus, to support certain ways of life, or communities, is to support certain sorts of values and, by extension, to lend support to different types of communities is to uphold value pluralism. Such a pluralism can be understood in two distinct senses. On the one hand are values of solidarity, cooperation, respect and so on, that are based essentially on the interactions between members of the community. In theory, they require no other object, resource or good in order to be upheld and can be derived from the social relationships between the community's members. On the other hand are values of participation, equality or learning, for example, that do require the provision of goods and resources external to the social relationships between community members – access to mobility (in order to go to places where you can participate in community affairs), money to 'pay your way', schools or related institutions, and so on. These different types of values are connected together in the life of a community but modern society has tended to separate them out into independent 'spheres' which distribute different kinds of goods on the basis of different kinds of values. The problem for liberalism in this construction is how to reconcile the tension between the embedded nature of values in a community's way of life and the separate control of those spheres in which communitarian goods are distributed.

In contrast to managerialist theories, liberal radicalism has had no formal association with political power. Its philosophical commitments have acted as important frameworks for political struggles for equality of opportunity, anti-discriminatory codes of conduct and laws, and for challenging the values and assumptions of state institutions. Below, we examine the liberal concept of 'equality' and its contribution to some of the political movements for equality of access and opportunity.

Liberalism and the paradox of equality

The supremacy of liberal theory in twentieth century British politics is remarkable, given that an avowedly liberal government has not been elected to power since the First World War. Until the election of the Thatcher government in 1979, liberal conceptions of equality, freedom, justice and opportunity had remained the dominant themes of political debate and dispute about welfare policy and practice since the implementation of the Beveridge plan and the inception of the modern welfare state. Indeed, the Beveridge plan itself represented a debate within liberalism about the extent of its commitment to equality and freedom, a debate that confronted some of liberalism's central theoretical problems.

Beveridge's plans for a total overhaul of the social insurance system represented, as we have discussed, an attempt at the social coordination and management of economic life. In this regard, they were aimed at supporting specific ways of life within the British nation-state. In particular, they were a means of repairing and strengthening the contours of capitalist accumulation and growth, maintaining a coherent framework of social reproduction and reinvigorating the status and fitness of the nation in a competitive world economy. The social insurance scheme thus combined a political economy – an organised system of accumulation and wealth-creation – with a social economy – an organised system of rights, statuses and entitlements and their division and allocation under appropriate authorities. Some aspects of the social economy – such as support for particular relations between genders – are highly visible in the Beveridge report, whilst other aspects – such as the cultural and ethnic relations characterising a diverse population – are obscure. The relationships between the social economy and the political economy are central to the modern welfare state, as can be seen in the roles that Beveridge outlined for men and women during postwar reconstruction. In that reconstruction, he argued, 'housewives' would have 'vital work to do in ensuring the adequate continuance of the British race and British ideals in the world' (Beveridge, 1942: 53, para. 117; cited in Harris, 1977: 402).

Beveridge was expressing sentiments that were commonly (but not universally) held at the time: that women and men had different roles to play in the fulfilment of social life. The normal condition of women was to be married housewives and they should be treated by society according to their entry into this role. The normal condition of men was to be employed and, whether married or single, they should be treated by society according to their entry into this role. Early drafts of the Beveridge Report side-stepped questions of provision for women's different life circumstances, viewing these as examples of 'special needs' – married women, 'unmarried wives', 'domestic spinsters' and 'unsupported mothers' (Harris, 1977: 395). In consequence, Beveridge's later proposals are filled with the contradictions that the distinction between men's and women's roles entails. For example, Beveridge proposed that married and unmarried women be treated differently. Employed single women would contribute to the social insurance scheme in the same way as employed men; married women would be eligible under a 'housewives' policy' that provided benefit through their husbands' contributions; 'unmarried wives' (i.e., co-habitees) would have access to part of the housewives' policy but would be excluded from important features of it – including the widow's pension and furnishings grants. There were also plans for a dependant's allowance during a husband's unemployment or sickness and domestic help for housewives who fell ill, but not vice versa.

The plans were criticised by a number of women's organisations. The Married Women's Association argued for equal treatment of married men and women, with the latter becoming full, independent contributors rather than depending on a husband's contribution. The National Council of Women argued that it was wrong to discriminate between single and married women but not between single and married men and also proposed that women should receive payment for housework – this proposal was especially apt given that Beveridge himself had argued that women would be performing 'vital work' of national importance in the home. The civil servant Mary Hamilton urged Beveridge to pay more attention to the 'domestic spinster' caring for elderly relatives who also did not fit in with Beveridge's original scheme. On the question of 'deserted housewives' – that is, women who no longer had a husband's support but who remained married – Beveridge could find no solution and suggested that they be excluded from the scheme altogether, relying instead on the public assistance authorities – a proposal vigorously contested by the Married Women's Association (Harris, 1977: 403–5).

Two points in particular are worthy of note, here. The first is that these debates and disputes go to the heart of what 'equality' and 'freedom' mean in liberalism. The second is that liberalism, although formally a political theory, has always rested on a moral foundation.

Liberalism has never attempted, in any respect, to secure substantive equality. That is, it has never promoted the goal of enabling the development of a truly 'free and equal' society where everyone has access to equal resources for participation in the society's communal and institutional networks. It has always proposed that freedom from *too much* of the *wrong sort* of authority and control can be attained within a society marked by severe inequality. Thus, Beveridge was adamant that means-testing and casework approaches to social assistance (with some exceptions, such as deserted wives) represented undue interference into private life and should be resisted at every turn. For Beveridge, then, peeking and probing into individuals' circumstances as a means of organising assistance is too much of the wrong sort of authority. On the other hand, making married women dependent on their husband's income and contributions is just enough of the right sort of authority. In general terms, the social frame-work of the Keynesian welfare state is an example of liberalism's para-doxical concept of equality: equality is, and should be, *stratified*. All persons within a given stratum should be treated equally, but there is no necessity to treat people equally across strata. This paradoxical equality is often missed in assessments of the Keynesian welfare state. Contrary to popular opinion, the welfare policies of the postwar era have never comprised a 'redistributive' system in any meaningful sense. The Keynes-ian welfare system is a means of distributing the poor's income among the poor (with a percentage being raked off by the rich). It is not and never has been a means of redistributing the total wealth of a society in order to achieve goals of social and economic equality. As Beveridge himself made clear, the abolition of poverty could be achieved by 'a redistribution of income within the working classes, without touching any of the wealthier classes' (cited in Harris, 1977: 393). This does not imply, according to Beveridge, that the incomes of the wealthy should not be redistributed. None the less, the insurance focus of the scheme is designed to manage the income of the working class so as to provide welfare services for the working class. It is, in reality, a technocratically supervised, distributive, rather than redistributive, system. A great deal of the political pressure for equality of opportunity in the postwar period, to which we turn next, has reinforced liberalism's paradoxical equality. The demands for equal access to employment, for equal pay for equal work and for equality of represen-tation and entitlement have comprised demands for entry into the strati-fied society, rather than a radical overhaul of the society and its systems of stratification.

Liberal political theory rests on a moral foundation. That is, in spite of Berlin's agonistic objections, it supports particular value-positions and their realisation through social and institutional codes, behaviours and systems. The moral support takes the form of maintaining and valuing certain ways of organising social life over others and upholding divisions within that organisation, or, in other words, maintaining a system of social stratification. Most commonly, the stratification system is claimed to be meritocratic – based on the reward of ability and talent. The political movement for equal opportunities is a classic case of this liberal logic.

Although a distinction has been made between 'liberal' and 'radical' ap-proaches to equal opportunities, in our view the two approaches represent a 'conservative–liberal' approach and a 'radical–liberal' approach since neither perspective mounts a fundamental challenge to – indeed, they provide support for – a liberal conception of social order. The 'conservative–liberal' approach focuses on the development of objective procedures to enable individuals to realise their innate talents within institutions broadly as they exist at the present time. The 'radical–liberal' approach focuses on changing the structural conditions that result in social and cultural discriminations within institutions broadly as they exist at the present time. The two approaches can be distinguished by the commitment to *equal treatment* versus the commitment to *equal outcomes* or *equal shares* (Young, 1992). Both approaches value the cultural and social diversity of the modern political order and seek to make recognition of the diversity and plurality of value systems a condition for legitimate government. Equal opportunities agitation and ensuing policy – deriving largely from feminist and anti-racist struggles – constructs oppression as an aggregate or summation of disadvantages and discriminations. Challenging the aggregation entails the promotion of procedural justice, consciousness-raising, positive discrimination and, in some formulations, a politicisation of the decision-making processes that lead to particular discriminations (Jewson and Mason, 1992). Equal opportunities policies are based on the proposition that a change in stereotypes, extra support for the most disadvantaged (cf. Rawls, 1971) and a validation of the different cultural characteristics of diverse social groups can lead to a fairer and more effective organisation of existing institutional structures – of employment, welfare, policing, education, and so on. Jewson and Mason (1992: 222) summarise this fundamentally liberal viewpoint in relation to paid work:

> 'Equal opportunities' cannot be said to exist until the representation of black people and women in the various divisions of the labour force reflects their presence in society as a whole.

Presumably, the proposition can be extended to include proportional representation of genders and ethnicities in household labour, educational and cultural institutions, and formal and informal caring services, as well as being expanded to deal with other demographic characteristics of the population. In proposing such a view, the equal opportunity movement upholds the modern liberal ideal of a singular and enlarged public sphere in which specific disadvantages and discriminations can be resolved. It also upholds the notion that overlaying that singular and enlarged public sphere is a stratification system (in Jewson and Mason's case, based on the divisions of labour) to which individuals should be allocated regardless of ethnicity or gender (and so on). It is, in short, an effort at universalising, across all cultural and social characteristics, liberalism's paradoxical equality.

In viewing inequalities and oppressions primarily as technical issues that arise through the malfunctioning of social institutions, the equal opportunities movement draws on a long tradition of liberal protest and an equally long tradition of liberal theorising. The struggle for women's entry into the franchise in the late nineteenth and early twentieth century, the struggle to ease the burden of poverty through welfare provision throughout the middle period of the twentieth century, the struggle to change racist attitudes and practices through race relations legislation and the Commission for Racial Equality from the 1970s onwards, have all aimed at the ongoing reform of a social order conceived, at base, as liberal democratic. In other words, they have accepted the inevitability of the institutional networks of imperialist and capitalist societies and have sought to expand the democratic principles through which, ostensibly, those networks operate. At the same time, they rest on the idea that society is a unity in difference: that society's institutional networks comprise an organic whole such that positive action in one area supports positive outcomes elsewhere. Social stratification is understood as an inbuilt feature of the social order: 'equality' is the representative distribution of racial, gender, cultural and other social groups in that stratified order. Thus, 'freedom' is the capacity to enter into the stratification system without let or hindrance from others and the right, individually, to move up (and down) the strata.

Concluding remarks

In this chapter we have provided a brief overview of the varieties and historical development of liberal perspectives on society and social welfare. Liberal conceptions of welfare are derivations of their theories of social order. Such conceptions construct 'society' either as the dynamic progress of an overall human destiny or as the differentiated integration of natural capacities and talents whose realisation results in a stratified organisation of social and economic institutions. Liberalism is often mistakenly associated with the preservation of traditions and the status quo whereas the diversity of its philosophical and theoretical commitments reveals that progress and development are central pillars of the liberal paradigm. Across the one hundred and sixty years since liberal philosophy first conjoined itself to political power, the concepts and logics through which the paradigm has theorised social welfare have changed dramatically. From the crudity of its public–private division to the complexity of its agonistic value commitments, liberal social theory has attempted to justify major distinctions in the roles, responsibilities and powers of political and communal institutions. These distinctions are the basis of a liberal conception of social order and their maintenance and support is, in turn, the basis of liberal social theory. When there is sufficient individual freedom from institutional interference and when the powers of institutions are reduced to the minimum practicable level, then the autonomous development of human talent and ingenuity will find its own means and resources for securing wealth and well-being. 'Welfare' in liberal philosophy is not something that is provided but something that is achieved and developed through the free and independent actions of an uncoerced individuality. In turn, the welfare of each individual promotes the well-being of the entire society by increasing the sum total of freedom in which its members live. Such a social theory, as we have noted, contradictorily construes 'equality' as the right to be unequal: as the equal right to enter into institutions marked by systematic inequalities in a stratified social order. In theory, liberalism promotes an equality of opportunity that is rooted in an inequality of outcomes. In practice, as we have also noted, it has promoted and, in some formulations continues to promote, inequalities of opportunity as well. It is in this sense that we characterise liberal social theory as a paradoxical theory of human equality.

2
Marxism

In the previous chapter, we showed that liberalism as a philosophical and theoretical perspective encompasses a very wide range of nineteenth and twentieth century writers and thinkers. Liberalism as a political project, however – that is, as a form of government and direct influence over the administration of society – is confined essentially to the period from 1832 to 1914. Liberalism, whilst undeniably Marxism's fraternal enemy in political struggles over welfare and the state, has a history that is almost exactly the mirror image of Marxism: liberalism accedes to a long period of power (approximately 80 years of almost continual political influence, if not always direct political dominance) followed by a philosophic history excluded from power; Marxism emerges in a long philosophic history and proceeds to a period of direct and indirect political power. The end of the liberal project – that is, the entanglement of liberal philosophy with liberal political power – occurs at precisely the moment that the equivalent Marxist project begins.

Thus, the history of the Marxist political–philosophical project is different from that of liberalism: the project did not really 'end' for Europe until 1989, with the demolition of the Berlin wall and the break-up of the Soviet empire – although the twentieth century is filled with premature predictions of its demise. But the historical difference should not obscure the fact that Marxism and liberalism shared important beliefs and assumptions about social and economic progress and about the future realisation of the free society. The achievements of liberal-democratic movements in securing social and economic changes are acknowledged by Karl Marx (1818–83) and Friedrich Engels (1820–95) as necessary, constituent stages on the road to communism. Marx and Engels, severely critical of liberal ideology and theory as they were, did not dismiss the historical significance of the political, social and economic revolutions that had been inspired and led by liberals. Rather, they rejected liberalism as partial, ideological and motivated, serving the interests and satisfying the demands of only a small section of the population: the bourgeois class. The struggle of liberalism against tyranny and for political equality emphasised the freedom of the individual, the inevitability of progress and the power of human reason. Marx and Engels sought to turn liberal political philosophy and theory on its head and begin not from abstract principles and ideals but from the real conditions of people living with the effects of nineteenth century capitalism.

Marxism and Enlightenment

The year is 1848. In Ireland, thousands of people are starving to death. Thousands more are migrating to swell the slums and warrens of English cities. Manchester, Liverpool and all of the other rapidly expanding urban centres of English capitalist production are paradoxical places. They have pleasant shopping centres, leafy suburbs and grand architectural monuments to the rich and powerful. They also seethe with poverty and pollution, disease and dissent. In France, King Louis Philippe has abdicated the throne and Paris is burning behind barricades erected by the people against government forces. In Germany there is rebellion, counter-rebellion and slaughter. All over Europe dissatisfaction with political and economic oppression erupts here and there into insurrection and war. In the English parliament sits a Whig government, glowing with ideological fervour over its free-market theories and policies, determined to keep control over economic life and expand the riches flowing into the coffers of the bourgeois class. Its Poor Law system of welfare relief maintains the shackles of stigma and penury around those unable to find, or unable to carry out, paid labour. In London, a young philosopher, Karl Marx, and his colleague and patron, Friedrich Engels, present to the Communist League, a small group of left-wing radicals, a manifesto for transforming the world: the *Manifesto of the Communist Party*. It is a document filled with ominous warnings for the complacent bourgeoisie, rich in the rhetoric of revolution, a document that is at once both a legacy of and a challenge to Enlightenment philosophy. From its opening portent – 'There is a spectre haunting Europe – the spectre of Communism' – to its closing call to arms, it is both a brilliant piece of political propaganda and the key that unlocks the whole of Marxist theory. Marx and Engels (1991 [1848]: 192) appeal to the working class to throw off the yoke of bourgeois domination, thus:

> The Communists disdain to conceal their views and aims. They openly declare that their ends can be attained only by the forcible overthrow of all existing social conditions. Let the ruling classes tremble at a Communistic revolution. The proletarians have nothing to lose but their chains. They have a world to win.
>
> WORKING MEN OF ALL COUNTRIES, UNITE!

The proletarians have *nothing* to lose because they possess *nothing*. They have been robbed of all means of independent subsistence, forced off the lands that supported their ancestors, squeezed into filthy, overcrowded slums without access to clean water, clean air, adequate food or decent shelter. Bereft of all human dignity, compelled, in order to have any life at all, to work long hours for a pittance in atrocious conditions at the capitalist's bidding, the proletarian has nothing except a brain with which to think and hands with which to toil. The proletarian's life is a miserable, degraded struggle against starvation, disease, exhaustion and accident. The proletarian has nothing at all to lose from revolution. For Marx and Engels, it was inevitable that capitalism would be smashed in a violent confrontation between those who owned society's wealth and those who produced it.

The *Manifesto* represents a turning point in nineteenth century political theory. It does not bury what preceded it but instead weaves together the strands of radical and critical philosophy into new patterns and makes new connections between the theory of history and the theory of politics. It represents a political statement of Marx and Engels' philosophical system: historical materialism.

Historical materialism is rooted in two post-Enlightenment sources: Hegelian idealism and the materialism of Feuerbach. Marx and Engels' perspective on historical change incorporates elements from each of these sources but ultimately rejects both as one-sided bourgeois philosophies. Georg W.F. Hegel (1770–1831) proposed that the movement of human history corresponded to the emergence of human freedom and, in particular, to the emancipation of human consciousness. History is understood as a sequence of stages in which the categories of human thought are made real (are 'realised') in forms of social and political organisation. Each 'stage' of history (Christianity, the Reformation, the French Revolution and constitutional monarchy) comprises an advance in the 'self-consciousness' of humankind or the evolution of Spirit (*Geist*). For Hegel, each such stage – and the social and political arrangements associated with it – represents a new plane of human consciousness and thus, claimed Hegel, physical being is determined by consciousness: history is human consciousness realising itself in the world. Ludwig Feuerbach (1804–72) was a strident critic of Hegel, claiming that the latter had made the human being into an object of thought rather than viewing thought as a product of the human being. For Feuerbach, 'man' is the source and origin of all things – thought, belief, invention, economy – and is led falsely to believe that his destiny is preordained by gods or laws of consciousness. In contrast to Hegel, Feuerbach proposed that consciousness is determined by physical, corporal existence: history is the trail of consciousness left behind by how humanity lives.

Hegel and Feuerbach epitomise the early nineteenth century debates around a form of philosophy called 'historicism'. Such philosophy is characterised by two important concepts; one is the notion that history has a *telos* (a meaning and direction) and the other is the notion of totality. In historicist thought all forms of collective life are understood as manifestations of a society's ability to produce and transform itself: 'the idea that individuals or social categories had a rendezvous with destiny or a historical necessity' (Touraine, 1995: 62, 64). Historicist thought is the expression of an idea of progress, proposing that historical change, even revolutionary historical change, is inevitable. Progress is the reconciliation of social divisions and the realisation of the wholeness or unity of humankind. Distrusting the individualism of natural law theories, historicist thought is preoccupied by a loss of community (or unity) engendered through the process of modernisation. It seeks the grounds for a new social order in which the individual is integrated into the collective. Through this strand of thought, personal freedom comes to be identified by participation in, and solidarity with, the social body. Historicism was an important element in the philosophy of Saint-Simon (1759–1825), whose criticisms of the French Revolution principles of liberty and equality were to inspire many later theorists, including Marx and Engels. Saint-Simon attacked the notions of liberty and equality contained in the Declaration of Rights in France, following the revolution. He viewed the 'Rights' as individualistic, atomistic and leading only to competition, economic anarchy, poverty and inequality (Hobsbawm, 1982: 11). Defining the revolution as a class struggle, Saint-Simon developed a model of social systems where changes from one kind of system to another are understood as a result of the organisation of the productive system and property relations (1982: 11).

Marx and Engels objected to both the idealist and materialist versions of historicism on the grounds that each abstracted the real, living person from the actual conditions under which their corporal and conscious existence occurred. For Marx and Engels, 'man' is not a figment of philosophy whose nature can be spelled out in the pages of a textbook but an active agent, involved in real relations with other people, operating under particular conditions of existence. To understand the reality of historical change, contend Marx and Engels, it is necessary to begin by examining the ways in which human relationships are organised and, in particular, the ways that these relationships serve the ends of the production and reproduction of the human species. Thus, Marx and Engels propose that, as in nature, history is subject to 'laws' that govern social progress and change. But these laws are themselves 'historical' in two senses. In the first sense, they only become apparent, they only become available for conscious reflection, under certain historical conditions: it would be impossible to understand the laws of motion of capitalism before capitalism had emerged in history. Thus, there is no timeless 'law' of capitalism like there is a timeless 'law' of gravity: there are only historical laws of capitalism that become effective under the historical conditions of capitalism. This means, in the second sense, that the 'laws of motion' of different historical systems are different: history is not the unfolding of a universal law of 'being' or 'consciousness', for the 'being' and 'consciousness' of real people is a product of their own activity:

> As individuals express their life, so they are. What they are, therefore, *coincides* with what they produce and with how they produce. The nature of individuals thus depends on the material conditions which determine their production. (cited in McLellan, 1982: 43)

Although, for Marx and Engels, there are universal principles of social change – the struggle between oppressor and oppressed, the divisions of property between those who own and those who are forced to work the means of production – each epoch of history is an entire way of life in and of itself. In each epoch, the character of individuals and the relationships between them are expressed through a 'mode of production', that is, a way of organising the means to live and reproduce. Rather than distinguishing those who were 'enlightened' and those who were not, those fit to take part in their own governance and those too deviant, different or uneducated, Marx and Engels proposed that even these distinctions were a product of the capitalist mode of production. The very notion that there existed an enlightened class and an unenlightened class was an ideological mystification of capitalist exploitation and served to prevent the spread of true knowledge of the capitalist system. Whereas, for liberalism, Enlightenment provided access to the true reality of the world, for Marxism the reality of the world provided access to the true Enlightenment that would arrive only with the proletarian revolution. Just as liberalism reflected an incomplete faith in Enlightenment so also, but for very different reasons, did Marxism.

Marx and Marxism

Marx and Engels' theoretical perspective developed during the industrial revolution when the emergence of the industrial working class threw up the 'social question' that dominated political discussion throughout most of the nineteenth century. The transition from an agricultural economy based on feudal social relations to an industrial economy based on capitalist wage-relations generated massive social upheaval (Hobsbawm, 1995a [1975]) – migration from the countryside to towns and cities, the obsolescence of old craft skills, community structures and cultures, the reorganisation of government and massive increases in commodity production and consumption. The poverty of the newly constituted urban working classes was viewed with alarm as a source of political unrest and social problems, intensified by the periodic economic crises afflicting the nascent system of industrial capitalism. Marx and Engels' philosophy and politics were developed and revised in the light of these political and economic circumstances. At the same time, after 1848, Marxism emerged as a political movement almost in its own right – there were already references to a 'Marx Party' and 'Marxian' views by the early 1850s (Haupt, 1982: 266) – with the consequence that its theoretical structures were interpreted, debated, negotiated and reinterpreted across a wide range of organised (and unorganised) groups, sects, parties and movements, leading to many varieties of 'Marxism'. Marxist political theory developed during the most vigorous period of working class struggle and agitation and went through a series of modifications as circumstances threw up new problems to solve and new conflicts to analyse.

Mass working class movements were already established in Britain, and were gaining ground in continental Europe, by the 1840s. There were strikes, insurrections and skirmishes involving both organised and spontaneous worker agitation throughout the decade both in Britain and continental Europe culminating, in 1848, in revolutions in France, Germany, Hungary, Austria and Italy and a Chartist insurrection in England. The revolutions and insurrections were viciously crushed by military and police forces, resulting in the slaughter of thousands of workers. Draconian laws and penalties were swiftly introduced to give the state and its armed forces the necessary powers to prevent further uprisings.

The social conditions of the impoverished workers, the iniquities of capitalism and the historic mission of the working classes, had also been incorporated into radical political theory by the 1830s. In Germany, Wilhelm Weitling and in France Pierre Proudhon castigated the economic system that depended on depriving the mass of the population of any rights to the fruits of their labours. Weitling had taken up Feuerbach's views on human nature to argue that degradation of the masses was itself sufficient to cause a communist revolution. Proudhon had asked, in the title of his (1840) pamphlet, *What is Property?* To which he replied 'Property is Theft'. Robert Owen (1771–1858) in England and Charles Fourier (1772–1837) in France had proposed utopian socialist schemes for cooperative worker ownership and control of the means of production. The intellectual and political climate of mid-nineteenth century Europe already contained many of the ideas and beliefs that Marx and Engels crystallised first into a historical philosophy and later into a theory of capitalism. Marxism is a historical, political and economic theory at the same time: each strand draws on the others to generate a critical theory of capitalist society.

Historical Marxism

In the 1830s and 1840s, as we noted above, historicism was the foundation on which radical and critical philosophies were constructed. Marx and Engels' writings at this time are dominated by the attempt to sort out the implications of historicist thinking for revolutionary theory and practice. The Marxism of *The German Ideology* (1845–6) and the *Communist Manifesto* (1848) is an evolutionary Marxism, tracing the long march of humankind's emergence from its 'primitive', tribal roots to its (projected) 'communist' social order. It is in these works that Marx and Engels elaborate their famous account of the revolutionary transitions from one mode of production to the next. The sequence that carries human society forward to capitalism and then communism is guaranteed in the very structures of each society and, in particular, in the relationships that characterise their modes of production.

For Marx and Engels, production is the basis not only of individual human life but of collective social life as well. Every society has to produce food, goods, shelter, and so on, in order to reproduce both its individual members and its social system. The way in which production is organised is called the *mode of production*. A mode of production is a combination of the means of production and the relations of production. The means of production include labour, land, tools, etc., organised in particular ways. So, for example, in the feudal economy land is organised on the basis of a 'strip' system – where serfs each work different strips of land individually or in groups – together with 'common' lands, where each person has rights to use the same forests, grazing grounds and so on. Similarly, independent craftspersons own the tools of their own trade and apply them to tasks for which they are paid a fee. The relations of production describe how property, production and labour are organised and how workers are brought into contact with the means of production. In feudalism, the productive land is owned by the feudal lord who allows the serfs to work the land in exchange for a portion of the produce they generate. The word 'serf' describes the relationship between the lord (the owner of means of production – land) and the peasant (who works the means of production – the land – in order to stay alive).

In *The German Ideology* and the *Communist Manifesto* Marx and Engels depict four modes of production in history. The first is primitive communism, characterised by a simple division of labour, the existence of negligible quantities of property and a social structure that is effectively an extension of the family and kin relations.

The second is the ancient community, where a class of citizens which owns property through the ancient state, and also property in its own right, is counterposed to a class of slaves who comprise part of that property. Within the citizenry are gradations of rank, or class, dependent both on the quantities of property possessed and status in the still-important familial hierarchies. The division of labour is more developed, with distinctions between town and country and between industrial and merchant wealth creation.

The third is feudalism, where ownership of land is the central division between two major classes but the division of labour is also structured by the division between town and country, with distinctions of status and rank opening up not only between princes, nobles and serfs but also between masters, journeymen, apprentices and a 'rabble of casual labourers'.

The fourth – and final exploitative – mode of production is capitalism. In capitalist societies, the mode of production is characterised by the private ownership of the means of production – land and labour, but also factories, machines, raw materials, and so on. The classes are divided by the fact of individually and privately owning or not owning these means. Capitalism thus simplifies the relations between the classes and, according to Marx and Engels, results in a confrontation between only two hostile camps – the bourgeoisie (ruling class) and the proletariat (working class). The bourgeois class owns the means of production, the proletarian class owns nothing but its labour power which it must sell to the capitalist in order to survive. All other groups between these two hostile camps, such as peasants or shopkeepers, were, for Marx and Engels, transitional groups who would become incorporated into the proletariat as capitalism developed.

The organisation of production not only determines the manner in which wealth is created and appropriated. It also determines people's knowledge and understanding of the reality of their situation. Furthermore, the division of ownership of the means of production combined with the division of labour, establishes fundamental antagonisms and conflicts of interest at the heart of the system. In simple terms, the capitalist has an interest in exploiting the labour of the proletarian to the full in order to maximise profit; the proletarian has an interest in increasing his or her wages to the full in order to accrue the maximum price for their labour. Social inequality and class struggle, even in this simple sense, are built into the organisation of capitalist production. Moreover, the struggle between hostile classes cannot be resolved: the interests of the protagonists are contradictory, not merely different. The proletarian has no vested interest in the capitalist system or any of its institutions, indeed, has a vested interest in its ruination. The struggle thus leads to the development of a range of political structures – most importantly, state structures – for managing and conducting that struggle.

In outlining this historic schema, Marx and Engels were thoroughly entrenched in the major philosophical paradigms of mid-nineteenth century Europe. The theme of evolution – as we noted in Chapter 1 – dominated many of the debates about society, politics and economics. Historical Marxism is a version of this evolutionary paradigm in social theory and philosophy. At Marx's graveside, Engels eulogised Marx in precisely these terms: 'Just as Darwin discovered the law of evolution in organic nature, so Marx discovered the law of evolution in human history' (cited in Foster, 1968: 27). Marx and Engels' historical theories of social change provide the framework in which their economic and political analyses of capitalism are situated.

Economic Marxism

Following the failure of the European revolutionary uprisings in 1848, Marx turned his attention to the mammoth task of explaining the 'laws of motion' of capitalist development. As we have noted, for Marx and Engels the self-destruction of capitalism is inevitable: it is built into capitalism. This auto-destruction is embedded in the economic, as much as the political and historic laws of capitalism. In trying to account for the revolutionary failures and describe the conditions necessary for success, Marx and Engels' prolific works examined the different conditions obtaining in different countries, the different stages of capitalist development, of bourgeois political structures and of trade union organisation. Marx and Engels considered that the homogeneous conditions caused by capitalist wage-relations would be more important than the existence of national identities, so that an international revolutionary workers' movement would eventually liberate all of humanity. In the meantime, Marx produced perhaps the most powerful critical account of the operations of capitalist economies ever written.

The relationship between the two hostile classes in capitalism is structurally antagonistic because it is intrinsically exploitative. The exploitation of the labouring class takes place through the private appropriation by the capitalist class of *surplus value*, or profit. Under capitalism, the worker's labour power has become a commodity, from which value is derived. According to Marx, surplus value is derived from the ratio between *necessary* and *surplus* labour, known as 'the rate of exploitation'. Marx explains this process by claiming that the conditions of industrial production allow the worker to produce more in an average working day than is necessary to cover the cost of his or her subsistence. Only a proportion of the working day needs to be consumed to produce the equivalent of the worker's own value, that is, what is required for the worker to reproduce him or herself. Whatever the worker produces over and above this is surplus value. For example, if the length of the working day is eight hours, and if the worker produces the equivalent of his or her own value in half that time, then the remaining four hours' work is surplus production which is taken by the capitalist (Giddens, 1971: 49).

The search for profit is an intrinsic and necessary feature of capitalism; money becomes capital when it generates profit, so capital can exist only if more capital is being accumulated, and more surplus value being extracted. However, there is a tendency for the rate of profit to fall. This happens because capitalism is a system based on *competition*; capitalists have to compete with each other and, to stay ahead of the competition, must, periodically, modernise the production process in order to reduce the costs of production. This involves spending money on technological development, buying new machinery and so on. But such modernisation has undesirable consequences for the capitalist. First, and most obviously, it eats into the capital that is needed to generate more capital. In spending money on machinery, the capitalist, initially at least, eats into his or her means of generating profit. Second, since 'profit' is the value derived from the margin between necessary and surplus labour, then most profit can be made when there is much more labour than machinery. As the capitalist increases the ratio of machinery to labour, the source of the capitalist's profit is reduced. During this process some enterprises will go bankrupt, some will be taken over by other enterprises and some will survive intact. To try to counter the tendency for the rate of profit to fall, capital intensifies the exploitation of labour through such measures as cutting wages, extending working hours and intensifying the labour process. The decline of the rate of profit is accompanied by a decline in investment and a decline in consumer spending together with job-losses. This process continues until unemployment reaches a high level, the wages of those in employment decline, and thus the conditions for an increased rate of surplus value are created. Investment then picks up and expansion recommences. Therefore, exploitation of labour by capital, and economic crisis, are 'built into' the capitalist system. Economic crisis is an endemic and necessary feature of capitalism and not a result of inefficiencies in the system (Giddens, 1971: 52–5).

However, each time capitalism enters a crisis, some of the smaller enterprises are taken over by the larger enterprises such that there is a tendency towards the growth of giant monopolies. In early capitalist crises, when there are thousands of small enterprises, the effects of a crisis are spread over thousands of localised bankruptcies, takeovers, and so on. In the later crises, however, the system is dominated by massive economic giants whose fall is much more catastrophic than the localised impacts of early crises. They are worse because when the giants collapse they each individually ruin a much larger portion of the total economy and there are correspondingly fewer enterprises who are large enough to take over the fallen giants. Thus, each crisis is worse than the previous one and the 'laws' of capitalism determine that, eventually, the entire economic system must fall in a massive, world-shattering economic crisis.

The exploitation of labour has two further features, for Marx, which are derived from the 'commodification' of labour. First, Marx viewed production as a social process, characterised by social relationships between people. Selling products as commodities in the market disguises the social and human characteristics of their production and reduces them to the appearance of impersonal objects existing independently of the people whose labour created them. For example, when buying a stereo system you might consider its sound quality and whether it is being sold at a reasonable and affordable price, but you are unlikely to consider whether the young, female workers from industrialising countries who most likely put its electronic components in place were employed under reasonable conditions or forced to both work and live in labour compounds for their entire 'useful' lives, paid a pittance of a wage which is sent to support poverty-stricken families and told when to eat, sleep or wash by the factory owner. When you buy a tin of beans, you are not likely to wonder if the tin was mined by a malnourished eight-year-old boy in Bolivia, paid in cocaine, and replaced by another young child a few years later when he becomes too ill to work. When you purchase linoleum, you are not likely to reflect on the illness caused to workers in petrochemical and other toxic industries, which locate themselves in poorer countries such as Mexico where environmental, health and safety regulations are virtually non-existent. You see a product, an object, not the social relations that enabled its production. The product could not exist without this level of exploitation under capitalism: capitalism is dependent on this type of exploitative relationship in order to produce anything at all. The mystification of social relationships – their objectification under the status of 'commodities' – is a key factor in the Marxist analysis of capitalism (Foley, 1991: 101–2).

Second, in the course of producing something, people engage in a creative activity and invest something of themselves in it. However, the end product belongs not to the worker but to the capitalist, and it then

enters the commodity circuit. The product takes on a life of its own. However minimal is the creative energy that goes into making the product, it
is never entirely absent. The separation of the worker from the product of
her or his labours comprises a form of self-alienation: people become
alienated from their own acts of creation. The alienation of people from
their inherent self-creative capacity results in their alienation from fellow
human beings and by extension from humanity as a whole. Private property – the private ownership and acquisition of commodity-objects – therefore creates an essential alienation which can be overcome only through
the former's abolition (Petrovic, 1991: 11–16).

Marx sustained this argument through a detailed analysis of the economic dynamics of capitalism in the four volumes of his major work *Capital*.
The analysis of the dynamics of capitalist production and development
focuses on the way that the systemic features of capitalism result in a structural inequality of power between a dominant class and a subordinate
class who are reduced to the status of commodities by the need to sell their
labour power in the market. In developing this analysis Marx was
concerned to explain the mechanisms by which inequality and injustice
arose and were reproduced within capitalist societies. The main thrust of
the analysis is a critique of the classical liberal view that social reproduction is carried out by numerous atomised individuals engaging in free and
equal market exchanges. The concept of individualism in liberal theory
was one of Marx's main targets, for he saw the notion of 'individualism'
as a mystification of the social character of production.

For Marx, human beings never produce simply as individuals, but as
members of a definite form of society, feudal or capitalist, for example.
Producing something involves relationships with other people and these
relationships are structured by the economic organisation of society. In
capitalist societies, individuals are not at all free and equal as argued in
liberal theory, for these societies are based on class domination and exploitation. The idea of the free individual and the free market disguises the
class character of inequality and the necessary relation of exploitation on
which capitalism depends. Whereas liberalism attempted to distinguish
the political economy from the social economy, Marxism proposes that all
economic activity is fundamentally social and cannot exist without an
organisation of social relationships in a specific mode of production.
The separation between 'economy' and 'society' in liberal theory and
politics is a mystification, an ideological distortion, of the real character of
capitalism.

Political Marxism

The German Ideology traces the origins of the state and other social institutions, such as the law, church and family, to the division of labour. The
state is seen to act in opposition to the real interests of all members of
society by constituting an 'illusory community', which then serves to

disguise the real struggles that classes wage against each other. In the course of history each method of production gives rise to a typical political organisation furthering the interests of the economically dominant class (McLellan, 1983: 146). Marx and Engels describe 'the executive of the modern state' as 'but a committee for managing the affairs of the whole bourgeoisie'. The idea that forms of state, political and legal institutions, religious and philosophic beliefs arise out of the division of labour and reflect the struggles embedded in the relations of production comprises Marxism's base–superstructure distinction, which is most clearly expressed in Marx's short 'Preface' to *A Critique of Political Economy*:

> The sum total of relations of production constitutes the economic structure of society, the real foundation, on which rises a legal and political superstructure and to which correspond definite forms of social consciousness. The mode of production of material life conditions the social, political, and intellectual life process in general. (1986 [1859]: 187)

The economic *base* of society consists of the specific relationships between the owners of the means of production and the dispossessed labourers, and the divisions of labour through which material production is organised. The *superstructure* of society consists of the ideological forms through which the conflict of interests between the two hostile groups of owners and labourers is fought out. Struggles over political representation, freedom of worship, the right to associate in independent unions or take part in public decision-making, and so on, simply reflect the fact that the mode of production is founded on a basic, irresolvable division of power and wealth. The mode of production itself generates political struggle as a constituent feature of its operation. In particular, the capitalist mode of production creates the technological and organisational framework for the satisfaction of all human needs but, by denying the real potentials of what capitalism can achieve, it creates also its own 'gravediggers'. Ultimately, according to Marx and Engels, there is nothing that can be done to prevent the demise of capitalism, for the conditions of its eventual destruction are built into its successful expansion.

The capitalist mode of production, based on a distinction between ownership and non-ownership of the means of production, requires that one class lives off the fruits of the labour of another class. It requires, therefore, that a class of dispossessed workers – proletarians – be brought into existence. In order for the system to work (in order to ensure that workers are willing to work for wages) capitalism must cause the dispossession of the proletariat, and in order for it to expand, more and more people must be dispossessed, so that the size of the proletarian class grows.

Industrial capitalism thus provides the conditions whereby the oppressed class of dispossessed workers becomes the majority class by a very large margin. However, capitalism does not simply increase the size of the dispossessed class, it also leads directly to the politicisation of that class, it forges the proletarian class into a self-conscious, politically organised

force for historical change. It does this not simply by oppressing the proletarians, but by the ways that they are used in the service of capitalism.
Capitalism in Marx's day depended on amassing large numbers of
workers in cities and towns and putting them to work in newly constructed factories and sweatshops of production. It encouraged the elimination of distinctions and divisions within the proletariat – replacing
time-honoured craft skills by machinery, for example – and reduced the
proletariat to the simple common denominator of 'labour'. By doing away
with distinctions among workers it engendered work as a universal
experience – in short, as virtual enslavement to the machine – throughout
the whole working class. Thus, the experience of being 'working class' was
the same in every job, in every region, in every country: capitalism created
the proletariat 'in-itself'. At the same time, however, capitalism also
requires that the working class is a disciplined class, a class that lives
according to the rhythms of production, a class that is organised as a
coherent factor of production. It requires that the working class functions
more or less as a single, giant unit in the cogs of the capitalist system. In
this way, capitalism creates the conditions and the experiences through
which proletarians can realise their true place and their true power in the
capitalist system: it leads to the proletariat becoming conscious of its
organised power in the production of the goods required to satisfy human
needs. Capitalism sets the stage for the proletariat to recognise its common
interests in seizing the means of production from the bourgeois class and
turning these means to the service of its own needs. It thereby creates the
conditions in which the proletariat emerges as a 'class-for-itself', fully
conscious of its position in the capitalist mode of production, organised as
a disciplined force and united around the simple fact of capitalism's
complete dependence on its labour.

Marx and Engels counterposed their analysis of the 'reality' of capitalism to the cherished doctrines of liberal philosophy and theory, producing critiques of the repressiveness of the Prussian state (which Hegel had
characterised as a virtual heaven-on-earth) and poverty in the nations of
Europe. Of particular note was their condemnation (following Saint-
Simon) of liberal concepts of 'rights', 'freedom' and 'individualism'. The
bourgeois revolutions, particularly in England and France, they argued,
far from guaranteeing freedom through an established system of individual rights, maintained people in atomised, alienated relationships to
each other, with overriding self-interest destroying social cohesion. These
political writings are concerned to envisage 'a truly free association of citizens in a state conceived, on the Hegelian model, as the incarnation of
reason' (McLellan, 1983: 143). In direct opposition to liberal political
theory, Marx proposed that rights, as properties of individuals, do not
guarantee freedom but, rather, its limitation. Of liberal conceptions of
'freedom', Marx (1843) wrote:

> The right of man to freedom is not based on the union of man with man, but on
> the separation of man from man. It is the right to this separation, the right of the

limited individual who is limited to himself. . . . The right of man to property is the right to enjoy his possessions and to dispose of the same arbitrarily, without regard for other men, independently from society, the right of selfishness. It is the former individual freedom together with its latter application that forms the basis of civil society. It leads man to see in other men not the realisation but the limitations of his own freedom. (cited in McLellan, 1983: 145)

'Freedom' cannot exist where the institution of private property divides people against each other, and where the state disguises this division, legitimating inequality in the process, through the appeal to individual freedoms based on rights conceived as individual properties.

At their most propagandist, Marx and Engels claimed that capitalism was doomed, that its inexorable logic of accumulation, proletarianisation and the limitation of freedom was simultaneously the logic of its self-destruction. In their more analytical works, however, they acknowledged that the logic of capitalism was in reality a system in struggle and counter-struggle, that the classes mobilised forces, developed strategies, responded to circumstances in order to further their own interests. Whilst the overall political theory suggested the inevitable overthrow of the capitalist base and its superstructures, in the real world of struggle the classes manoeuvred against each other, using whatever resources they had at their disposal, in order to secure advantage in the conflict.

Marxist revisions

As industrialisation proceeded across the West the numbers of industrial workers grew exponentially, and with this growth came the organisation of labour and socialist movements. The development of working class consciousness and political activity across many countries encountered many difficulties as activists and intellectuals struggled to address the various different economic and political characteristics within and between nations. Marxism as a political movement had an often indirect but major impact on working class political action across the industrialised world during the latter half of the nineteenth and early years of the twentieth centuries, primarily through the organisation of three successive International Workingmen's Associations (IWA). The first was established in London and spanned the period 1864–72. The second was established in Paris in 1889, and the third in 1919 in Russia, following the successful Bolshevik revolution in 1917. The second and third Internationals took a specific line on the significance of Marx and Engels' work, notably emphasising the 'objective economic laws' that determine historical change. In this regard, although the second IWA collapsed with the onset of the Great War (re-emerging as a very different organisation after the war in opposition to the Comintern in Soviet Russia), it helped to lay the foundations for Soviet scientific socialism (Drachkovitch, 1966). Whilst the IWA was still in operation, however, Marxism began to break into several distinct schools of thought and action, some of them in direct opposition to the economic determinism and 'scientism' of the IWA's position. These include 'Austro-Marxism' (cf. Adler, 1978 [1904–27]; Hilferding, 1981 [1910]), amongst others, and 'Western Marxism' associated with Korsch (1970 [1923]), Lukács (1971 [1923]) and Gramsci (1971 [1929–35]). One of the defining characteristics of the development of these schools of Marxism is the extent to which they have incorporated Marx and Engels' writings into other philosophical frameworks (and vice versa) with the aim of more clearly understanding people's role in the creation and re-creation of revolutionary movements. They reject the notion of a homogenised mass proletariat that is led towards a scientific socialist ideology simply through the 'laws' of economic development and are much more open to understanding the place of culture and experience in the development of socialist consciousness. In short, they seek to 'radicalise' the Marxist tradition by overturning the focus on scientific objectivity that had been heaped on it through the second IWA and, later, by Lenin and Stalin. Radical Marxisms are concerned with the ways in which the world is constructed by human beings, how it is made and remade in the daily routines and actions of people, and with how the world in which we live is 'imprinted' with our social relations. In other words, how do the social relations among people come to take on real forms – in institutions, the media and culture, in the objects and commodities that surround us? Rather than subsuming questions of race, gender, and so on, under pseudo-scientific economic 'laws', radical Marxisms attempt to develop more constructive philosophies of social change and social theories that consider more complex determinations acting on social institutions and social relations. Even where they reaffirm the primacy of the economy in determining consciousness (as Althusser, for example), this is seen never as a direct economic impact but always as a mediated effect.

The radical Marxist tradition has been influenced strongly by several distinct philosophical schools. These include the critical theory of the Frankfurt School, especially Benjamin (1973 [1940]), Horkheimer and Adorno (1973 [1947]), Marcuse (1964), and Habermas (1976, 1984, 1988), existentialism, especially through Sartre (1976), and structuralism (Althusser, 1969 [1965]; Althusser and Balibar, 1971). Although the contributions of these schools have been very different, they have encouraged the growth of often looser and potentially more inclusive theoretical frameworks for understanding capitalism, its dynamics and uneven operations. Radical Marxisms developed in conditions that were utterly different from those prevailing in Soviet Russia. Whereas the Russian Communist Party had to develop policies for organising and supervising a diverse, diffuse and largely peasant, semi-feudal economic system, the various socialist and communist organisations in Europe were concerned to develop policies and strategies for working within and against fully developed capitalist economies.

The Italian Marxist Antonio Gramsci, for example, explored the means by which the capitalist state maintains its rule – and, by extension, how a workers' state might secure rule. This ruling, he argued, was not based merely on the bourgeoisie's capacity to use force but on its capacity to engineer sufficient consent for its dominance from other important social groups, thereby creating a powerful 'bloc' supporting the bourgeoisie's political interests. The leadership exerted by the bourgeois class was achieved by building a web of political alliances, by disseminating particular ideologies and by creating a network of institutions that could be represented as necessary to the maintenance of order, prosperity, social well-being, and so on. In these respects, Gramsci emphasised the importance of cultural – as well as political and economic – forces in sustaining the capitalist system. This leadership Gramsci called 'hegemony', a concept intended to indicate that the bourgeois class was active in building and maintaining its dominance, not merely defending it.

Working in a very different tradition, Louis Althusser argued that the state served to maintain capitalist social relations by imposing a dominant ideology on society through a network of 'Ideological State Apparatuses'. Notable among these were schools, the media and the institutions of the welfare state. By representing social life *in* capitalism as natural and inevitable, the dominant ideology 'interpellated' (or 'hailed') the working classes into their prescribed roles *under* capitalism. This interpellation naturalised the social roles of men and women, upper and lower classes, the wage-relation, the neutrality of the law, and so on, so that their existence appeared normal and unchallengeable.

The critical theory of the Frankfurt School, in reality a collection of divergent perspectives, attacked the concept of 'Reason' in modern philosophy and, consequently, the value of the Enlightenment in securing freedom from myth and oppression. Horkheimer and Adorno (1973) argued that modern reason had transformed into its opposite and had been placed in the service of domination. Hitler's concentration camps and Stalin's gulags, they noted, were justified on the basis of the highest ideals of Western philosophy – the perfection of humankind, the learning of political philosophy through labour, and so on. At the same time, their operations were exemplars of the efficient use of resources, time and technology. If 'Reason' could be put to such ends, they argued, then it was a tool of domination, not a means of emancipation. On the basis of this analysis, Marcuse (1964) characterised both capitalist and Soviet-communist systems as 'one-dimensional', stifling individuality, creativity and freedom, saturating social life and personal experience with instrumental attitudes and values, especially through the status accorded to science in modern cultures. Marcuse's ideas were reformulated by Habermas (1976, 1984), who argued that instrumental reason was only one type of rationality operating in the modern world and that it could be subordinated to, or at least mediated by, other types of rationality. In particular, Habermas proposed that the 'instrumental rationality' of science could be brought into public, democratic control through the application of 'communicative rationality' to modern institutions. Communicative rationality, which structures our everyday 'lifeworld', is based on at least the possibility of agreement between people and can therefore be used as a means of reaching decisions about the ends to which 'instrumental rationality' should be put.

There is not the space here to explore the extensive details of radical Marxisms, but two points should be noted before we move on to their effects on contemporary debates over welfare. First, from their inception, the various radicalised Marxisms have recognised that the 'proletariat' is not – and probably never will be – a homogenised mass of people who share a single consciousness. Anti-capitalist forces come in many different guises, such that struggle around the capitalist state is not merely the mechanical realisation of an over-arching historical law that predetermines the death of capitalism. Second, the different institutions characteristic of capitalist systems, whilst certainly imbued with the logics of capital accumulation and struggle over wage labour, are not structured only by those logics. Instead, they operate according to several distinct principles and rationalities that have their own independent consequences for the organisation of social and economic life. In particular, such institutions are mediated by cultural dynamics that are divisive and iniquitous in much more complex ways than the division of ownership of the means of production.

Welfare and the paradox of Marxist emancipation

The radical Marxisms we have outlined above encouraged a series of reconstructions and reformulations of Marxist theory from the 1960s onwards. Four dimensions of the reconstruction and reformulation are of particular note in Marxist accounts of welfare. First, there was work applying Marxist theory specifically to the relationships between social policy, the welfare state and the imperatives of capital accumulation, class control or class struggle. Second, the notion of *contradiction* within capitalist societies was emphasised. Both of these reconstructions were centred on theorising the nature and dynamics of the state in capitalism and emerged in a series of books, articles and pamphlets in the mid to late 1970s, at the beginning of the retrenchment in welfare provision. Third, there was increasing interest in the 'cultural' Marxism of Gramsci, especially at the Birmingham Centre for Contemporary Cultural Studies. Finally, there were further revisions resulting from feminist and anti-racist struggles and critiques, resulting in attempts to explain social divisions other than class within a Marxist framework. Both of these latter reconstructions were centred on theorising the intersections between different forms of domination in capitalist societies.

The political economy of welfare (i): class, capital and socialist struggle

The political economy of welfare comprises two related theoretical perspectives: theories of the production and reproduction of capitalist social relations and structures through the institutions of welfare, and additionally through the practices of welfare workers which we examine here; and theories of the systemic crises and contradictions of welfare states, which we examine below. The basis of the political economy of welfare is the proposition that the welfare state is a form or dimension of the *capitalist* state. In other words, the welfare state is not a neutral arbiter of social problems or a structure with the primary goal of ensuring the well-being of the population, but rather an apparatus of the capitalist system underpinned by the imperative of capital accumulation. Specific social policies – housing or social security policy, for example – and the specific practices of the agents of welfare – social and community workers, for example – represent arenas of class struggle in capitalism. Ginsburg rejects the view that the welfare state represents, in any simple sense, a 'victory' for working class struggles. According to Ginsburg (1979: 12), the welfare state does not merely represent concessions won by the working classes from the bourgeois class – a larger 'piece of the cake' in a capitalist system that is becoming progressively more 'socialist'. Nor is the welfare state only the outcome of capitalism's need to reproduce labour power by ensuring at least a minimum of provision for the working class. Rather, the welfare state exhibits a 'dual character' (1979: 19, *et passim*), simultaneously mitigating the bare exploitation and oppression of the working classes whilst also processing and deflecting their demands and struggles.

Gough (1979: 62, 152, *et passim*) also rejects the idea that the welfare state is a 'concession' or a bribe to the working classes consequential on their political and economic struggles. According to Gough, the welfare state simultaneously 'embodies tendencies to enhance social welfare, to develop the powers of individuals, to exert control over the blind play of market forces; and tendencies to repress and control people, to adapt them to the requirements of the capitalist economy' (Gough, 1979: 12). The welfare state acts to enable the 'dominant capitalist class' to formulate and realise its long-term interests (p. 62) by securing capitalist relations of exploitation over time (p. 13). Social policies, here, are understood as examples of, or as specific manifestations of, the bourgeoisie's struggle to maintain its dominance and to reproduce the working class as a willing and able labour force.

Corrigan and Leonard (1978) and the London–Edinburgh Weekend Return Group (LEWRG) (1980) focus on the experiences and practices of people who work in or depend on the welfare state – teachers, social and community workers, NHS employees as well as 'clients' of welfare services. Both adopt elements of Gramsci's theory of hegemony to argue that the welfare state is a means of engineering consent for capitalism. This is achieved, on the one hand, by dividing the population into discrete groups – clients, parents, state and private employees, and so on – whose interests are dealt with through different services, institutions and agencies. Thus, the welfare state performs an important divisive function, making it appear that the common problems of living in capitalism are really unique problems of particular social groups. On the other hand, the welfare state acts as a powerful ideological force, promising 'treatments' for individual problems and privatising what are in reality social problems, such as poverty. Corrigan and Leonard and the LEWRG are especially concerned to highlight how the practices of public sector workers and the recipients of their services can begin the process of overturning the powerful ideological and institutional structures that secure the domination of the bourgeois class. Corrigan and Leonard emphasise the importance of 'strategic' struggle within the organisations (especially the local organisations) of the welfare state and the importance of building alliances between different groups and interests in order to challenge the divisive ideology of the welfare state. The LEWRG (1980: 102) propose that welfare workers, in alliance with their clients and community groups, can construct 'counter-organisations' against capitalist domination of welfare state structures and thereby 'prefigure' socialist organisation in the midst of capitalism.

The political economy of welfare (ii): contradictions of the welfare state

The political economy of welfare, especially in the work of Gough and Ginsburg, acknowledges Marx and Engels' claim that 'crises' are a normal feature of the capitalist economy and that its dynamism is rooted in contradictory relationships between classes and between economic, political and social life. Similarly, although the political economy of welfare, especially in Gough's case, claims that social policy and welfare are subordinated to the imperative of capital accumulation, the perspective rejects the idea that this subordination is direct and unmediated. The concepts of crisis and contradiction are given much more extensive treatment in the work of O'Connor (1974, 1984), Habermas (1976) and Offe (1984). O'Connor's work explains state policies on the basis of the notion of 'fiscal crisis'. In simple terms, the argument proposes that, as more and more demands for state provision are met out of state-directed funds, the interests of the capitalist class are more and more undermined: the 'function' of the state in supporting capital accumulation is contradicted by the 'function' of the state in securing the social conditions for the reproduction of labour power and the system enters a crisis. Habermas argues that a social system (a society) consists not simply of an economic system that periodically undergoes a crisis, but of a number of interacting societal subsystems. These are the economic subsystem, the political subsystem, and the socio-cultural subsystem, each of which may enter into a crisis of its own and each of which may have an effect on the other subsystems. Here, we focus on the work of Claus Offe (1984), whose analysis of the contradictions of the welfare state parallels Habermas' theory and is the most developed of these accounts.

Offe's political theory of crisis is based on the premise that the social formations of advanced capitalist societies are organised around a central principle: the exchange principle. This principle is universal, dominant, but also 'recessive' because the logic of accumulation produces phenomena incapable of integration in the social formation in accordance with the principle of exchange, and which are irrelevant to the creation of surplus value. Following Habermas, it is argued that the fundamental societal contradiction is that between social production and private appropriation. Of crucial importance are the non-market structures which are necessary to maintain the dominance of the exchange principle but which serve, ultimately, to undermine it. The state straddles these contradictions and tensions, devising ever more strategies in an attempt to achieve balance between them. The state itself is not a monolithic unity, but is differentiated in terms of both its structures and the agents who occupy these structures. As a result of these factors, the state is in a permanent condition of managing actual or potential crisis.

The model Offe (1984) develops to explain this position proposes, like Habermas, that the capitalist system consists of three subsystems, each governed by a specific logic or rationale. These are: the economic, where capital accumulation is secured and the logic of exchange relations prevails; the political–administrative, governing rights, resource allocation and so on, governed by political organisational principles; and the normative, encompassing the sphere of culture, values, motivations and socialisation. The three subsystems exist in tension with each other by virtue of the disparities between their functional principles. The tensions require that actual and potential conflict between the subsystems must be managed so as to maintain the reproduction of capitalist exchange relations. This is the task of the political administrative system, which must ensure the dominance of exchange relations across the total system and prevent both the political and normative subsystems from undermining this dominance: it stands between the other two and operates to ensure that a crisis in one system – a crisis of accumulation, for example – does not spill over into a crisis in the other – a crisis in the values of the normative system, for example. The political administrative system is thus split into two parts addressing two other subsystems that function according to different principles. The economic system operates according to the *exchange* of values in the process of accumulation; the normative system operates according to the *sharing* of norms in the process of legitimation. The political–administrative system operates through both coercion and concession as it provides benefits and services in response to demand and regulations to secure a separation between the economic and normative systems.

In 'Social Policy and the Theory of the State' (1984: 91), Offe remarks that the essence of a sociological approach to the state in society consists in the question, What is it that keeps a social system as it is, and what is it that leads to its changing? In capitalist societies, system stability and reproduction cannot be left to 'capital', since it exists only as an abstract category – in the empirical world capital-as-a-whole cannot see or organise a common interest and thus conditions for exchange and accumulation must be organised by the political–administrative system. To try to fulfil this imperative the state must secure sufficient consensus for its policies whilst simultaneously utilising regulatory principles external to the market in such a way that the economic system does not become overly politicised, losing its privatised nature. The state must maintain accumulation, cope with the social consequences of private production and maintain attitudinal and behavioural patterns of compliance with capitalist exchange. Social policy plays an important role in this process: for Offe, 'social policy is the state's manner of effecting the last transformation of non-wage labourers into wage labourers' (Offe, 1984: 92).

Offe argues that, during the period of industrialisation, traditional patterns of working to stay alive are destroyed. People find that their skills and work habits become redundant and their traditional work opportunities diminish. In consequence, labour power is 'disorganised' and mobilised: craft guilds and associations break up and there is mass migration from rural to urban areas. However, it is not sociological simply to assume that, with the breakdown of previous patterns, people will automatically choose to sell their alienated labour power to a capitalist in return for money wages and thereby become proletarians. Sociologically, it is necessary to identify the means by which the switch is achieved. It is true that a certain amount of 'passive' proletarianisation occurs during the period: faced with the prospect of starving to death, a number of people will opt for wage labour as an alternative. But, in theory, a range of alternatives is also open – migration to re-establish previous patterns, begging, establishing alternative economies, pillage, plunder or revolution, for example. The rise to dominance of wage labour, Offe claims, cannot be assumed but must be explained. For, not only must people be brought into the wage labour relation, they must also be contained within it.

The process of proletarianisation is the business of social policy. According to Offe, social policy provides three services in the transformation of work into wage labour. First, it delivers the cultural motivation necessary to persuade workers to opt for wage labour over alternative means of subsistence by providing a system of socialisation organised through schools and family interventions as well as by establishing norms through available media. Second, it provides and regulates a network of institutions that enable people to reproduce themselves as fit and able workers, including exemptions from having to work when too old, too young or too sick, or when they are in education or training, for example. Offe argues that it is important for the state to take on this role in a capitalist society because, left to themselves, the 'informal' institutions of community and family are potentially subversive. If these latter had the means to provide their own exemptions then people might go sick and not return, might retire at thirty, stay at school forever, and so on. In consequence, there has to be a degree of central control over the conditions for the reproduction of the working class. Finally, the state must, at least to a degree, intervene in the labour market to ensure that there is an approximate balance over time between the quantities of dispossessed workers and the availability of wage labour opportunities. Without this balance, the workforce may choose to engage in alternative forms of subsistence in competition with, or even contradiction to, capitalist wage-relations. 'Understood in this way,' writes Offe (1984: 98), 'social policy is not some sort of state "reaction" to the "problem" of the working class; rather it ineluctably contributes to the *constitution* of the working class.' The state must achieve 'labour power' as a commodity to be exchanged in a competitive economic system and at the same time instil shared norms into the population to shore up capitalism's stability. It must act to constitute a working class that will struggle against the state and the wider capitalist system of which it is a part. Social policies are the vehicles or means for realising this contradictory pattern of social development, they are not solutions to contradictions lying outside the state.

Gendering Marxism

The resurgence of feminism in its 'second wave' in the 1960s stimulated two sources of challenge to Marxist accounts of social change, exploitation and inequality. One source was women's direct experience of the structures and practices of left-wing movements for emancipation. The other was the public emergence of a range of creative intellectual debates over the causes and consequences of women's socio-economic position and political status, both inside and outside the movements. Women activists in a range of left groupings became increasingly fed up with the assumption that they would make the tea, type the leaflets, address the envelopes, stick on the stamps, do the shopping, cook the meals and look after the children, whilst men got on with the work of developing, planning and executing strategies for political action. In short, the gendered division of the private sphere of reproduction and the public sphere of political action appeared to reproduce itself in the movements that promised emancipation. Theoretically, women interrogated critically the ways that a proletarian revolution and subsequent socialist organisation of society might lead to their emancipation. After all, following the Bolshevik revolution, when money became tight under the pressure of civil war and an international trade blockade, the first cuts were made to welfare services for women. Revolutionaries like Alexander Kollantra had chronicled the sexism encountered by women in the years following the revolution. Much later, material smuggled out of the Soviet Union indicated that women were struggling under the double burden of full-time work and full-time responsibility for domestic labour and family care, as we noted above (Women and Eastern Europe Group, 1979; Mamonova, 1984). As they were deemed formally to have been emancipated by the revolution, complaint of inequality was a crime and the continued inequality experienced by women was officially silenced. Heterosexual relations were considered to be the only legitimate form of sexual relationship and equality for lesbian, gay and other sexual orientations did not even reach the political agenda. Second wave feminism's critiques of political parties, institutions and ideologies did not apply only to Marxism. The explosion of feminist work across the 1970s and 1980s by women of many different political and intellectual persuasions established a climate of critical appraisal and prompted a major revision of many masculine orthodoxies. It became apparent that the very questions asked about welfare and the state, and the assumptions underpinning theories of welfare, were blind to women's experiences, perspectives and actions.

For example, welfare is commonly theorised as a single system of entitlements to which citizens have, more or less, universal access. The development of welfare programmes, and the development of the welfare state in itself, here represents the outcome of a long haul of struggles and reforms which simultaneously provide some measure of protection for the poor and effect a greater control over them. This type of argument is put forward by Gough and Offe, above. But feminists point out that welfare programmes have never expressed a singular development. Rather, they have always embodied, at least, a dual structure: one dimension relating to men, another to women.

Both entitlement to, and assumptions underpinning, welfare provision display gendered dimensions. For example, the assumption that welfare programmes somehow simply 'provide for need' ignores the fact that providing welfare requires someone to deliver the provision – and that usually it is women who undertake this activity. Many perspectives on welfare miss the most obvious forms of (gender) division in welfare policy and practice.

Finally, a related assumption is that there is a fundamental distinction between the world of welfare and the world of private life. That is, it is assumed that 'welfare' is 'provided' by 'the state'; that the state or some other institutional structure has 'taken over' the functions and roles of families or communities or other informal support networks; and that, in so doing, it has created a system of unnatural dependencies on external agents, or handouts, or institutions, etc. The welfare state is castigated by the right and by the left for its usurpation of personal autonomy or responsibility and 'great debates' rage over where society will end up unless we deal with our own problems, stand on our own two feet, take control over our own destinies, and so on. But examining *who* is doing the welfare work, *where* it takes place, *what* are the differences between the world of public welfare and the world of private care, it turns out that, for many women, the all-powerful, all-interfering welfare state is more conspicuous by its absence than by its presence.

On the basis of this critical questioning, two areas came under immediate scrutiny in feminism's second wave encounter with Marxism: the family and domestic labour. The debates around these issues have been influenced by Engels' (1884) thesis in *The Family, Private Property and the State*, that women's oppression in the family arose with the institution of private property and is reproduced due to the requirements of the reproduction of capitalist relations. In a scathing attack on bourgeois morality, Marx and Engels (1991 [1848]: 190) had previously proposed that 'Bourgeois marriage is in reality a system of wives in common' and that 'it is self-evident that the abolition of the present system of production must bring with it the abolition of the community of women springing from that system, *i.e.*, of prostitution both public and private'.

It is not clear whether Marx and Engels actually asked any prostitutes whether they would like to be abolished or whether they assumed their own invective was sufficiently convincing to persuade prostitutes that abolition would be the best course of action. None the less, Marx and Engels' treatment of women's place in capitalist society mirrored their treatment of other political and social forms. Women's situation was understood as a superstructural support for the social relations of production. Marxist feminism initially took up the 'superstructural' focus of Marx and Engels' work, proposing that gender inequality was rooted in specifically capitalist social relations, with gender divisions in the family and in paid work understood as ideological effects of capitalist class relations (Himmelweit, 1991a: 214). Theoretically, the grounds on which this perspective rested were shaky indeed, given that Marx and Engels' own work simply asserted that women's position was a superstructural effect and also that they expended no time examining the actual relations among and between genders. Similarly, the struggles of many trades unions and other working men's organisations to exclude women from certain types of work (in the higher paid occupations of heavy industry or mining, for example), combined with the gamut of different formal and informal regulations on women's behaviour appears to suggest that the 'superstructure' is not a single site where the 'effects' of capitalism are reflected, but is at least partially active in constructing those effects.

The 'superstructural' perspective was followed by attempts to theorise women's inequality through material processes in the same ways that men's class inequality was theorised in Marxism. This generated a debate about whether housework could be seen as work which generated value in the same way as paid labour. Since women's labour within the home does not produce a commodity for sale, and since women working within the home are not directly employed and subject to the laws of capitalist production governing waged work, the effort to fit domestic labour into traditional Marxist categories became increasingly tortuous, requiring the addition of concepts often borrowed from non-Marxist theoretical frameworks to maintain theoretical integrity. The debate was more than apt in the context of welfare theory because women provide the overwhelming majority of caring services in their homes, in their communities, and in the institutions of the welfare state. Precisely how the paid work of giving someone a bath in a day centre related to the unpaid work of giving someone a bath at home and to what extent either of these represented 'use' or 'exchange' values remains an unresolved problem (see below). Also, whilst a worker in a factory may complete a day's dull and repetitive work at the capitalist's machine, giving the capitalist, say, four of the eight hours as surplus labour, it is not clear who benefits from the 'surplus labour' of a welfare worker. A care worker could provide someone in need of help with bathing with a quick five-minute rub down or could spend an hour talking, consoling, and generally providing much more than the simple 'time' that is expropriated by the capitalist to generate surplus value. Whether the beneficiary of the fifty-five minutes 'surplus' labour is the capitalist or the person who needs help to have a bath in this context really is a moot point.

One solution was to argue that whilst domestic labour does not directly produce surplus-value it does produce use-value, consumed by potential and actual workers within the family, thus contributing to the reproduction of labour power. Debates here centred around whether domestic labour constituted a separate mode of production and housewives a separate class. Once again, however, it is not clear how many women's labours fit into this schema. For example, does a woman paid to clean a private house belong to one class for the few hours that she is in paid labour and then belong to another class when she cleans her own (or a friend's or relative's) house for free? The ultimately unsatisfactory terms of this debate and the difficulty of identifying the material basis of women's oppression within domestic labour led to arguments that the organisation of the family and the sexual division of labour is simultaneously conditioned by capitalism and by patriarchy. Himmelweit discusses Seccombe's proposal that gendered household forms have been

> conditioned by 'patriarchy', another powerful historical force, dependent on the existence of private property but distinct from and not determined by the capitalist mode of production. The nuclear family is 'patriarchal' in that men have the effective possession of household property, the control of family labour and sexual and custodial rights over wives and children. (1991b: 158)

Seccombe argued that the erosion of the patriarchal family – which, for Marx and Engels would occur because of the lack of property ownership characterising the condition of the proletariat – failed to take account of the accumulation of household property by the proletariat, which resulted in 'breadwinner power' and thus the basis for the reproduction of patriarchal relations. The emphasis on patriarchy as an autonomous force led to many debates about how to understand its relationship to capitalism. Again, the theory's complexity soared once non-capitalist modes of production were taken into account, for it became obvious that patriarchy structures relations within all modes of production and pre-dates capitalism. The difficulty of accounting for women's unequal status within traditional Marxist categories led some to reject the attempt altogether. Firestone, for example, argued for a conception of patriarchy as a sex class system, with men as the dominant and exploitative sex class. This strand of radical feminist analysis proposed that the emancipation of women could be achieved only through the overthrow of patriarchy, and identified separatist women's social and political organisation as a condition of effective struggle. Radical feminism was highly influential in focusing attention on men's use of violence as a means of controlling women, and women's sexuality as a key site of struggle. Prompting research and analysis of rape, domestic violence and the legal regulation of women's subordination, this perspective led, both directly and indirectly, to the establishment of refuges for women experiencing domestic violence, the political mobilisation of prostitutes and attention to their physical and psychological abuse against which there is no redress, and campaigns to change the treatment meted out to victims of rape or domestic violence by official agencies as well as the legal regulation of women's sexuality and autonomy.

In these ways, feminism's encounters with Marxism not only led to reformulations in order to include women in Marxist analyses, or a refinement of concepts to make them more accurate, but also shifted the terms of the debate, exposing how the categories of 'labour', 'value', 'class' and 'property' were based on male experiences of work and life. Of particular note here is the fact that for women's lives the distinction between 'work' and 'welfare' is highly problematic. It is not simply that women make up the bulk of paid welfare workers but, more importantly, that their daily work so often leads to welfare in and of itself. Thus, from the point of view of many women, 'welfare' is not a system, policy or structure, that needs to be worked 'in and against'. It is, rather, a routine feature of ordinary life that is worked 'on and for'.

Whilst the intellectual and political success of radical feminism had provided challenges for Marxist analyses of patriarchy, both of these theories were contested from the perspectives of black feminists, for whom the universalism of women's subordination contained in both Marxist and radical feminism meant that historical and contemporary experiences of racism were disguised and black women's specific situations unacknowledged. For black feminist writers, the pervasive racism and discrimination of contemporary societies meant that their experience of the home and domestic sphere, for example, could be very different from that of white women (hooks, 1989, 1991; Brah, 1992a). For some, the domestic sphere represented an important site for the political struggle against racism, and a place where there was respite from the racism of the public sphere (Amos and Parmar, 1984). Others recognised the inequalities between black women and black men, but argued that the struggle against racism united them, providing commonalities of interest and experience not shared by white and black women (Carby, 1982). Although acknowledging that patriarchy structured relations between black men and women, it was proposed that racism could not be conveniently swept under the carpet of capitalist or patriarchal domination. Debates about the historic subjugation of black men, women and children under slavery and colonialism, the role of white, Western women in reproducing relations of racism, the fundamental divisions of both material and cultural resources and practices based on racism, and the differential treatment of black peoples within all social, economic and political institutions, including the welfare state, pointed to the difficulty of incorporating all social divisions under a universal theoretical category, whether 'class' or 'women'. Meanwhile, as these debates within feminism were taking place, other attempts to theorise inequality and oppression on the bases of 'race' and ethnicity were being developed by writers drawing on Gramsci and influenced by the cross-fertilisation between Marxism and cultural studies.

Racism and capitalism

Marxist attempts to incorporate 'race' and ethnicity into its analysis were dominated initially, like the Marxist-feminist endeavours, by interpretations that viewed racial divisions through the same theoretical schema as class divisions. Thus the divisions between black and white workers were understood as creating class 'fractions' which disunited the working class to the benefit of capitalist employers who could more easily exploit their labour power (Denney, 1995). Whether this took the form of political divisions within the working class, or of viewing black workers as a reserve army of labour who functioned to keep overall wages down, the relationship between 'race' and class, like that between gender and class, was most frequently analysed with reference to its functional utility to the mode of production and the reproduction of capitalist economic relations. One of the most persuasive analysts in this tradition was the Marxist–Leninist C.L.R. James, who criticised Stalinism, analysed black struggles both in concert with and independent from proletarian struggles and regarded the Leninist vanguard party as the vehicle for class and racial emancipation (see Grimshaw, 1993). Across the 1970s and 1980s, the commitment to theorising the relationships between race and class was a source of innovation in Marxist analyses, although faith in the vanguard party all but disappeared from serious theoretical work. A number of influential writings on the state, class and race explored the emergence and consolidation of racism following the period of colonial immigration (Sivanandan, 1974; Miles and Phizacklea, 1979; Phizacklea and Miles, 1980). Situating racism in the wider contexts of the capitalist mode of production gave rise to attempts to explain working class racist beliefs and practices. The difficulty of explaining this racism in Marxist terms – as 'false consciousness' or as a phenomenon of the division of labour –

encouraged the view that 'race' and 'class' were not disconnected dimensions of individual identity, with the former always subsumed to the latter. Instead, 'race' and racism were seen as having their own dynamics that gave shape to the meaning and experience of 'class'.

Stuart Hall, for example, insisted that race and class should be understood not as separate entities, but as interconnected modes of experience: class and race form the structures through which black people's lives are shaped: 'It is through . . . the "modality" of race that black people comprehend, and begin to resist, the exploitation which is an objective feature of their class situation' (Denney, 1995: 314).

As Denney explains, Hall, drawing on Gramsci, argues that there is no homogeneous grouping of 'race' – in the same way that there is no monolithic grouping of 'the working class' or 'the ruling class'. Rather, what is important is the relationship, what Hall calls the 'articulation', *between* race and class fractions. At certain times, and under certain conditions, different 'class fractions' form political alliances around particular projects. The state, in this case the welfare state, has a crucial role to play in the construction or mobilisation of alliances or hegemonic 'blocs'. At the same time, authority is exercised within and by the state through such alliances. Hall's theoretical approach to the study of racism focused on the relationships between 'race' and class in the construction of such alliances, introducing a Gramscian cultural emphasis into the political-economy perspectives that had dominated many Marxist writings on 'race'.

Hall's interests lay in examining the ways that the state maintained and reproduced relations of inequality through the cultural mobilisation of consent for the status quo. In *Policing the Crisis*, Hall and his collaborators (1978) focused on the attempt by the New Right, or Thatcherism, to construct a 'hegemonic' project. This project sought to mobilise a bloc of interests around the rejection of the social democratic structures of the postwar period through a discourse of anti-statism, anti-unionism, anti-collectivism and the 'enemy within'. Through the claim that Britain was becoming 'ungovernable' – by blaming union militancy, increasing crime rates, increasing welfare dependency, left-wingers, 'alien black elements' and falling moral standards – the New Right were able to construct an ideological 'crisis' that required decisive action on the part of the state. The Thatcherite project is referred to as 'authoritarian populism' because whilst it draws on popular prejudices and discontents to attract support and legitimacy, the central apparatus of the state is considerably strengthened (cf. Hall, 1982).

By creating a 'crisis' the state obtains consent for its increasing authoritarianism, particularly its repressive and oppressive policing of those constructed as the cause of the crisis – black youth, welfare claimants, unions – legitimating the most coercive measures towards these groups. The drift towards authoritarianism is not, however, peculiar to Thatcherism. Rather, it has been developing across the past century as Britain's global political and economic power has decreased. The response of the state is to use a variety of means to orchestrate and maintain consent for its policies – consent, and hegemony, are never fully secured but constantly have to be achieved. The role of the media in representing black people as the convenient 'enemy within' formed the substance of much of Hall's work in the 1970s, where the 'alien', 'criminal' or 'pathological' representation of black people allowed the state to appeal to the protection or consolidation of 'great' British values, of a 'racially' unified image of 'Britishness' which tried to erase class differences and mobilise different social classes against the common 'black enemy'. In this way, racism is institutionalised and accumulation crises displaced as domestic, moral problems which require, for their resolution, a strong state prepared to act against those constructed as the problem (Morley and Chen, 1996: 12).

Ways of seeing 'race' are not disconnected from the treatment of 'races' in the institutional structures of contemporary capitalism. In recalling a specific construction of 'Britishness' the Thatcherite project provided ideological resources for discrimination both in the formal and informal contexts of welfare provision. In 'informal' terms there has been an increase in the social and cultural separations between racialised communities. The separations between (white) British communities and (black and Asian) British communities are sustained in part by persistent racial abuse and harassment and in part by local housing and development policy, for example (Ginsburg, 1992a). The racialisation of cities and communities is matched by racialisation in the labour market, where the practices of employers, training agencies and schools discriminate on racial grounds. In education and training, the emphasis on 'vocational' subjects for 'low achievers' can serve as a means of distinguishing by 'race' who will be allowed to take up what courses and train in what subjects. Similarly, the widespread racism in British employment is reproduced in the training schemes offered to unemployed youth (Wrench, 1992) whilst the racialisation of social work results in the over-representation of black people in social work's controlling institutions and practices (Dominelli, 1988). In each of these cases, the intersection of 'race' and 'class' cannot be described accurately as the linear determination of racialised experiences by an 'economic base'. The relationships between race and class, in Hall's terminology, comprise 'modalities' of lived experience that are never fixed, but take on different forms in different historical circumstances. In turn the 'articulation' of these relationships at particular times and in particular places provides new means for sustaining wider political projects, such as Thatcherism's authoritarian attack on unions, local government and other forms of collective democracy, the centralisation of political power and the privatisation of social problems.

Concluding remarks

Struggles within and against the state do not 'reflect' the conditions and contradictions of the capitalist mode of production in any simple sense.

Indeed, in many ways, such struggles motivate and maintain political relationships that are specific to a given cultural formation: the racialisation, sexualisation and stratification of economic and social institutions are dynamic conflicts that distribute rights over, statuses in and access to participation in a very wide range of routine everyday contexts. Racialisation, sexualisation and stratification are not in themselves fixed conditions into which people are placed by an overarching system, they are *processes* of division and distribution, control and determination. If the bourgeois class can be said to 'rule', then it rules not only as an economic class, but also as a gender or sex class and a race class as well. This does not mean that Marx and Engels' dictum – that the state is a 'committee' for managing the interests of the bourgeoisie – is necessarily wrong in its entirety. What it does mean is that those 'interests' cannot be reduced simply to the division of ownership and non-ownership in the means of (economic) production. If 'classes' are defined around this division, and if emancipation is conceived in terms of its dissolution, the processes that sustain other important and iniquitous social divisions are obscured. Again, this is not to deny the importance of class stratification in determining people's life-chances in capitalist societies. It is, rather, to emphasise that the social institutions by which those life-chances are organised, distributed and controlled are not merely the 'superstructures' of economic conflict: they also take part in and reproduce equally important struggles around other social, cultural and political divisions in modern society. The struggle for class emancipation contradictorily exposes the divisiveness of the institutions, networks and cultural relations whose non-class dynamics maintain inequalities of race, gender and sexuality. In this sense, Marxism represents a paradoxical theory of emancipation.

PART TWO

AGAINST ENLIGHTENMENT: QUESTIONS ON POWER AND KNOWLEDGE

Preface

As we have seen, the eighteenth century Enlightenment is said to represent a radical departure from orthodox, religiously inspired interpretations of worldly phenomena. In the dominant institutions of learning, statecraft and religious observance of medieval Europe the acceptance of Divine purposes in the organisation of human affairs was a powerful principle of political order. All truths, all knowledge, all purposes and meanings behind human and natural phenomena were subject to Divine plans and intentions. Mere mortals could never ultimately comprehend these intentions but, by complying with the dictates of God on Earth – stipulated by the church – they could be followed and approximated. For the very exceptional, chosen few there was the possibility of 'Divine revelation' in which God might speak a truth directly to a mere mortal.

The Enlightenment narrative tells of the replacement of this institutionalised belief system with one emphasising 'Reason' and the limitless capacity of human knowledge. Enlightenment philosophy suggests that what occurs in the world is subject to entirely knowable and explainable laws that can be discovered and used in directing the progress of human society and securing human mastery over the natural and social world. It is in the discovery of such laws and their subjection to human purposes that knowledge of and power over the world can be combined. Histories of science and progress have charted the great discoveries and the march of philosophical systems as histories of the accumulation and refinement of knowledge, as a long road that has led from ignorance and superstition to understanding and truth. Against this narrative of Enlightened progress both neo-liberalism and poststructuralism propose that 'Reason' and the scientific method have acted not as instruments of emancipation but of domination: that the contemporary world is dominated by Reason in a political sense. Reason is or has become a vehicle through which power is exercised and on the basis of which the populations of European societies have been reduced to acquiescent, dependent or 'docile' individuals.

Neo-liberal analyses, influenced by the philosophy of Friedrich Hayek, reject the Enlightenment belief in scientific knowledge as a guide to social action. Viewing the modern faith in science (especially, but not exclusively, positivist social science) as misguided, neo-liberalism contends that the communal and traditional structures and practices which ensure successful social reproduction have been undermined. The idea of Reason – meaning the faith in technical and scientific knowledge as the only appropriate way of understanding the world – has implied that the character of the social world and its institutions can be identified properly and that, in consequence, a single body, such as the state, can put a vast amount of knowledge together and act upon it. Hayek argues that this is impossible: knowledge is not a quantity that can be acquired and held in the mind, it is dispersed throughout society in such a way that all the concrete details of what exists in the world are too numerous to grasp. The totality of what there is to be known is beyond the intellectual capacity of the human mind. Hayek's detailed expositions on the distinction between 'scientific' and 'tacit' knowledge form the basis of his argument against state planning. The state cannot draw upon Reason and scientific knowledge because such knowledge is only partial, encompassing only a small portion of how the world is actually organised and ordered. In consequence, it cannot, therefore, provide a useful guide for social planning or action. The Enlightenment gave rise to the ideals of equality and social justice, and to the belief that they could be achieved through rational planning and state intervention. Such ideals have resulted in a greatly expanded state power, distorting wealth-generating mechanisms, limiting individual freedoms and creating a servile and irresponsible population.

Poststructuralist analyses suggest that the 'progressive' histories of ever-expanding Enlightenment are glosses on how scientific and rational belief systems came to be embedded in modern institutions. Such belief systems view the progress of scientific discovery as if it were a self-evident progression from a set of (false) beliefs to a set of (true) axioms. Other ways of drawing this history exist which suggest a very different interpretation of the Enlightenment and its effects on human social life. It is by recharting and reinterpreting these accounts of rational and social progress that poststructuralist perspectives challenge conventional theories of social welfare. In particular, they point to the relationships between knowledge of social life and power in social institutions, observing that the techniques and methods for controlling, administering, monitoring and managing a population and its behaviours and needs are constituent features of our definitions, classifications and knowledge of those behaviours and needs. The dominance of the Enlightenment narrative is a feature of the social power that is exerted through the institutions and hierarchies of science and social administration, not an indication of its truth as a historical account.

Although poststructuralism shares with neo-liberalism a rejection of Enlightenment beliefs in scientific knowledge as a neutral force for progressive social development, the rejection takes very different theoretical forms. Both Hayek and Foucault have positivist social science as their target; both, for different reasons, seek to overturn the theoretical underpinnings of Marxism, considered as an exemplar of Enlightenment thought; and they share a common objection to the notion of historical teleology – the idea that history proceeds in a particular direction, towards an identifiable end-state. Similarly, both scorn the notion that society comprises an underlying unity that can be known through the application of the methods of science, and both make the critique of scientific knowledge one of their central philosophical targets. They also share a concern with the complicity between knowledge and power, pointing, in different ways, to the administrative power regulating the actions and freedoms of individuals in modern Western societies. As Hayek saw the faith in science as leading to a totalitarian political system, so Foucault saw it as a 'blueprint for totalitarianism' (Jay, 1984: 527). Yet they diverge considerably in their understandings of how knowledge connects with power. For Hayek, as in neo-liberalism more generally, the state represents the site of coercive power, a power it has acquired through the mistaken faith in its capacity to utilise knowledge and plan accordingly. Hayek maintains a distinction between 'tacit' and 'scientific' knowledge, the former understood as an evolutionary phenomenon underpinning conduct, the latter understood as a specialised type of knowledge that can be supported or rejected. For Foucault and poststructuralist analyses inspired by his work, power is seen as widely dispersed through the social body, and is intrinsically tied to ways of knowing the social world. Knowledge is historically contingent – ways of knowing shift over time – but more than this, 'knowledge' as a thing-in-itself does not exist, it is a product of discourses which are complicit with power regimes. There is no pure, autonomous 'knowing', tacit or otherwise, but only discourses which construct the objects of their knowledge. Thus, for Foucault and those following him, power and knowledge are inextricably linked: to 'know' is to exercise a *way of knowing* that produces objects and subjects, facts and fictions, truths and untruths.

3

Neo-liberalism

'Neo-liberal' philosophy, political economy and policy formulation has been instrumental in generating a series of political responses to the perceived crisis of the Keynesian Welfare State in the 1970s, a crisis containing both economic and political dimensions. Britain, for example, had been beset by economic problems since the end of the postwar 'boom' period in the 1960s. Throughout the 1960s and 1970s there had been a steady decline in Britain's share of world exports of manufactures, as well as falling investment and productivity (Leys, 1983; Gamble, 1985). As a result, unemployment rose, thus adding to public expenditure through the payment of unemployment and other benefits. The steady expansion of the public sector had already increased public expenditure to one-third of the Gross Domestic Product with corresponding increases in taxation. Inflation was also rising: by 1976 it had reached over 26 per cent, and the combination of rising unemployment and inflation served to undermine the legitimacy of Keynesian economic theory (Leys, 1983: 80–6). These economic problems were exacerbated by the oil crisis in 1973, then followed by an international recession. The Conservative government of 1970–74 responded by adopting measures to reduce both public expenditure and the power of the trade unions as a means of creating a basis for a free market economy in preference to a Keynesian mixed economy. However, one of the earliest major legislative measures, the 1971 Industrial Relations Act, generated intense opposition from the trade unions, numerous strikes, and the declaration by the government of five states of emergency. The Conservatives were unable to pursue their preferred policies and, following a major confrontation with the unions, especially the National Union of Mineworkers, were defeated by the Labour Party in the 1974 general election. Following this defeat Margaret Thatcher replaced Edward Heath as leader of the Conservative Party.

The Labour Party took office facing numerous economic problems, including a huge balance of payment deficit, high inflation, rising public expenditure and an antagonistic trade union movement. Labour's *modus operandi* involved trying to restore the relationship with the unions by establishing a 'social contract', where discussions between government, trade unions and business aimed at securing the cooperation of unions in various counter-inflationary measures, particularly in relation to wage restraint. In return for cooperation, the government repealed the 1971 Industrial Relations Act and improved job security through the Employment Protection Act. Other measures included putting the taxation system on a more progressive footing, initiation of nationalisation programmes and commitments to increase the 'social wage' – collective services and social security benefits. However, economic difficulties increased and in 1976 a sterling crisis led to a major devaluation of the pound, forcing the Labour government to seek a loan from the International Monetary Fund. The conditions of borrowing stipulated a deflationary approach to economic policy and, under the weight of economic pressures, the Labour government's strategy was unsustainable. By 1978 the trade unions were refusing to accept a fourth year of wage restraint and a series of strikes signalled the collapse of the social contract (Leys, 1983: 80–8).

Throughout the 1970s neither the Conservative Party nor the Labour Party was able to halt apparent economic decline, and both parties saw an increase in political activity from their radical wings. The new right were organising in the Conservative Party, arguing for a complete break with the economic and social foundations of Keynesianism, whilst the socialist left was organising in the Labour Party. There was, in short, widespread rejection of the conventional postwar wisdom of a happy marriage between the Keynesian Welfare State and advanced capitalism. Not only did the Keynesian Welfare State appear to have exhausted its problem-solving potential, it was seen by many to constitute part of the problem – its structures and practices had generated consequences which required radically different solutions.

For many in the Conservative Party, neo-liberalism provided intellectual analyses of postwar problems which offered such radical solutions. The success of neo-liberalism in penetrating the political and policy agenda since the 1970s therefore arose in the context of the crisis of Keynesianism and the political and economic problems associated with it. Neo-liberalism has aimed to provide both a moral and intellectual case for capitalism, arguing that social democracy, as concretely manifested in the Keynesian welfare state, is economically and socially ruinous. In the case of the leading theorist of new right thought, Friedrich Hayek, whose work has been extremely influential in shaping the policy agenda in both the West and the newly marketised economies of the ex-Soviet bloc (Wainwright, 1994), social democratic structures are seen as prefigurative of a fully developed socialism leading inexorably to an authoritarian political state.

Hayek was a life-long opponent of the social, economic and philosophical doctrines influencing the growth of social democracy in the West. He had been educated at the University of Vienna, which, in the early decades of the twentieth century, saw an extraordinary growth of new ideas and debates cutting across the disciplines of philosophy, economics, psychology and social and political science, revolving around questions of scientificity, subjectivity, language and culture in the development of knowledge, and the role of rationality and irrationality in human behaviour. Hayek's position as director of the Austrian Institute for Economic Research between 1927 and 1931 saw the beginning of his argument with scientific positivism (cf. the discussion of Beveridge in Chapter 1). The Austrian Institute was home to a form of economic theory which stressed the role of subjectivism in economic processes. His early immersion in the intellectual debates between logical positivism, Austro-Marxism and subjectivist economics were to exert a powerful influence on his social philosophy, which took an urgent and poignant turn with the rise of national socialism and Nazism in Europe in the 1930s. The persecution of Jewish, travelling, homosexual and mentally disabled people during the 1930s, the diaspora of Jewish intellectuals, and the outbreak of war was the context in which Hayek turned his intellectual energy to understanding what organisation of socio-political structures could prevent the tragedies witnessed during this period.

Whilst Nazism was gathering force in Europe, Hayek was in post as Professor of Economic Science at the London School of Economics, where he had been engaged by William Beveridge, and where he was to debate vigorously with Maynard Keynes. The contemporaneous dominance of Fabian socialism and its penetration of liberal thought was a source of great concern to Hayek. As his intellectual position became increasingly marginalised, so that by the 1950s Austrian subjectivist economics barely existed any longer, Hayek's writings became more and more prolific. Eventually, they found a home in an Institute set up in 1956 specifically to propagate them, and to develop social and economic policies based upon their ideas, this being the Institute of Economic Affairs (IEA). Its early members had been involved in the Mont Pelerin Society, established shortly after the Second World War as a forum for liberal intellectuals to share their ideas and fears concerning postwar socio-economic development. The IEA continues to devote itself to the production of policy alternatives to postwar state organisation and remains an important participant in debates on different aspects of welfare provision. There is now a number of Institutes world wide performing this function and, in Europe, IEA-inspired Institutes have been established in Brussels, Paris, Stockholm, Italy and Spain (Green, 1979: 153–4).

Other Institutes devoted to the dissemination of liberal principles include the Adam Smith Institute, the Institute of Directors and the Institute for Policy Studies, which form an interlocking network, with members from one group sitting on boards of others, acting as consultants and working within several organisations which, jointly, have been instrumental in propagating policy proposals, analyses and debates about welfare reform (Kavanagh, 1987). During the early 1970s many members of the Conservative party, including Keith Joseph and Margaret Thatcher, took up the ideas associated with Hayek and other neo-liberal writers and, following the 1979 Conservative election victory, various 'new right' academics were taken on by the government as policy advisers. The 1970s saw the creation of an influential grouping within the Conservative Party which decisively broke with the 'one nation' Toryism associated with the 'wet' wing of the party, and who can be seen as forming a party within the party. The policy shift that followed the 1979 election, often described as 'anti-union, anti-welfare and anti-egalitarian' (Leys, 1983: 89), was christened 'Thatcherism', after the then Prime Minister, Margaret Thatcher, and represented a major reorientation of British social policy (Gamble, 1988; Jessop et al., 1988; Hay, 1996). Whilst Hayek's ideas have not been taken up by governments in any 'pure' form, or in a way that encompasses the intentions of Hayek and those who develop his ideas (Green, 1996), they have provided intellectual legitimation for a political sea-change in global policy agenda. Hayek's 'revolt against [French] Enlightenment' amounts to a sustained critique of some of the founding assumptions on which the social democratic welfare compact between state, society and economy was constructed in the postwar era. An examination of Hayek's brand of liberalism and its elaboration in new right philosophy is therefore a prerequisite for understanding the contemporary character of social policy and welfare.

The importance of Hayek's work in changing welfare policy needs to be understood in relation to other significant theoretical currents in neo-liberal theory which have all contributed to a major reappraisal of postwar institutions and practices. A number of different theoretical schools has been engaged in the analysis of postwar social and economic organisation including Milton and Rose Friedman's free market economics, public choice theory and the moral philosophy of the IEA itself, which has published extensively on welfare issues. These positions, located within a neo-liberal view of the state–society relationship, have sustained a formidable barrage of criticism directed at the Keynesian Welfare State. The chapter begins with an outline of Hayek's work, which, unlike the other perspectives examined here, develops an extensive philosophy on which to rest a theory of welfare. We then discuss the work of Milton Friedman, whose formulation of monetary theory has been a formative influence in economic policy and, together with Rose Friedman, in emphasising the issue of choice in public and private services and provision. The Friedmans' critique of state welfare gained authority at the same time as public choice theorists added to the critical appraisal of political and bureaucratic structures. We go on to explore attacks from public choice perspectives on both the possibility of public institutions delivering 'user friendly' services and on the distortion of the political process occurring when the state is extensively involved in such provision. Finally, we outline some recent applications of neo-liberal theory to questions of cultural change, illegitimacy, and family formation.

A counter-philosophy of welfare

Hayek's lifelong objective was to construct a philosophy of freedom through a restatement and reformulation of classical liberalism. Alarmed by the growing popularity of Fabian socialist ideas in the 1930s and then by the influence of Keynes' economic theory following the publication in

1936 of *The General Theory*, Hayek began work on a detailed critique of the concepts of reason and social justice. These two concepts remained centrally important to all of Hayek's subsequent and prolific publications, as he considered that they provided the basis for crucial political developments during the twentieth century – developments whose results, Hayek argues, have been catastrophic. His assessment of modern socio-political institutions draws on neo-Kantian philosophy, jurisprudence and Austrian micro economics. His rebuttal of socialist and social democratic currents of economic and political theory emphasises the importance of ideas as a basis for policy development and political mobilisation, and he thus strove to provide a counter-philosophy capable of informing alternative developments, stating that 'Policies must grow out of the application of a common philosophy to problems of the day' (Hayek, 1960: 5).

The central principle informing Hayek's work is 'freedom', defined in a negative sense as an absence of coercion upon the private activities of individuals. By coercion Hayek (1960: 20) means 'such control of the environment and circumstances of a person by another . . . that he is forced to act not according to a coherent plan of his own but to serve the ends of others'. Hayek's philosophical individualism is inextricably linked to his negative concept of freedom since, for Hayek, preserving the freedom of private individuals is the overriding concern of liberalism. Thus, virtually all of his works have been concerned to argue that the collectivist, state-planned socialism of the British Fabians, which gained considerable intellectual ground during the 1920s and 1930s, was a fundamentally misconceived project, and the postwar Keynesian Welfare State completely antithetical to the preservation of individual freedom and the 'spontaneous order' which is both dependent upon, and in turn protective of, such freedom.

Hayek proposes an important distinction between two types of society: a 'spontaneous order' (the liberal society) and a 'constructivist', state-directed society (social democratic and communist). The politics and philosophy of liberalism derives from 'the discovery of a self generating or spontaneous order in social affairs . . . an order which made it possible to utilise the knowledge and skill of all members of society to a much greater extent than would be possible in any order created by central direction' (Hayek, 1967: 162). Hayek's epistemology is located in a strand of post-Kantian critical philosophy in the sense that he rejects the proposition that subjects can know the world-as-it-is, in its essential or unmediated state. He also eschews the notion that any phenomenon, natural or social, contains 'inherent properties'. Thus, he rejects positivism in any discipline and stresses the role of cultural factors in the development of knowledge (Hayek, 1952, 1979, 1988). However, Hayek goes further than the post-Kantians by arguing that although knowledge of the world is mediated by mind and subjectivity, the amount of knowledge we can ever have access to is a tiny fragment of what there is to be known. This is the starting point of his theory of knowledge which, in turn, is crucially important in understanding his position on the relationship between markets, democracy and freedom.

Social evolution and knowledge

Hayek's theory of knowledge is based on a critique of French Enlightenment rationalism, which latter, he argues, translated directly into political structures inspired by the ideals of social justice and equality (Hayek, 1944, 1982:II, 1988). His theory begins with an attack on the concept of reason. The idea of 'reason', he argues, presupposes that the necessary character or properties of phenomena can be known to the human mind, thereby making a metaphysical guide to human action possible. Hayek's argument is that this is impossible – we can never, in fact, fully understand the world. Instead, Hayek argues that knowledge is an evolutionary phenomenon characterised more by fragmentation than coherence. Knowledge is dispersed throughout society: the myriad concrete details which exist in the world are impossible to grasp in their entirety. Consequently, the totality of what there is to be known lies outside the capability of the human mind to discern.

The most important form of knowledge possessed by human beings is, for Hayek, 'tacit' knowledge. Tacit knowledge develops during the evolutionary process in the course of human cultural practice, and is largely unstated and unexplainable in abstract terms. All social life depends on this tacit knowledge, which is concretely manifested in social and moral rules, customs and norms. Although often unarticulated and not consciously grasped, tacit knowledge is transmitted through learning the 'rules of conduct' taught by churches, families and other social institutions, for example. On the basis of the theory of tacit knowledge, Hayek develops his concept of a 'spontaneous order'. This concept is then counterposed to Platonist traditions which assume that knowledge is explicit and that the use of reason can bring coherence to the world, in the sense that such knowledge can be utilised as a basis for social planning and direction. Hayek opposes then, the dominant strand of thought associated with 'the Age of Reason' – the post-Enlightenment faith in a positive science as a progressive force which could understand, and consequently eradicate, social problems. Here, Hayek is providing a critique of a central aspect of Enlightenment thought – the notion of the human Subject – where people are constructed as fully conscious agents capable of total self-knowledge. For Hayek this is a myth – knowledge is accessible only in partial, fragmented form: it is impossible for us to access 'the real' and to achieve a correspondence between reality and our knowledge of it (Hayek, 1952, 1982:I, 1982:II, 1988).

Instead, Hayek argues that all order in the physical and social world arises from the spontaneous formation of self-regulating structures. In the course of evolution, tacit knowledge becomes embodied in certain practices and institutions. In turn, these latter are the products of the natural selection of rules of action. Hayek sees this development as a process of cultural adaptation through competition: of the multiple sets of practices and rules which develop during the evolutionary process, those allowing for the most functional adaptation to the external environment become dominant (Hayek, 1982:I, 1982:II). All evolution is seen as a process of continuous adaptation to unforeseeable events, contingent circumstances that cannot be predicted. Against 'those philosophers like Marx and Auguste Comte who have contended that our studies can lead to laws of evolution enabling the prediction of inevitable future events' (Hayek, 1988: 25–6), Hayek offers a critique of historicism – the belief that there is an overall pattern to history or laws governing its progress – arguing instead that history is uncontrolled and directionless.

The notion of 'tradition' is therefore important to Hayek since tradition is what transmits the 'successful' cultural rules and norms to generations through time. Cultural rules and norms constitute the conditions for the optimum promotion of general human reproduction and welfare. Hayek builds this concept of human culture from his theory of the 'spontaneous actions' of individuals and counterposes it to a concept based on a theory of 'purposeful design'. Aspects of human culture, such as values and laws, arise, for Hayek, as adaptive strategies in the evolutionary process, and those which become dominant embody the tacit knowledge necessary for successful social reproduction.

The spontaneous order that prevailed in the eighteenth century embodied a set of 'commercial morals' which operated universally in the Western world (Hayek, 1988). They were sustained by a process of socialisation, in the family, community and economic life, which latter in turn was geared to the functioning of the small enterprise in a competitive market economy and upheld by a limited state structure. These institutional and social arrangements were, for Hayek, highly successful, and had evolved through processes of adaptation rather than being 'deliberately designed'. However, they were already subject to influences which would undermine them, influences stemming from the development of Rationalism in the sixteenth and seventeenth centuries (Hayek, 1982:I). The shift in social thought represented by, in particular but not exclusively, French Enlightenment philosophies set in train a series of events which would dissolve these arrangements, disturbing the delicate (spontaneous) balance between tacit knowledge, social institutions and markets.

The rise of social reform movements in the nineteenth century and the spread of socialist ideas result from the re-emergence of the repressed 'primitive instincts' of solidarity and altruism which existed in 'primitive' society. Such instincts and the reform movements which express them, Hayek argues, are dysfunctional in recent history because they lead to attempts to plan modern societies and to control the distribution of income and wealth for political purposes. The reform movements were inspired by the French concept of liberty which incorporated notions of equality and social justice with the result that the 'English' conception of individual freedom was gradually displaced. Since the end of the eighteenth century the classical liberal view has been systematically undermined by an intelligentsia whose inspiration has been Rationalism, reinforcing the belief that social institutions and structures could be successfully planned and directed, thus undermining 'the foundation of the moral and political belief in freedom' (Hayek, 1960: 72, 1982:I).

Since Hayek views social institutions as the unintended outcomes of the actions of individuals pursuing various ends, the attempt to plan and organise such institutions in advance constitutes a limitation on the ends that may be pursued and thereby a constraint on the freedom of action. Planned and organised institutional arrangements – the expansive state, the regulated market – function, albeit indirectly, to coerce individuals into pursuing certain ends rather than others, engaging in particular activities rather than others, thereby destroying the spontaneity which, for Hayek, is the very basis of freedom (Hayek, 1960: 56, *et passim*).

Knowledge and markets

Hayek is a micro economist who argues against the methodology of macro economics. It is the notion of economics as a predictive, objective science which he objects to and, in discussing the methodology of the social sciences, he argues that the belief in science as a neutral, objective force for progress is one of the great mistakes of the French Enlightenment philosophies. At the heart of this critique are Hayek's (1952, 1979) views on subjectivism and human knowledge, according to which there is a fundamental and irreconcilable difference between the objects of study of the natural and social sciences. Thus he rails against 'the tyranny ... which the methods and technique of the Sciences in the narrow sense of the term have ever since exercised over the other subjects' (Hayek, 1979: 20).

He rejects the claims of macro economics to be able to predict economic behaviour through the development of aggregate categories and instead stresses the role of interactions and subjectivity in economic processes: 'Unless we can understand what the acting people mean by their actions any attempt to explain them, that is, to subsume them under rules which connect similar situations with similar actions, is bound to fail' (Hayek, 1979: 53). He begins the critique of macro economics by making a distinction between the economy and the market, or 'catallaxy'. The term 'economy' describes a set of deliberately coordinated actions designed with particular goals in mind, whereas a market system refers to numerous interrelated economies in which individuals pursue their own individual, multiple ends (Hayek, 1982:I, 1982:II, 1988). These may be purely selfish, private ends, but the overall result is the increased well-being of all – a result that could not have been deliberately arranged. Thus, 'catallaxy' refers to 'the special kind of spontaneous order produced by the market through people interacting within the rules of the law of property, tort and contract' (1982:II: 109).

Hayek's thesis is that central state planning will always remain inefficient compared to market processes because in a centrally planned economy there is no mechanism to compensate for the role played by competition and the price system, which, Hayek argues, perform the critical function of transmitting tacit knowledge throughout fragmented markets.

The prices and wages systems are the mechanisms that coordinate the millions of activities making up an economy. They do this by signalling information to producers, consumers and resource owners – the price mechanism indicates needs, preferences and availability. Only the price mechanism can fulfil this function because of the social dispersion of tacit knowledge and, additionally, the subjective dimensions of economic behaviour. Price and, hence, value for Hayek, is not an objective condition inhering in the quality of an object but is, rather, a reflection of the preferences and decisions of individuals. Value is rooted in a subjective process that can never be precisely charted. The ideas and concepts held by people are an important influence on economic outcomes which macro economics can never grasp (Hayek, 1979). By ignoring this fact, macro economics constructs a view of the economy at odds with the reality of economic life. Hence, for Hayek, aggregate economic categories, for example, national income, aggregate demand, output etc., are to be treated with extreme caution because these categories ignore a complex set of relationships that cannot be counted as fixed 'constants'. Because, for Hayek, economic activity is a dynamic 'process of discovery', then all aggregates depend upon the micro economic activity of agents – which by definition contain a strong subjective element and therefore remain largely unpredictable. This concept of value is opposed to the objectivism of, for example, Ricardo and Marx, where value is seen to be derived from labour. Hayek argues that such a perspective constructs essential aggregates, independent of human subjective actions and preferences, where, in fact, none exist.

The question of 'labour' is treated by Hayek not as a matter of production but as a question of wages in the market. This is because, in order to satisfy basic needs, people must earn money. However, to do this requires knowledge of where one's skills or labour might be required. Given that no individual could possibly know all of the prevailing conditions and characteristics of the production process and employment relation, Hayek argues that, as with the relationship between price and value, a social mechanism is needed to match skill availability with skill requirement. Once more, the market is seen as the best mechanism for achieving this match, thereby generating income and creating wealth. Thus, the market plays a central role for consumers and producers in the discovery of and provision for new needs and desires; it is the means by which knowledge is encoded and transmitted by agents: by taking individual decisions and realising subjective preferences, all the dispersed knowledge that is unavailable to individual agents is ultimately utilised; and it enables the distribution of wages and incomes by matching skills and tasks.

Competition is seen to be a key element in this process because of Hayek's insistence that the sheer volume of information dispersed throughout society could never be centrally coordinated in an effective way. This restates the problem of how the optimum utilisation of the knowledge, skills and opportunities that are dispersed among millions of people can be utilised (Hayek, 1982:III: 68). For Hayek, competition simultaneously encourages the development of new products for which there is a demand and lowers costs due to the need for efficient production. Competition, wages and prices within the market system, which is the key mechanism, enable a lucid response to the uncertainty of economic activities and social needs to be made, as well as enabling the most efficient utilisation of resources in the economic process. Competition within the market, whilst allowing for the maximisation of economic production and individual preferences and goals, also secures social solidarity through the interdependence of individuals. The 'primitive instincts' towards collectivism which characterised earliest societies are replaced by solidarity promoted by the division of labour in the course of evolution towards competitive capitalism. Thus, for Hayek, the market provides the conditions through which overall social welfare is realised.

Inequality and freedom

To the extent that the market is distorted by centralised planning and state intervention, the natural path of social development is deflected, with the consequence that moral values are undermined, the socialisation process ceases to operate effectively, the function of the head of the family in accumulating capital is impaired, and there emerges an erroneous faith in the scientific control of social development together with an overestimation of human capabilities.

By 'morals' Hayek means traditional 'tenets of religion, such as the belief in God, and much traditional morality concerning sex and the family . . . but also the specific moral traditions . . . such as private property, savings, exchange, honesty, truthfulness, contract' (Hayek, 1988: 66–7). Thus, morality consists in a set of pro-family and pro-capitalist attitudes which were culturally transmitted via church, family and other social institutions. Under the influence of Cartesian and Rationalist philosophy – which posited that truth must be proved, and therefore that which cannot be proved must be open to doubt – this moral framework came under siege (Hayek, 1952, 1982:I, 1988). The moral tradition of eighteenth century England, for example, had flourished 'merely because it had worked', not because any adequate justification for it existed. The faith in reason led to a belief that people could rationally plan the structures of society and the path of social organisation, thus creating the legitimation for the interventionist state and subjecting traditional moral values to dispute and uncertainty.

Whilst market process will generate unpredictable and unequal material outcomes, Hayek argues that the overall benefit outweighs individual disadvantages. In modern, pluralist societies, people's activities will be directed by subjective preferences and values. The multiplicity of aims found in the market allow individual freedom and the values associated with it to flourish. By its interventionist nature, according to Hayek, the twentieth century state is a coercive and unnatural apparatus whose very existence gives rise to two crucial consequences: a restriction of individual freedom and a parallel decline in individual responsibility. For Hayek, individual freedom is a moral principle which 'needs to be accepted as an overriding principle of government and all particular acts of legislation' (Hayek, 1960: 68). Liberty is considered not as a particular value but 'the source and condition of most moral values' (Hayek, 1960: 6). With the decline in individual freedom comes a corresponding decline in individual responsibility as the state takes on an increasing role in providing for the population's welfare. The latter requires large-scale intervention in economic affairs, stifling individual initiative. In order for societies to continue to adapt successfully the state must refrain from such intervention. The ensuing inequality, which Hayek admits follows logically from the minimalist state, is considered as the inevitable outcome and unavoidable correlate of individual freedom. This is because only *formal* equality, that is, equality before the law, is compatible with such freedom. Any attempt to institute *substantive* (material) equality leads directly to the coercive curtailment of action and goals and thus the destruction of liberty. For Hayek, substantive inequalities in the market can never be considered morally unjust because 'injustice' requires that an outcome be intended. Market outcomes are unintended consequences of impersonal processes, and this leads Hayek to argue that the notion of social justice is a 'mirage', an illusion premised upon a fundamental misunderstanding of the notion of justice.

Justice and the welfare state

> We do not object to equality as such. It merely happens to be the case that a demand for equality is the professed motive of those who desire to impose upon society a preconceived pattern of distribution. It is this which is irreconcilable with freedom. (Hayek, 1960: 87)

The preservation of liberty requires abstract, general rules which allow individuals to pursue their various interests with a minimum of interference. Hayek's view of law and justice rejects concepts of natural rights and natural law, advocating instead a procedural theory of justice in which justice is measured by the Kantian test of universality. If a particular law is to be considered just, it must be universally applicable. Such laws are called 'just rules of conduct' by Hayek, because they act as guides to conduct, and are 'end-independent' in the sense that they lay down only a general framework for action rather than specifying particular outcomes. These 'end-independent' rules preserve society as a 'spontaneous order'. In order to be just, the legal system must treat all citizens alike and must ignore differences and inequalities in individuals' material circumstances. Hayek is concerned that this conception of law and justice has been replaced in the postwar period by laws informed by the concept of 'social justice'. Such a development arises out of the attempt to redress inequalities through legislative measures and therefore to treat social groups differently (Hayek, 1982:II). The attempt has resulted in the subordination of rules of just conduct to public law, with individuals becoming increasingly subject to state authority.

In Hayek's view, there is no justification for allowing the state to redress substantive inequalities. This is, firstly, because market outcomes cannot be considered unjust. For an action to be unjust requires that someone intended such a consequence. However, as material inequalities are the unpredictable result of anonymous forces, not the responsibility of a motivated agent, they cannot be considered unjust. Secondly, it is Hayek's view that the assumption of greater powers of direction by the state, and the use of those powers to implement legislation to benefit certain groups ('end-dependent' rules) is antithetical to the application of general rules equally to everyone ('end-independent' rules) which latter are required to preserve freedom. It is crucially important, for Hayek, that rules of law merely provide a framework for action which applies to all people without exception, rather than specific measures directed at particular social groups. Hayek contends that social justice has been aimed at the latter and is thus, in reality, distributive justice. No single agency is capable of dispensing social justice, for there is no agency against whom to claim it. The state, as the arbiter of such justice, effectively becomes the organisational mechanism of distribution.

The demand for social justice for certain groups of people results in legislation which aims to manipulate outcomes, and this corrupts the legal framework which preserves individual freedom. During the twentieth century the acceptance of social justice as a legitimate value has become so widespread that 'almost every claim for government action on behalf of particular groups is advanced in its name' (Hayek, 1982:II: 65). Those who promote ideas of social justice are socialist, in Hayek's view, because they demand state intervention in income distribution. Hayek argues that although the appeal to social justice originated with socialism it has now been embraced by all political, educational and humanitarian movements, including a large section of the Christian clergy. The idea of 'social justice' has therefore claimed the moral high ground. Against this, Hayek proposes that state intervention leads inevitably to state planning and authoritarian control, corrupting the classical liberal framework most conducive to the preservation of freedom. Rather than supporting the 'rules of just conduct' contained in the universalist legal framework, rules developed to serve social justice endow the state with ever-increasing power over its citizens. Citizens become objects of state administration as more and more private activities are brought within its jurisdiction, leading to an almost completely administered society with a consequent loss of freedom of action (Hayek, 1982:II: 134–49).

As well as the dangers to individual freedom, achieving particular material results for different social groups is considered dysfunctional for further reasons. In order for resources to be redistributed, some criteria of merit or need will have to be developed. However, achieving consensus on these criteria is impossible, as not everybody will agree on the relative importance of categories of needs or the merits of particular types of work. In the latter case Hayek is referring to the futility of incomes policies, which interfere with normal market processes that signal relative values for skills and labour. In the former case, Hayek is concerned about the effect on the democratic process and the rule of law.

Absolute need or poverty has been abolished by capitalism, according to Hayek. Relative poverty will continue as long as inequality continues. The best way to deal with relative poverty, Hayek argues, is to allow the accumulation of aggregate wealth which 'trickles down' to those in the bottom socio-economic groups, eventually raising overall living standards. However, the proliferation of special interest groups requesting government intervention is likely to destroy the conditions which ultimately benefit the poor. It is impossible, according to Hayek, to guarantee protection to all disadvantaged groups because of the increasing state apparatus, increasing state expenditure, and increasing central direction and intervention that would be required. The only 'just principle' is not to grant any form of special protection to any group. The principle of justice must be universally applied but interest group activity destroys the notion of universalistic equality before the law.

This problem of interest groups is manifestly at its worst in Britain, Hayek (1982:III) states, because the principle of parliamentary sovereignty gives unlimited power to a group of elected representatives whose decisions are conditioned by the need to 'bribe' groups of voters by granting special concessions paid for through the tax system. Because such concessions are thought to be socially just, the process becomes routinised and creates expectations that government will intervene in all aspects of income distribution and redistribution. When income distribution becomes determined through the political process, pressure groups of all sorts look to the state for certain privileges leading to increasing political intervention in economic processes. It is for this reason that Hayek objects to the idea of social rights. He makes a distinction between civil rights (the right to vote and to own property) – and substantive rights associated with the concept of 'positive freedom' – the freedom to realise one's potential and to control one's environment. This latter concept Hayek attributes to socialist thought. Hayek argues that the development of socio-economic rights, legitimised by notions of social justice, is inimical to the concept of negative freedom and procedural justice, which Hayek sees as necessary to the reproduction of the 'spontaneous order'. Hayek finds it extremely threatening that socio-economic rights, which he argues originated with the Bolshevik revolution and are a concrete expression of Marxist politics, have been legitimised within the Universal Declaration of Human Rights adopted by the General Assembly of the United Nations in 1948. Going through the rights laid out in this declaration, which are aimed at ensuring that all citizens can participate fully in social life, Hayek writes that such rights can exist only in a society totally directed and administered by the state. The state must have such all-encompassing powers to enforce these rights that it effectively becomes a totalitarian state, in the sense that the 'rules of just conduct' which guarantee individual freedom disappear, along with personal responsibility for decision-making and action in many spheres of social and economic life (Hayek, 1982:II).

Therefore, the development and spread of rules that determine material rights lead to an erosion of the rule of law. The growth of taxation to fund the welfare state requires that, whilst people are considered equal under general law, an egalitarian economic system controlled by the state involves treating people differently, thereby breaking the rules of general equality. The Keynesian Welfare State is seen as leading to increasing regulation of citizens, increasing taxation, increasing distortion of market processes, and a gradual erosion of liberty which is both practical – the welfare state is producer-oriented at the expense of consumers – and psychological – people forget what freedom really means and develop a dependent and 'servile' psychology (Hayek, 1960, 1967). When people expect the government to provide for all needs, individual responsibility for self-maintenance declines. Thus, the effects of claiming 'social justice' as a reason for the state to intervene to redress income inequalities are, for Hayek, disastrous:

> Nobody with open eyes can any longer doubt that the danger to personal freedom comes chiefly from the left, not because of any particular ideals it pursues, but because the various socialist movements are the only large organised bodies which, for aims which appeal to many, want to impose upon society a preconceived design. This must lead to the extinction of all moral responsibility of the individual and has already progressively removed, one after the other, most of those safeguards of individual freedom which had been built up through centuries of the evolution of law. (Hayek, 1982:III: 129)

The remedy for this state of affairs requires, first and foremost, that the legal system maintains only general, universal rules. This is the paramount requirement for curbing the arbitrary powers of the state, thus preserving individual freedom. The state must abandon attempts to legislate in favour of particular groups on the basis of appeals to social justice and return to a residual role in welfare provision. Hayek does not suggest, or try to justify, the removal of the state from all welfare activities as some contemporary commentators suggest that the new right advocates, but the role he would allot to state intervention in welfare would be strictly minimalist. The income maintenance system should be residual and selective and tax rates kept to a minimum so that people are encouraged to work harder by being able to keep more of their earnings.

For Hayek, legitimate activities of government in the field of welfare must correspond to and be informed by the liberal principle that government must not have a monopoly on services. Not only does this increase the centralised power of the state, it also discourages private and charitable service provision. Resources for social and welfare provision must be raised through a uniform, flat rate taxation system, thus preventing the tax system being used as a means of income redistribution. In order to engender responsibility in the electorate, it should be made clear to all voters that they cannot shift the burden of paying for social or economic welfare on to others. This can be achieved, Hayek argues, only by making everybody contribute equally to public expenditure so that individual voters are aware that they will have to pay for services (Hayek, 1982:III). Minimalist state provision, and the removal of socio-economic rights, would help to arrest modern society's rush along the 'road to serfdom'. By removing social rights much of the activity of pressure groups is made redundant thereby restricting the expansion of state activity through the logic of the 'vote buying' process (Hayek, 1960, 1982:II, 1982:III). At the same time, the state must withdraw from interference in economic processes in the form of incomes policies, minimum wage laws or employment protection legislation, thus reducing the role of trade unions in economic and political life. These prescriptions, forming the basis for a legal framework which enables both individual freedom and economic prosperity, have been of great influence in economic, political and social-welfare theory.

The superiority of free markets

Like Hayek, Friedman argues that liberty can best be guaranteed through the market and that state intervention harms both economic growth and individual freedom. He develops his case through a combination of economic arguments designed to show the superiority of the free market over Keynesian managed economies, and political arguments designed to show the superiority of the market over the state in the organisation and coordination of social life.

The crisis of Keynesian political economy

Friedman's work has done much to undermine the validity of Keynesian economics, and hence the intellectual and moral legitimacy of state intervention in the economy in the postwar period. His major work is a detailed empirical examination of the history of monetary policy in America which, specifically, reinterprets the causes of the 1929–33 depression (see Green, 1979). Friedman argues that the stock market slump was critically worsened by the actions of a state agency, the Federal Reserve System, whose incompetent actions resulted in the eventual crash of the market. He argues that the depression was a result of government, rather than market, failure. The political critique of the American state developed by Friedman is extended to examine the postwar welfare state in Britain and elsewhere.

According to Friedman, Keynesian economic policy failed in the 1970s because of the combination of escalating inflation and unemployment which proved to be the most significant challenge to the assumptions of postwar economics (Green, 1979: 64–5). The appearance of stagflation in the 1970s – a stagnant economy combined with high inflation, a combination that should not occur according to Keynes' general theory – was of utmost importance for social and economic policy. If the theories on which Keynesian demand management was based were so seriously flawed, the entire set of assumptions upon which the Beveridge Report was based – state management of the economy leading to sustained growth and full employment – would collapse, confirming the doubts expressed by Hayek and others who had argued consistently that state intervention in economic processes would not deliver the goods. It was argued that the economic ills of the 1970s were in no way a crisis of capitalism *per se*, but, rather, the result of the application of Keynesian techniques or, in other words, a result of the political administration of capitalism. For Friedman, an important factor in the control of inflation is the amount of money circulating in the economy – it is this which needs to be controlled, not the plans and initiatives of business and enterprise. Government borrowing becomes important because of its inflationary potential. Hence controlling public expenditure, in the long run, is a priority as a measure to control inflation, in order to prevent inflation growing faster than the rate of growth of the economy.

The combination of high inflation, increasing unemployment, a large publicly managed and financed sector of the economy absorbing a rapidly increasing proportion of GDP and a very low rate of economic growth all served to expose the inadequacies of Keynesian economic policy (Gamble, 1985). In this circumstance, two policy priorities gained political significance. The first was the control of the money supply, the second was the creation of wealth through incentives contained in tax policies: it was argued that lower tax rates would result in substantially decreased activity in the unregistered and illicit economy and substantially less tax evasion. Lower taxes would, in fact, result in increased revenue for the state.

This position was summed up by Hoskyns, writing in *The Times* in 1985, who argued:

> to get out of the recession we need more investment; to have more investment we must cut taxes; to cut taxes we must cut public spending; to cut public spending we must cut unemployment; to cut unemployment we must cut wages; and to cut wages we must devise a new poverty line based on real needs, or in other words, cut benefits. (cited in Levitas, 1986: 90)

The legitimation of cuts in benefits is achieved by advocating an absolute concept of need. The concept draws on Hayek's critique of distributional justice – that needs have gradually become legal rights. However, the concept of 'absolute need' and the prescriptions for creating economic growth by reversing the dysfunctions of Keynesianism, also have a political dimension that is inextricably linked to the economic case for free market capitalism. This dimension is developed by Milton and Rose Friedman.

Freedom, markets and the state

Whilst monetarist philosophy is frequently presented as a technical solution to economic problems, in fact it depends on a particular conception of the state–society relation. If monetarist solutions to the crisis of Keynesian economics are to be effective, they must be applied through policies that go beyond technical economic aspects: the political institutions and social rights of the postwar period also must be radically transformed. Monetarism cannot be effective within the 'social democratic compromise'. This issue has underpinned the work of Milton Friedman, whose arguments parallel those of Hayek in important respects.

Friedman (1962) and Friedman and Friedman (1980) argue that socialist political and economic structures inevitably undermine and, ultimately, abolish individual liberty. In particular, Friedman focuses on the gradually expanding meanings ascribed to the concept of equality – from equality before the law, to equality of opportunity, to the notion of equality of outcomes. It is the latter usage of the concept which is seen as particularly threatening and which Friedman (1962) argues has been adopted as a guide to policy in Britain. The argument against equality of outcomes has several dimensions.

First, inequality is seen as an inevitable outcome of market processes in capitalist societies. Life is seen as a lottery, in which we all receive a ticket at birth. What happens to us depends upon our innate capacities and luck. The natural inequalities engendered by market processes result in less overall inequality than other social systems. Markets generate inequality but, through their efficiency in transmitting information to market participants, the distribution of income is less unequal than in other societies. More importantly, Friedman (1962) argues, the overall level of social wealth increases through the private activities of individuals engaging in market processes and ultimately this benefits the poor. The forms of freedom compatible with preserving such activities are equality before the law and equality of opportunity. Friedman argues that 'fairness' of material outcomes has been advocated increasingly by intellectuals. The application of this perspective to economic and welfare policy leads to the problem of an extended state apparatus which attempts to ensure 'fairness' in outcome through directing the activities of individuals in the market (minimum wages, protective legislation, prices policy, and so on) and through the tax system to effect income redistribution.

A second theme is that extensive state intervention in welfare has created a class of bureaucrats who have a vested interest in further expansion of state activities. However, the provision of state services benefits powerful producer groups at the expense of consumers, who come to depend on the continuing provision of such services, eventually losing all individual initiative and personal responsibility for self-maintenance. The consequence of this imbalance and dependence is the breakdown of the moral fabric which the Friedmans (1980) claim holds society together. Allied to this cultural deterioration are the ever-increasing costs generated by the vested interests of the welfare bureaucracy. Rising taxes are required to pay for rising costs, thus undermining incentives to work and creating more and more state direction over the lives of individuals. The market, it is argued, keeps costs down and is sensitive to consumer needs.

A third theme is that social insurance is seen as a tax on employment and can therefore generate unemployment by artificially raising employment costs. However, the greatest threat posed by social insurance is that it is seen as a means to foster socialism by raising taxation without public debate. This is said to be socialist inasmuch as it is directed by the state and denies people control over their own income. By paying taxes for benefits people are deprived of the opportunity to make alternative arrangements through the market and have no choice other than to take what the state provides.

The Friedmans argue that choice in welfare will increase personal liberty, strengthen social and community bonds and enhance the competitive capacity of the whole economy. Minimalist social security provision would encourage employment growth and add to personal savings and security for many workers (Friedman, 1962: 155). Traditional forms of welfare support – the family, voluntary sector and market – which were 'crowded out' by state provision, would flourish again, thereby reviving individual initiative and responsibility. The role of the state would decrease and with it the threat to individual freedom that it poses. A much reduced set of state powers in social life would allow the market to perform its natural functions of wealth creation and the preservation of freedom, and this is the primary reason for the Friedmans' sustained attack on social democratic structures. The practice of 'collectivism' serves the interests of producer groups and inevitably leads to the development of vested, special interest claims against society and the state which ultimately threaten the democratic process itself (Green, 1987: 81).

Ungoverning markets: regoverning morality

Just as the outcomes of market transactions are said to be directed by an 'invisible hand', so a similar argument has been applied to the processes of political action. The idea of an 'invisible hand' in politics has been the subject of detailed work by the 'public choice' school. Part of the focus here has been an analysis of the political pressures which lead to an increase in the money supply, forming part of the critique of social democracy. The issue of ungoverning markets is at the same time a moral issue addressing social questions of community structures, family responsibility and personal obligation. Neo-liberal critiques of social democracy tie together processes of government, individual morality and choice.

Public choice and the welfare state

Known as the economics of politics (Buchanan, 1978), public choice theory applies economic analysis to political processes and institutions. The focus of analysis is the 'demand side' of the political market and the 'supply side' of bureaucracies, and of interest is the ways that individual preferences influence collective decisions – in particular, the relationships between voter preferences and political outcomes. The political arena is conceptualised as a market, voters as consumers of policies and political parties as firms, selling their policies to voters. In this arena, the 'vote motive' is considered to replace the profit motive. The public choice school argues that voters have neither the expertise nor the information to select from the range of options presented to them. What we are offered is a ragbag of policies put together as a package designed to appeal to a number of different interest groups (Harris and Seldon, 1979). The 'ragbag' character of policy packages is inevitable since, in order to be elected, parties have no choice other than to try to appeal to a variety of interests. In other words, they must try to offer the greatest possible inducements to the greatest possible numbers. In consequence, there is an in-built bias in the democratic polity towards increasing expenditure (and therefore political control over the economy) by governments.

The supply side analysis begins by challenging the presupposition which is seen as inherent in the works of Fabian socialists – that public institutions will be staffed by neutral, disinterested public servants whose primary aim is to serve the 'general good'. Working from a model of human activity as rational and utility-maximising behaviour, the argument presented is that employees of state bureaucracies have a vested interest in expanding services, which leads to pressure for increasing state intervention and expenditure. This is considered undesirable both because of the inflationary potential and also because individual preferences cannot be ensured – the consumer has no control and no redress in regard to the services provided. They are producer-oriented at the expense of consumers. In consequence, it is claimed, socio-political institutions must be redesigned so that behaviour can be channelled towards a 'common good'.

Public choice arguments, applied to welfare issues, have been taken up most vigorously in the United Kingdom by Harris and Seldon at the IEA (1979: 68–9). They studied electoral choice over some twenty years and argued that market transactions are always superior to state action. A series of consumer surveys carried out by Harris and Seldon between 1963 and 1978, the results of which have been scrutinised critically by Bosanquet (1983), are said to demonstrate that politicians and bureaucrats promote expansion of monopolistic structures. This results in a situation where people are so heavily taxed to pay for the monopolies that they cannot afford to subscribe to alternative forms of provision and, as with the Friedmans, voluntary innovation has been 'crowded out' by the public sector. Monopolistic services tend to lack any mechanism of consumer accountability and thus cannot serve their consumers very well. However, in the absence of alternatives, the consumer cannot withdraw from these services. The analysis is used to criticise conceptions of the state as benef-icent. The solution is seen as the de-socialisation of the public sector (Seldon, 1979) and a return to residual, means-tested provision. Only in this way can the oppression of the state be checked. Harris and Seldon express this point forcibly:

> The welfare state has gradually changed from the expression of compassion to an instrument of political repression unequalled in British history and in other western industrial societies. (1979: 204)

This startling conclusion is drawn on the basis of the claim that the involvement of government in the provision of goods and services dis-plays the character of the 'invisible hand' through the need for political parties to 'bribe' voters by offering different benefits to different groups. This cannot, however, serve voters well because as consumers they become trapped in inefficient and monopolistic services geared towards the interests of their producers. In turn, the vested interests of producer groups result in further demand for the expansion of the public sector, with consequent higher levels of taxation.

Back to the future: communities and welfare

A series of publications from the IEA has developed policy-oriented analy-ses based upon the Hayekian, Friedmanite and public choice positions outlined in this chapter (Hanson and Mather, 1988; Davies et al., 1993; Dennis and Erdos, 1993; Green, 1993; Lal, 1994; Himmelfarb, 1995; Morgan, 1995). Influenced by the underclass debate in the United States (Murray, 1988, 1990, 1994), neo-liberal theory has recently focused atten-tion on personal, moral and social questions of illegitimacy, unemploy-ment and crime, whose increase in both America and Britain is considered to result from the attack on traditional values, attitudes and patterns of authority launched by the counter-culture and new social movements, particularly feminism, of the 1960s. Much of this work has focused especi-ally on the moral problems of welfare provision and the need to use policy to counteract the erosion of individual and community responsibility, and many of these concerns overlap with arguments presented by ethical socialists. Green's publication *Community Without Politics* draws attention to views shared by those of differing political persuasions regarding welfare dependency and community responsibility. There is a degree of acceptance that:

the problem of welfare is moral in nature. It is having harmful effects on human character, encouraging the breakdown of the family, crowding out voluntary associations on which the moral order of a free society rests and, as if these were not serious enough, it also fails to accomplish its chief declared aim of reducing poverty. (Green, 1996: 112)

Re-emphasising the themes of 'freedom' and 'responsibility', Green, for example, proposes that 'the mainspring of a free and democratic society is the individual's sense of personal responsibility' (1996: 112), which latter is characterised by self-control, independence from government and duty towards fellow citizens. This sense of personal responsibility arose within a moral framework which, increasingly, has been eroded during the twentieth century through the emergence and consolidation of state welfare. The eighteenth and nineteenth centuries, for Green, exemplified the moral attitudes and social institutions compatible with maintaining personal and community welfare. The division of responsibility for welfare was shared among families, who took the primary responsibility, charities, voluntary and mutual aid associations, supporting the family, and the state, providing a minimal safety-net. Much of Green's research (cf. 1993) has been on the associations which flourished as 'non-political public services' in the nineteenth century in Britain. Along with a philanthropic ethos of social and moral reform, welfare provision was based on a mixture of stigma and deterrence, mutual aid and character improvement. In support of his assessment, Green cites the self-help principles associated with Samuel Smiles' tract *Self-Help, Character, Thrift and Duty*, as well as the emphasis on improving moral attitudes and character espoused by the Charity Organisation Society – an important precursor to modern social work. Combined with a duty to benefaction on the part of its patrons, together these principles and attitudes formed the basis for a satisfactory welfare system. According to Green, two primary benefits arose from this emphasis on moral reform and personal responsibility. The first was that it rendered possible a 'community without politics' – a moral community where social solidarity springs from an obligation to help others in an ethos of mutual respect between helper and helped. The second is that it encourages a concept of duty without rights – everyone has a duty to help the less fortunate but no one has a right to receive help (1996: 113–34).

The expansion of state responsibility for welfare in the twentieth century – the rise of the 'therapeutic state' – has destroyed the moral framework within which civic associations were situated. The paternalism of the state and its organisation of welfare creates a 'permanently dependent population' who assume rights to resources. The dependence amounts to a 'victim mentality', where people are treated as victims of circumstances with a right to redress and compensation by the state. Green argues (1996: 84–112), that this mentality results from the spread of socialist and counter-cultural ideas amongst the intelligentsia in the 1950s and 1960s. This has taken two routes. Britain has established a 'victim citizen' through mainstream social policy's attempts to equalise material conditions, de-stigmatise the receipt of welfare and associate lack of resources with exclusive and partial citizenship. The United States has constructed the 'victim-with-attitude' through the impact of the cultural revolution led by the middle classes. Here, feminist, militant anti-racist and liberal intellectual movements denigrated unskilled work and traditional patterns of authority, creating a climate of group discrimination, hatred and contempt. The implications are both cultural – leading to family breakdown, lack of personal responsibility for one's own problems and a reluctance to work – as well as structural – the legal system becomes increasingly politicised as measures privileging particular groups are enacted. The upshot of these cultural and policy shifts in both countries is the destruction of the moral framework which brought out the best in individuals. Instead, contemporary society is saddled with a welfare system that appeals to the worst, rather than the best, in human nature.

Green's response to welfare 'victimism' is to restore the social solidarity generated by moral community and civic association through legal, organisational and cultural measures. The legal system must be placed above and outside party-political interference whilst at the same time establishing the complete independence of charitable and voluntary organisations from government, rather than the present system where the latter are little more than 'sub-contractors to government'. These measures, alongside the retraction of government from all but the barest of safety-net provision, would enable a return to the civic virtues and associations existing prior to the welfare state.

To restore personal responsibility in family life, three activities would be criminalised and vigorously enforced: threatening violence against the mother to prevent her from revealing a child's paternity, failure on the part of a father to register the birth of a child, and failure to pay maintenance. Green is particularly concerned with what he sees as the abdication of family responsibility on the part of men, writing that: 'It is a male responsibility to use a condom. The clear message the law should send is that any man contemplating sex outside marriage must be prepared to face the consequences of his actions' (1996: xviii).

A series of further measures concerning illegitimacy are proposed, to be implemented alongside a wholesale reform of the taxation and benefits systems. The aim is to send a strong moral message to society at large through public policy. Green's emphasis is very much on children conceived outside marriage, as divorced and widowed mothers are exempted from the proposals, and he emphasises that abortion and homosexuality are not on his agenda. The measures that Green proposes are intended to contribute to a change in cultural practices and to reverse the rights-based character of much public provision and political and social thought in favour of a moral, social and legal framework based on the notion of duty. Legal and public policy must contribute to a transformation of ethical principles and moral behaviour in order to restore the civic arena and its values and associations to the centre of social life.

Feminism, families and the state

The emphasis on illegitimacy and male responsibility for children forms the substance of Morgan's (1995) analysis of changes in family structure and the role of policy in supporting certain types of family formation. The traditional two-parent family – a married couple and their children – is in danger of extinction, Morgan argues, for two major reasons. First, there has been a fundamental shift in British social policy in which the lone parent has become the focus of policy development, to the detriment of the two-parent family. Second, this shift is a result of the influence of the feminist movement on cultural and social norms and practices, lifestyles and policy making. The social consequences of this situation are, for Morgan, disastrous, having seriously detrimental effects on children's health and educational achievement, leading to increased delinquency, and generating large numbers of predatory males, detached from social and kinship ties. This latter development is seen as comprising the conditions which lead to the creation of a 'warrior class'. Such dysfunctional outcomes derive from the breakdown of the traditional family unit, a situation which threatens the foundations of democratic societies. For Morgan, the traditional family is the bedrock of liberal democracies. Citing from a text entitled *Feminism and Freedom*, Morgan (1995: 152) draws on anthropology to claim that: 'Not only has there never been an open, democratic society not based on the family, there has never been any society of any sort not based on the family.'

This traditional family has been under attack from feminists for some considerable time, an attack based on the claim that patriarchal dominance and control over women and children characterise family relations. Liberating women from such control – private patriarchy – requires liberation from the patriarchal family. As more and more women disengage from marriage, the important role of the family in providing cultural stability and social integration is correspondingly weakened. Echoing Hayek's views of the family as a morally and legally based institution whose purpose is to uphold functional norms and values, Morgan (1995: 153) writes that 'Fatherhood, that "creation of society", exemplifies the rule-making and rule-following without which no culture is possible'. The breakdown of the traditional family constitutes the greatest threat to the basis of the cultural arrangements underpinning social organisation in democratic societies. This breakdown is in evidence in the numerical increase of lone-parent families, in particular the rise in numbers of births to women who have never been married. Between 1971 and 1991 the number of lone-parent households in the UK doubled to comprise a fifth of all households. In 1971 women who had never married formed the smallest grouping of lone-parent households; by 1991 they comprised the largest category (Morgan, 1995: 3–4). Whilst the majority of births to single women are in fact registered by both parents, Morgan points to the frequency with which parents are registered at separate addresses, and the greater incidence of relationship break-up amongst never-married parents compared to their married counterparts. Morgan argues that this rise in illegitimate births needs to be situated in the context of a notable decline in births to married women, who now tend to marry later in life and to have fewer or no children, so that births outside of marriage now constitute a large percentage of all births.

Another factor in what Morgan describes as a 'casualisation of relationships' is men's disengagement from financial responsibility for their children. The majority of lone parents are reliant upon the state for financial support, with the proportion of lone parents in paid employment dropping throughout the 1980s whilst the labour participation rates of married mothers increased, so that 'by the 1990s the proportion of lone mothers with a child under 5 in employment was almost half that of married mothers ' (Morgan, 1995: 6). Data for the end of the 1980s indicated that 39 per cent of lone parents had received maintenance payments from former spouses or partners, 29 per cent receiving regular payments (p. 7), leaving most women with few financial resources other than state benefits. The biggest category in this position are mothers who have never married, 93 per cent being in receipt of state benefit in 1986 (p. 7). The cost of all lone-parent support amounted to £8.5 billion in 1994, approximately 9 per cent of the social security budget (including means-tested and universal benefit).

One of the impacts of the feminist movement, according to Morgan, is that the situation of lone parents has dominated the policy agenda, with 'the family' being redefined as a mother–child dyad rather than the father–mother–child triad. A general cultural shift towards validating the changing family form has penetrated academia, policy think-tanks and state departments. A highlighting of the poverty of lone parents has resulted in a widespread perception that they comprise the group in greatest poverty. This perception, Morgan argues, is quite wrong; couples with children actually constitute the largest group at the bottom of the income scale. Detailing provisions of the taxation, benefits and local authority housing allocation systems, Morgan (1995: 6–24) proposes that lone parents are better provided for than low-income couples or couples where the male is unemployed. Social policy has, for Morgan, shifted away from the notion of family policy where the family comprises two parents, to a model of policy built around the needs of lone parents. The state has been instrumental in undermining resources to, and support for, two-parent families, who are disadvantaged relative to one-parent families throughout the taxation and benefit systems in particular, so that one-parent families receive 'more at every level of earnings than the married couple with children' (1995: 3).

Traditional families are disadvantaged in the policy process by construing family poverty as women's poverty, paralleling a conceptual shift that, as Morgan contends (1995: 26), has been described by feminist commentators as one in which 'the consequences of greater public economic provision for lone mothers is that dependency shifts from men to the state', creating what they have called a 'state patriarchy'. As public patriarchy allows women to exert more power over their lives, many feminists see it as a condition to be encouraged. Morgan (1995: 26) cites the following comments by feminist writers as examples of such approval:

> [the] feminisation of the state launches a new offensive in the gender war. It is now an orthodoxy that one of the primary duties of the state is to protect women's interests against men's.

> [what the state] can do is shape a society that makes a place for women and children as family units, self-sufficient and independent.

Thus, the state, through the policy process, is seen as playing a pivotal role in undermining the legal, economic and moral foundations of the traditional family. It has become both culturally acceptable and economically viable for women to parent without men, for not only does the state penalise traditional families financially, labour market conditions are resulting in a major displacement of men from paid work at the same time that women's employment prospects rise. Labour markets together with taxation and welfare policy result in a situation where it becomes increasingly difficult for men to support a family, the upshot being that:

> Lone mothers are unlikely to be employed and unlikely to marry or re-marry, as long as they are supported by adequate welfare. Many lone mothers are of lower than average intelligence, so the jobs open to them would be low paid. The combination of the destabilisation of male earnings with expanded welfare programmes has been destructive of marriage, particularly amongst the poor. A woman may be no worse off, or even better off, without the father of her children. The increase in the resources made available to lone parents coupled with the confiscation of resources from families has resulted in rising numbers of sterile marriages, as many married couples feel they are unable to afford to have children at all. (Morgan, 1995: 50)

The link between moral and economic considerations about marriage is of crucial importance. Not only are women encouraged to 'go it alone' but also men's decisions concerning marriage are conditioned by the obligations attached to the breadwinner role, so that unemployed men are less likely to marry than employed men. Male joblessness also greatly increases the chances of divorce. Surveying a range of evidence, Morgan argues that the disengagement of both men and women in lower socio-economic groups from marriage has a number of seriously dysfunctional effects upon children raised by lone parents and, particularly, on young men, who are more likely to drift out of regular and socially sanctioned networks into criminality. Fatherless youths are a group likely to engage in crime and, as marriage and parenthood have traditionally been stabilising influences on delinquent youths, the effect on men of remaining detached from entry into marriage and creating a family is grave (1995: 113). The growth of deprivation together with a widespread lack of the social and moral integration afforded by the traditional family will result in a society where peripheral men will 'pose daunting problems of cohesion and control' (1995: 153), with the simultaneous emergence of what Gilder describes as 'a police state to suppress the men and of a child care state to manage the children' (cited in Morgan 1995: 146). Such an outcome is laid by Morgan at the door of the feminist movement, the 'anti-family' thrust of policy being 'the result of the imposition upon society of a model designed to promote minority political objectives' (1995: 154). Recreating the conditions for the traditional family formation which plays a crucial role in maintaining the social fabric of liberal, democratic societies requires, at the very least, that social and fiscal policy is neutral in respect of one- and two-parent families; at best, that it supports and promotes the nuclear unit.

Concluding remarks

In large part, the connection between classical liberalism and neo-liberalism rests on the moral critique of the state and state welfare. Whilst accepting many of the same beliefs and principles as its nineteenth century counterpart, neo-liberal philosophy and theory has rejected Enlightenment assumptions about science, reason and progress. Neo-liberalism has lost liberalism's faith in human perfectibility, in the progressive Enlightenment of all humanity and in the eventual subjugation of all natural and social forces to the power of human reason. Not only has neo-liberalism rejected the possibility of realising this state of affairs, it has also rejected the value of striving to bring it about. Thus, many neo-liberal perspectives on welfare and the state draw on Hayek but not Berlin, on Oakeshott but not Santayana. Neo-liberalism proposes that social order is both precarious and contingent, that the relationship between freedom and subjection, tyranny and democracy is delicately balanced. Yet, instead of searching for the balance that will harmonise society and bring about the (future) liberation of all, neo-liberalism proposes that imperfectibility and unpredictability are the basis of human societies. In this sense, neo-liberalism *has given up on the liberal project*. 'Welfare' is understood simply as a revitalisation of market relations, a subordination of everyday life to transactions in an unregulated economy, and a revalidation of those institutions – the family, community and charity – that are considered to substitute for what markets cannot provide.

Thus, neo-liberalism presents both a negative and a positive assessment of the organisation of welfare. Negatively, neo-liberalism proposes that the increasing centralisation of responsibility for individual welfare in the political state has undermined the moral foundations of civil society – notably the family and the community. At the same time, the legal foundations of the social order have been corrupted to serve the interests of political power. Law no longer refers to procedural conduct – 'rules of just conduct'. Public law has become a means of achieving substantive ends through manipulation by powerful interest groups who come to hold an

increasing stake in the expansion of state power. The tyrannical infringe-
ment on individual freedom resulting from state intervention is paralleled
by a distortion in the natural operations of market economies. The tacit
knowledge by which information is distributed through the market is
rendered increasingly redundant by state regulation of economic life.
Given the unpredictability of historical development it is illusory to
suppose that a political state can steer an economy to 'deliver' welfare
through planning and administration. Positively, neo-liberalism proposes
that voluntary innovation and individual responsibility are the basis of
moral order and that, consequently, the promotion of welfare consists in
the depoliticisation of everyday life. In place of the 'right' to benefit, neo-
liberalism substitutes the 'duty' to support, and in place of the desire for
'equality' it substitutes the value of 'freedom'. A society that truly
promotes welfare is not one that seeks to administer 'social justice', by
defining in advance what market outcomes are desirable, but one that
preserves the 'spontaneous order', by making rules and laws that are 'end-
independent' and treat all citizens alike regardless of material inequalities
between them.

4

Poststructuralism

The debate about welfare that gathered pace throughout the 1960s and 1970s was fuelled by the explicit rejection of a number of logics underpinning the politics of social policy. The rejection is based on two problems unsolved by Marxist and liberal models of social administration. The first is that social policies give rise to contestation, deflection and political divisions around their goals, means and practices. The second, related, problem concerns the nature of 'the political' itself. In both the Marxist and liberal traditions, political questions are posed almost exclusively in terms of the state. Yet there remain important political questions about social policy outside of the relationship between the state and individual or collective well-being including, in poststructuralism, the relationships between knowledge of social life and the diffusion of power through society.

The poststructuralist analysis of welfare hinges on these two sets of problems – on the relationship between power, resistance and practice, and on the political nature of knowledge about social and personal life. The analysis strikes at the core assumptions of Enlightenment theory because it unpicks the connections between systems of knowledge about the individual and the social on the one hand, and political practices involved in managing and administering policy programmes on the other. In order to understand the poststructuralist critique of welfare it is necessary to understand the social and political contexts in which the perspective emerged and the nature of the questions to which it gives rise. With this in mind, we begin by examining poststructuralism's relationships to the 'crisis of Marxism'. We then go on to discuss the ways that poststructuralism challenged dominant interpretations of social progress, before outlining important features of the work of Michel Foucault. As in all the perspectives we examine, there are variations in the ways that poststructuralist insights have been developed in the analysis of welfare and we outline some of these later in the chapter.

The crisis of Marxism

Poststructuralism represents a rejection of the major tenets associated with Enlightenment theories and philosophical traditions: those which envisage a universal subject (the working class, the rational actor), an essential human nature (species being, self-interest), a global human destiny or collective social goal. It involves a rejection of Marxism, liberalism and scientific modes of thought in which human history is claimed to represent a unilinear development. Poststructuralist analyses have called into question the central authority of science, philosophy and theory throughout Western cultures (Lemert, 1994).

Poststructuralism developed in France and the USA around a number philosophers – notably Michel Foucault, Julia Kristeva, Jacques Derrida and Luce Iragary. Derrida 'deconstructed' major traditions in Western social thought, showing their vulnerability to endlessly different interpretations and readings. The sense or meaning of such traditions derives from the impermanence and inconsistency of the concepts they develop: instability, not stability, is what underpins their meanings. These instabilities in the canons of Western philosophy expose the play of a cultural politics in the validation, centralisation or marginalisation of interpretations and readings. Derrida's work has been taken up widely in media and cultural studies, English and literary studies and has also influenced sociological analysis. Iragary and Kristeva produce critical readings of psychoanalysis and emphasise the importance of language and symbols in ordering and ranking our perceptions and experiences of identity. Both develop concepts of women's language or feminine meanings that they counterpose to the masculine traditions of philosophical analysis. Their assessments focus on the inherently political nature of meanings and symbols and have been influential in feminist and cultural studies (Sarup, 1993). Michel Foucault examined systems of power–knowledge in which human actions are both understood and organised. His work on prisons, asylums, science and culture emphasised the micro politics of power supporting discourses of deviance, madness, sexuality and the body. These writers provided important critiques of Enlightenment philosophy in both its liberal and Marxist versions, becoming important figures in post-1960s New Left social and political theory.

It is important to begin with this political note because in French social and political theory Marxism was the dominant theoretical paradigm to emerge after the Second World War. Roland Barthes, Jean-Paul Sartre, Louis Althusser and Jacques Lacan all embraced elements of Marxism – even when, as with Sartre and Lacan, they did so through other philosophical systems. Disillusionment with Marxism, however, began early, with recognition of the brutality of communism in the Soviet Union and the repression and massacres over which the Soviet state presided. The Soviet invasion of Hungary in 1956 caused the further disaffection of many European Marxists. In France, in particular, the suspicion was directed towards the organised focus of political French Marxism, the French Communist Party (PCF), whose centralised, autocratic and rigid structures isolated and demoralised many radical activists as well as deterring much of the non-radical working class. In the early 1960s, the New Left attempted to develop a 'left' politics unlike the bureaucratic, repressive model represented by the Soviet Union or the authoritarian, centralised institutionalism of Western communist parties.

The outbreak of political unrest across Europe in the late 1960s – notably in France, Germany, Italy and Czechoslovakia – involving coalitions of students, workers and counter-culture groups, indicated growing dissatisfaction with the established social order and growing disaffection from the postwar political settlement. In France, in May 1968, when students marched arm-in-arm with workers, and strikes, demonstrations and occupations erupted around the nation, a national, left-oppositional movement seemed to have arrived. Yet, even as the demonstrations were being organised and solidarity within the working class proclaimed, it became clear that the oppositional movement was sectional and fragmented rather than holistic and united. Important elements of the ideologies of production and class struggle bypassed the political agenda of women's groups, immigrant workers and non-French ethnic communities. The failure of the French Communist Party to mobilise nationwide support for the May protesters demonstrated that the party was more concerned to secure votes and respectability than to invest in alternative political action. Shortly after the first wave of unrest in May, counter-demonstrations were organised in a number of French cities – backed by Charles de Gaulle in Paris – and, although smaller in number and less vocal in their demands, they served to undermine the claim to national interest that the socialist activists had been seeking to secure. One outcome of these divisions and failures was to provide a warrant for the French state to ignore the wider demands of the protesters and draw up piecemeal, instance-by-instance settlements of isolated worker and student disputes (Harman, 1988).

The 1960s were also a period of ideological and intellectual revision. Daniel Bell's *The End of Ideology* appeared in 1962; Herbert Marcuse's *One Dimensional Man* was first published in 1964; Louis Althusser's *For Marx* was published in 1965. By the end of the 1960s, Marxist pamphlets and periodicals – such as *New Left Review, Black Dwarf* (themselves explicitly revisionist publications), and the *Socialist Register* – were increasingly dominated by debates over the role of consciousness and ideology in revolutionary change. The tenets of Marxist historiography were similarly revised through the publication of, for example, E.P. Thompson's *The Making of the English Working Class*, which first appeared in 1963, and the increasing acceptance of 'culturalist' interpretations of historical change promoted by, for example, Raymond Williams' *Culture and Society: 1780–1950*, first published in 1958, and *The Long Revolution* (1961). 'Second wave' feminist struggles found intellectual expression in, for example, Betty Friedan's *The Feminine Mystique*, which appeared in 1963, and the popularisation of Simone de Beauvoir's *The Second Sex*, first published in 1949 and translated into English and republished in 1964. The revisionism contested the established view of historical change as an almost mechanical unfolding of events, proceeding automatically from one to the next. Revisionist, feminist and anti-imperialist (after Fanon, 1986 [1952], 1969 [1961]) historians and political theorists undermined orthodox Marxist (and liberal) accounts of the ways that history is lived by different groups of people in different socio-cultural contexts. They drew attention to the relationships between the experience of institutional and communal life and the everyday political and cultural contexts which provide such experience with a historical meaning.

The 1960s in France were a testing ground for Marxist intellectuals and New Left activists. Widespread rejection of and estrangement from the French Communist Party in the 1960s had occurred alongside the rise of the counter-cultures emphasising subjectivity and micro and situationist politics, feminism and its insistence that the personal is political, the civil rights and Black Power movements in the United States, and the slogan of the American counter-culture 'If you're not part of the solution you're part of the problem'. As Hebdige (1996: 179–80) points out, these various movements contributed to the post-1968 explosion of a politics of subjectivity and distrust of formal, hierarchical political organisation administered from a bureaucratic centre, in favour of local, participatory, networks of action. The combined effect of the 1960s civil and political activism, the crisis of Marxist ideologies and the new histories of social change helped to generate a questioning of the very foundations of 'left' accounts of social and historical progress. They were instrumental in creating a 'crisis of representation': undermining the legitimacy of representative democracy, reinterpreting the historical origins of Western cultural traditions, and contesting the validity of scientific claims to absolute or universal truth.

Questioning the Enlightenment

The struggles in the 1960s were struggles around both knowledge and power. They contested the monolithic, progressive ideologies associated with the organisations of both the political establishment and mass opposition movements. In so doing they forced on to the intellectual and political agenda issues of political unity and social progress as questions in their own right: not simply *which* unity or progress is desirable, but *whether* they are achievable or desirable at all. In short, they undermined faith in a project of Enlightenment: a project in which an inclusive society would result from the rational organisation of social forces and political structures, including markets, classes, labour, investment, consumption, families and communities, parties, movements and trade unions.

Such a systemic, organic conception of the inclusive order and its associated political practice was challenged on two major counts. First, the capacity to describe, define and explain societies in these terms is rooted in the authority of certain discourses over others, in the vision of historical development and change that they promote. 'Knowing' that social forces consist of 'classes' or 'labour' or 'consumption', for example, requires that certain procedures or techniques of knowledge are used: procedures that differentiate and classify populations according to axes of wealth, ideology, interpersonal bonding, and so on. In turn, these procedures depend on others: procedures for measuring income, values or consanguinity, for example. An entire 'technology' of knowledge is needed in order to describe and define social experience through the concepts of class, consumption or labour. Second, the politics of the systemic-organic order privileges certain experiences over others, certain struggles over others: it constructs hierarchies of need, identity, rights and obligations that systematically marginalise the divergent political strategies and goals of diverse groups in conflict. In order to realise equality, emancipation, liberty within the organic-systemic order it was necessary to subordinate some struggles to others, to place some struggles in the service of others and to structure away the differences. Just as the techniques for classifying and measuring the reality of the social world constructed hierarchies and priorities, inclusions and exclusions, so too did the politics of universal emancipation, either through successive reforms of the state (as in liberalism) or through its seizure and ultimate abolition (as in Marxism). Increasingly, the critical questioning of universal ideologies and theories focused on the relationships between power and knowledge, on their interconnections.

The questioning, as we have noted, was pursued vigorously through the politics of feminism, anti-imperialism, ecology and the New Left, each of which named different problems and generated different political and intellectual revisions of the connections between power and knowledge. In their different ways, they subjected the suppositions of Enlightenment theory and philosophy to critical scrutiny, suggesting that the traditions of radical political theory were themselves exclusive and hierarchical: the emergence and social dominance of such traditions was at least in part a result of their institutional utility. The 'objectivity' they promised, for example, served particular purposes and not others, valuing some forms of knowledge and belief over others. This critical assessment of Enlightenment traditions was taken up by Michel Foucault, who re-examined the history of systems of thought in the West – the dominant Euro-American traditions of positivism, liberalism, science and art. His work is a sustained critique of Enlightenment epistemology, arguing that the latter prioritises the distinction between thinking or cognition (a system of knowledge) and acting or doing (a system of power), whereas the history of Enlightenment theory and knowledge indicates that there are only ways of acting–thinking, or power–knowledge (what Foucault calls *pouvoir/savoir*).

Knowledge and power, for Foucault, are inseparable: each enables the existence of the other. In particular, Foucault argues that particular types of knowledge are entangled in particular relations of power. In 1978, Foucault and his co-workers published *I, Pierre Rivière* . . . It was the text of a confession to murder, in 1835, by a young French peasant, Pierre Rivière, and documents by persons (lawyers, doctors, judges, witnesses, and so on) involved in his trial. Foucault and his co-workers suggested that the document raised questions about how any text is to be read and, in particular, how historical texts should be read. For example, the lawyers prosecuting the case argued that Rivière showed that he was rational in the actions of his murder and the intelligence and eloquence of his confession. Doctors argued that his actions and confession represented two examples of the same insanity. The lawyers argued that Rivière *must* be rational in order to commit the murder so coldly and tell it so coolly. The doctors argued that in order to do these two things he *must* be irrational or insane. These two opposing views were derived from the same evidence – Rivière's confession, primarily, together with a number of witness accounts and examinations. Briefly, the text of these documents indicates two important features of historical interpretation. First, it indicates the instability of meaning: a single 'text' carries many meanings and can be read in many different ways. The doctors, the lawyers, Foucault and his co-workers, all were able to interpret and judge Rivière's confession and other evidences differently. In poststructuralist terms, the text contained no intrinsic meaning but was itself a product of, and in turn gave rise to, a number of 'discourses'. The term 'discourse' refers to the relationships between meanings, definitions and statements and the institutional and social networks that give them their authority and validity (as 'professional', 'scientific' or 'aesthetic' meanings, for example). The second feature is that it indicates that struggle over meaning is a power struggle. The period in which Rivière's case occurred, argues Foucault, saw a series of shifts in authority and control over madness and crime, the family and sexuality and other sites of social order. The new discourses on reason and unreason – addressing motive, behaviour, attitude, mannerisms, appearance and many other details of individual and social life – consisted of struggles around the authority of meaning: which meanings would define the experience of 'madness' or 'crime', whose judgements and interpretations would settle or expand disputes over those meanings and definitions, what measurement, examination and assessment systems would validate the definitions and give the meanings their authority? What we may take for granted today as established knowledge about ourselves was the subject of intense struggles around different sets of meanings and interpretations. Further, the scientific, philosophic and professional discourses through which madness and crime, the family and sexuality, and so on, are construed in the present are themselves likewise engaged in struggles over definitions and the authority of meanings (Hall, 1992b: 291–5; Sarup, 1993: 65–6).

Poststructuralist critiques of contemporary welfare policy and institutions draw much of their inspiration from Michel Foucault, drawing attention to conflicts over classification and categorisation and to methods of policing and normalising social identities. Modern forms of social administration are characterised by these conflicts, methods, classifications and normalisations. They involve the operation of a vast disciplinary régime, diffused throughout the social body, but they are also resisted and contested in struggles over knowledge and power.

Michel Foucault: poststructuralist problematics

Foucault's work, as we have noted, investigates discourses of modern public and private experiences – sexuality, crime, madness, the body, for example. He traces the histories of each of these objects not through the great discoveries that scientists and philosophers have made about them. Instead, Foucault investigates the methods and procedures that have been used to judge, measure and assess their 'normality' or 'abnormality', their 'criminality' or 'insanity' and the ways that these distinctions are socially maintained. The methods and procedures include examining, comparing, categorising, correlating, testing and ranking events, establishing normal and abnormal cases, correct and incorrect responses, standards, deviations and patterns. According to Foucault, such a history exhibits neither the uninterrupted progress of true knowledge over false belief nor the replacement of irrational thought by rational philosophy. Rather, it exhibits a collection of culturally constructed and socially sanctioned strategies of political organisation and control: a matrix or network of power relations.

Foucault's books on the divisions between rational and irrational thought, on the birth of the prison and on the history of sexuality, each address questions of power relations in different ways. Some of the differences are methodological – *Madness and Civilization* and *The Order of Things* are both exercises in the 'archaeology' of discourse; *Discipline and Punish* and *The History of Sexuality* are exercises in the 'genealogy' of knowledge. We make some comment on these concepts before outlining some substantive themes in Foucault's work.

'Archaeology' and 'genealogy' are methodological standpoints. Each represents historical events in different ways. Foucault's 'archaeology' represented an attempt to read histories through 'discourses': that is, he proposed that it was possible for meanings and definitions formulated several centuries ago to 'speak' directly to the analyst of the present day. This is much like the archaeological excavation of pieces of pottery or the remains of human settlements. The archaeologist attempts to reconstruct what the objects meant and how they were used in the past, in the contexts in which they were developed. It is never possible to paint a complete picture because only shards and remnants remain; nevertheless, it is possible to reveal 'hidden' truths about the past. Foucault's archaeological studies attempted to 'dig up' the shards of meaning from the past (like the text of *I, Pierre Rivière . . .*) and reconstruct them in the present, showing what they meant and how they were used at the time. They focus on 'ruptures' in knowledge (like the emergent conflict between law and medicine in the Rivière case or the new classifications of and supervision systems for 'mad' people and 'paupers' in the nineteenth century). The ruptures signal the transition from one 'episteme' to another, where 'episteme' refers to a régime or system of knowledge that organises the relations among discourses. The focus on such ruptures is said to show what meanings and what definitions were in struggle and what sorts of relationships were formed between knowledges and institutions. They sought to reveal the 'hidden' (discarded and broken) knowledges of madness and deviance, for example.

However, the 'past' never reveals itself to the investigator in its own essential 'truth'. The complexity of past life has to be filled in with assumptions made or 'truths' accepted in the circumstances of the present. Each time the past is investigated, its meaning is transformed through the discursive networks of the present. Hence, knowledges are not discovered from the characteristics of the past, but are produced through the discursive conflicts of the present: historical study is a political act. In response to this problem, Foucault adopted the standpoint of 'genealogy'. 'Genealogy' considers history not as a 'site' where original meanings are to be found, but as a discontinuous series of events that are connected to each other through people exposing or re-covering them in the present. Foucault's genealogical studies begin from the authority of specific contemporary discourses, especially the 'psy' discourses of sexuality or the body: discourses of psychology, psychiatry and psychoanalysis, together with related discourses, such as sexology, therapy and social work. He then traces backwards through their conceptual and methodological 'lineages' to investigate the points at which specific components of those discourses came together or broke apart. This is much like the practice of family genealogy, where the family tree is traced backwards into an ever expanding network of closely and distantly related branches. Depending on the starting point, the branches will be traced in different ways and different relations will be exposed. There is no singular, universal, linear history of 'crime', 'deviance', 'madness' or 'sex': the political relations through which these objects of science and policy are formed result in the repression or subjugation of alternative knowledges and histories. The genealogist does not discover these relations but retraces them, making connections between the power to define and to speak and power to subjugate and repress.

The limits of reason

Madness and Civilisation (Foucault, 1982) notes that the history of 'Reason' in European social science has been written almost invariably as the progressive unfolding of the ideas of 'great thinkers' – Locke, Bacon, Descartes, Newton, Marx and Freud, for example. In contrast to this history of ideas, Foucault proposes that Enlightenment Reason, in its origins and contemporary application, depends upon procedures for identifying, classifying and containing its opposite. The birth of 'Reason' as the basis of our knowledge of the world was, in fact, a double event, with the creation of Unreason – or 'madness' – as its correlate. It is this obscured history (i.e., the history of the production of 'Unreason') that *Madness and Civilisation* presents. Here, Foucault investigates the historical relationships between the development of psychiatry, psychology and psychoanalysis, on the one hand, and the practice of internment – the exclusion of the mad from society – on the other. He notes that the appearance of madness as a special concern – an object of special sciences and social policies, a field of research and treatment – resulted from a combination of circumstances. These included the removal of the mad from eighteenth century houses of internment. Prior to the nineteenth century, 'madness' was not distinguished in any particular way from idleness, infirmity, destitution or delinquency: all represented categories of persons unwilling, or unable, to live within the bounds of the social order. The houses of internment, or 'correction', contained an undifferentiated collection of such persons. From the end of the eighteenth century onwards, the inmates of these 'houses' were dispersed into more specialised institutions which reclassified and reorganised their supervision and treatment. The segregation of the mad from the bad and destitute was undertaken on a number of grounds: that they were a disruption to and burden on other internees, thereby undermining the latter's 'recovery', 'training' or 'rehabilitation'; madness became an important category of medical discourse and an important object of 'psy' knowledge; madness became increasingly 'medicalised'; finally, new rules of moral culpability (new rules concerning the circumstances under which 'blame' or 'intent' could be assumed in law) divided 'madness' from 'destitution' and 'criminality'. The changes were inaugurated by philanthropists, the medical profession and the judiciary amongst others, sometimes with the aim of treating or helping the mad but as often to achieve other – administrative or economic – aims. For example, the removal of the mad from the houses of internment helped to improve the efficiency of the interned workforce, whilst the reclassification of rules of moral culpability defined a legal subject who could be committed to trial by reason and hence fall under the jurisdiction of men of the law rather than men of religion. The emergence of 'madness' as a social problem, targeted by state, professional and philanthropic movements alike, is one piece or fragment, however important, in an epistemic shift in systems of knowledge and control. Pauperism, destitution, unemployment, criminality and contagion emerged alongside of, and were instrumental in shaping, the nature of the 'problem' represented by madness.

The transformation from internment of and 'ignorance' about madness to its treatment and 'cure' is commonly represented as a shift from barbarism to humanism: as a great step towards civilising and compassionate care. Yet the ethic of 'treatment' did not cause the appearance of modern systems for administering and controlling the variety of contemporary phrenias, phobias, depressions, neuroses and psychoses. The divisions between and the definitions of these conditions followed on from the segregations, classifications and regulations governing idleness and employment, culpability and blame, for example. The nineteenth century birth of the asylum as a special place of retreat and treatment for the mad followed on from these changes. The mad were not segregated on humanitarian or therapeutic grounds and then interned in asylums for treatment. Rather, it was the 'visibility' of madness – the difficulty of subjecting the mad to trial by reason, the uncontrollability of the mad in the workplace, and so on – and subsequent concentration in asylums that gave rise to its various classifications, treatments and therapies. *Madness and Civilisation* sketches a complex interplay between legal, economic, medical and political interests in the isolation and classification of madness. All of these interests combined in the organisation and control of the mad across the eighteenth and nineteenth centuries, whilst each pursued a different goal: efficiency and uniformity in production, the rationalisation of criminal justice, the distribution of citizenship rights and the legitimation of new medical therapies and hierarchies. The system of classification and the social institutions which maintained them comprise a 'discourse' on madness or 'unreason'. The nineteenth century asylum and its twentieth century counterpart the 'mental hospital' comprise the physical space of organisation of 'Unreason'. Here were developed the parameters, patterns and variations of behavioural, emotional, cognitive and moral responsibility that exclude persons from both citizenship rights and entitlements and legal culpability, for example, property rights, political representation and criminal liability. In 'asylum', people were not in 'society'; the practice of asylum is a practice of exclusion.

Foucault's account of the growth of the asylum as a physical place concentrates on the means, the discourses, of exclusion and how these are expressed in the institutional and social organisation of political life. The discourses thus also define – at least negatively – the limits and conditions for social and legal *inclusion*, or, in other words, what counts as reasonable, responsible, rational participation in the daily substance of collective, organised life. Foucault's point is that embedding 'Reason' in the mundane operations of modern institutions was (and is) framed within the development of an entire apparatus of 'Unreason', including an array of officially sanctioned experts, a framework of institutions and agencies, a system of assessment and evaluation and rules for the (involuntary) incarceration and treatment of those judged to be mad. Such an apparatus touches the lives of everyone – at school and work, in hospitals and courts, as well as in specialised institutions – and serves to define who shall be excluded, how and on what grounds, as 'mad'. Thus, a system for processing madness or 'unreason' is simultaneously a system for identifying the presence or absence of reason – and by extension for defining what reason is – in the context of everyday life.

Foucault contests the idea that contemporary 'enlightened' systems for controlling and administering madness represent the substitution of humane treatment for barbaric containment or banishment. Instead, he argues that how 'unreason' is defined and dealt with today is the product of an epistemic shift in knowledge about the nature of humankind, its individual and social make-up. Rather than assuming that the 'psy' sciences now speak the 'truth' about madness, replacing the false beliefs and superstitions of the past, Foucault argues that 'truth' is historically variable and exists only within relations of discourse or 'epistemes'. 'Knowledge' about unreason objectifies 'madness' differently in different epistemes.

The disciplinary society

Discipline and Punish (1977) charts the transition in penal theory and practice from the tortures, executions and public confessions of the Classical Age (before the eighteenth century) to the modern system of imprisonment, surveillance and training (from the nineteenth century onwards). The book begins with an account of the public torture and execution of Damiens the Regicide in 1757. In great detail, the instruments of torture and the steps of execution are described for the reader to absorb. Foucault contrasts this account with the rules of conduct and daily activity for inmates in a juvenile prison, only eighty years later. The rules and regulations are precise in the extreme, noting the exact time (and exact amount of time) for the performance of every daily task, from waking to washing, breakfasting, toileting, working, cleaning, and so on. The prisoner's entire day is codified in minute detail.

Again, Foucault challenges the conventional view of this transition as indicating the progress of more humane and enlightened attitudes over barbaric and brutal philosophies of crime and punishment. Instead, for Foucault, it shows the advent of a new, extensive type of power – 'discipline'. As with Foucault's work on madness and reason, *Discipline and Punish* investigates how different societal interests combined in the development of the new penal system. The book's richest seam, however, is the detailed technical description of the procedures for implanting discipline into the operating frameworks of modern institutions – in prisons, especially, but also in factories, schools and workhouses, for example. These institutions, Foucault argues, are characterised by 'régimes of [disciplinary] power' which subject their charges to surveillance, training, subordination and normalisation. Indeed, their design and procedural details reflect precisely this 'subjecting' purpose.

The ideal figure of disciplinary power – the 'model' that exhibits most clearly its means of operation – is the panopticon, the prison designed by eighteenth century social reformer Jeremy Bentham, although the design was never in fact constructed. The appeal of the panopticon lay in its potential to produce trained, reformed and useful inmates with maximum efficiency. The panopticon – and the actual prisons built during the nineteenth century – held out such a potential because their design and operation embodied a number of basic, and simple, organisational principles. These included:

- the secure exclusion of deviants and delinquents from the rest of society;

- the direct visibility of the inmates to a central supervisor and the invisibility of that supervisor to the inmates;
- the isolation of inmates in separate cells;
- the routinisation of daily activity;
- a graded hierarchy (or ranking) of punishments and forfeits covering all infractions of rules; and
- a continuous process of recording and monitoring in order to chronicle the inmate's institutional career.

The important point to make here is that it is the continuity and multiple applicability of these techniques that mark out 'discipline' as a unique type of power. Although the prison–panopticon holds a privileged place in the history of discipline, the techniques for training and normalising inmates, with some variation according to context, took hold across the entire spectrum of public and private institutions. In clinics, hospitals, schools, factories, asylums, orphanages and workhouses the principles of isolation, routinisation, ranking, recording and visibility served both to define the nature of deviance, need, personal or educational development, sickness and recovery and at the same time to instil a régime of behaviours, compliances, regulations and moral-political codes into the institution's structures and practices. It is the *system* of normalising procedures – more or less continuous across modern institutions – that supports and gives meaning to the nineteenth century reforms of the penal system since these reforms are themselves elements in the development of discipline as a means of regulating and organising social life.

Foucault's objective in *Discipline and Punish* is not merely to describe the punishment of offenders and delinquents, but to account for the diffusion of disciplinary techniques throughout the social body, their 'penetration' deeper into the spheres of everyday life, their extension over a wider range of social and institutional contexts and, ultimately, the adoption of self-disciplining techniques by individuals. The transition from the torture of the regicide to the continuous monitoring and codification of the life of the imprisoned delinquent is simply the starkest example of a political reconfiguration of the body of the individual and its relation to power. This reconfiguration displaces the body as an object of external torture and substitutes for it an internally self-disciplining entity: a body that, through continuous surveillance and monitoring, through the application of endless rules of conduct, manner, attitude and appearance, could become 'useful', 'docile' and attuned to the administratively rational operations of modern political, economic and social orders. In both the smallest micro structures of behaviour – gait, clothing, expression, gesture – and the largest macro structures of the political economy – division of labour, military organisation, urban design – a 'calculus' of discipline has been developed and applied. The panopticisation of buildings and neighbourhoods, the 'time-tabling' of activity, the gradations of punishment, entitlement and treatment, and the hierarchies of knowledge (with 'science' at the top and 'myth' at the bottom) comprise 'micro technologies' of power. They reveal and conceal knowledge and information, they allocate people to spaces and times, they validate and invalidate norms and beliefs, they transform 'time' and 'space' into *useful* objects and insinuate the rankings, hierarchies and gradations into the everyday experiences and actions of entire populations. They co-relate the 'external' organisation of power and the 'internal' exercise of discipline and coordinate the interrelation of multiple centres of power. The power to judge, to police, to diagnose and treat, to educate and to assess and supervise *constitute* the disciplinary society. Such powers are not located in single institutions; 'assessment' and 'judgement' are undertaken by a range of different social actors – social workers and psychologists, teachers and supervisors, as well as members of the judiciary, are all involved in exercising the power of judgement over others. As the powers of judgement, assessment, supervision, and so on, become more and more entrenched in the maintenance of social order, so more and more people are drawn into the micro technologies. Powers to judge, assess or supervise are diffuse and decentred: no single, central authority regulates or bestows them. Instead, they are decentred and distributed throughout the social and institutional networks of the modern political order.

The discourse on sex

The Victorian era is conventionally renowned for its puritanism, for a moral conservatism about sexual and bodily matters. Yet, Foucault (1981) notes, at the same time, it is filled with talk about and attention to sex to an obsessive degree – in terms of private revelation (in psychiatry, psychoanalysis and, later, psychotherapy), cultural expression (in literature and the arts) and public action (in population surveys, statistics and social policies). In short, in spite of its supposed puritanism, the Victorian era contains a detailed history of the origins of modern sexuality: what it is to be a sexual self. In Foucault's reading, this fertile history furnishes two major critiques of social and political theory. The first is the critique of what Foucault terms the 'repressive hypothesis' of sexual control, the second is the critique of the 'juridico-discursive' concept of power. We deal with each of these in turn.

Since Freud, it has been common to think of sexuality in terms of repression, that is, as something unstable and unpredictable, requiring an elaborate array of codes, rules, canons and prescriptions in order to prevent inappropriate, anti-social, uncontrolled sexual excess. These 'prohibitions' on sexuality have been the subject of philosophical and political critique for the better part of the twentieth century. Critical theorists like Fromm, Reich and Marcuse castigated the repression of sexuality and proposed that challenging the codes and rules of sexual expression and conduct was consistent with revolutionary liberation from capitalist domination of personal identity. However, Foucault points out that, from the point of view of the development of sexual relations, the modern era is characterised by institutions and practices whose purpose is precisely to *produce*, not prohibit, sex, sexuality and sexual identity. These include large sections of the quasi-medical and psychotherapeutic professions whose status, income and professional goals are dependent upon the continual reproduction and reappearance of sexual trauma and sexual difference. At the same time, sex and sexual behaviour have been an important feature of social policies since the middle of the nineteenth century when statistics were first used as a means of recording, determining and predicting population changes. Here, sexual behaviour is treated as a procreative 'function' that needs to be controlled in the name of national health and strength. Similarly, artistic, literary and other widely available cultural genres have been important sources of sexual representation. Far from being 'repressed', hidden from view or denied, sex and sexuality have been the subject of very extensive scrutiny, exploration, analysis and representation. They have been objectified in scientific inquiry, in public policy and in political resistance.

The problem of sex and sexuality, for Foucault, is not the extent of their *repression or prohibition*, but the nature of their *production and reproduction*. The observation that sex and sexuality have been, throughout the modern age, the object of a wide-ranging and diverse series of discourses – medical, legal, political, cultural, and so on – leads Foucault to suggest that modern human sciences, laws and political strategies have themselves manufactured the very sexualities that they are said to have repressed. In turn, this perspective on the creation and recreation of sex and sexuality as central pillars of modern social life questions whether power itself is adequately represented by concepts of prohibition and repression: whether, in short, it is power that prevents liberation and incapacitates action. In particular, Foucault questions the 'juridico-discursive' concept of power which, he proposes, lies at the heart of modern constructs of the sexual self. The juridico-discursive conception of power attributes power to a central 'sovereign' source (the state, the ruling class, bureaucracy, and so on), proposing that freedom from domination involves wresting power from that source and giving it to someone else (the working class, the community, the people, and so on) who will then constitute the new centre of power. Yet, Foucault's historical analysis proposes that the power to manufacture and organise sexuality has no centre; that it is to be found in many different sites – in religions, sciences, arts, families and schools, for example – serving many different purposes and that it produces and reproduces many *different* sexualities. What follows from this recognition, for Foucault, is an emphasis on the *relations* of power that define and organise sexual identity and on the *strategic analysis* of these relations. Simply put, this means that rather than viewing power as the establishment of the total dominance of one group over another in everything from sexual to social reproduction, it is more appropriate, and more useful, to conceive of power as the shifting and unstable political relations between actors, institution and discourses.

Power–knowledge and practice

Between the analyses of reason, discipline and sexuality are three theses on power central to the poststructuralist critique of welfare. These are, first, that the modern disciplines of psychoanalysis, psychiatry, medicine, penal and social science have tended to portray their development as a history of growing humanity, proposing that today's treatments, therapies, psychological and social services are the result of benevolent philosophy and action. The philosophies and actions of our classical forebears, with their tortures, deprivations, executions and exiles, by contrast, are viewed as barbaric, pre-civilised, erroneous and even monstrous. But this binary division between 'good' modern practice and 'bad' historical practice misses the most obvious feature of the shift from classical to modern forms of medical treatment, policing and public administration. Namely, that the shift represents a change, not primarily in the humanitarian outlook of the reformers – and, by extension, the advent of a more 'enlightened', modern approach to deviance, sexual or mental difference. Rather, it represents first and foremost a reorganisation in the power-relations that sustain our definitions of what is normal and what is abnormal and how these should be treated. The shift represents the displacement of one type of power, which is exclusive (the province of a restricted rank of authoritative persons) and arbitrary (in that there is no necessary correlation between a crime and severity of its punishment, for example) for one which is general (the province of a very large number of officially sanctioned social authorities) and continuous (in that there is in every institution a rational calculation of power and how it can be most efficiently applied).

The second theme is the focus on peripheral and marginal sexualities, on petty illegalities and the minutiae of psychological differences. On the basis of mundane, routine and, at times, trivial actions, attitudes, intellectual and emotional variations has been built an extensive and increasingly penetrating system of monitoring and surveillance, socialisation and normalisation. From the moment of birth to beyond the moment of death the populations of modern societies are recorded, coded, categorised, classified and chronicled. Each individual is subjected to an evaluative régime in which every facet of 'normal' life is used by someone in order to bestow rights, assess needs and entitlements, judge educational, developmental and moral progress. A political-institutional network – ranging from General Practice through school, academy and workplace to the social and psychiatric services and the police – is arranged around the beliefs, actions and capabilities of the entire population. This continuous system of surveillance, assessment and judgement amounts to a 'Petty Assizes' of everyday life: a general and dispersed arrangement of judges – usually in the form of experts – conditioning each person's life-course.

The third theme follows directly from this observation: the assessments, judgements and sanctions that surround sexuality, deviance and madness are not the sole province of the state or capitalist ruling class and nor is the state the only or necessarily the primary beneficiary of the continuous political system. Certainly, the state plays a major role in enacting legislation, providing funds through taxation and other means, establishing targets and goals for the resolution of variously defined 'social problems'. Yet, in many ways, the systems of power described by Foucault are instituted not by openly coercive or repressive state agencies but by a very wide miscellany of civil institutions. They are systems of power (or 'micro power) that are inculcated into the behaviours, habits and practices of an entire society of people with the consequence that the rules, codes and procedures of regulation and control are experienced as 'normal' features of institutional and everyday life. The 'normal' and the 'abnormal' are each a product of the relations of power–knowledge that give them their specific meanings and contents and coordinate their social co-presence.

Poststructuralist applications

Foucault's theses on power–knowledge have been taken up in the sociology of welfare in a number of different ways. These include (under the influence of Derrida and Kristeva) analyses of the regulation of the *body, identity and difference* and the dependence of political cultures, programmes and ideologies on that regulation (Gatens, 1992; Pringle and Watson, 1992; Butler, 1993; Seidman, 1995). A second application has been the focus on *discourses* – of poverty, deviance, social work or welfare, for example – and the ways that such discourses establish rights, responsibilities, duties and authorities around categories of deviance or need. This way of taking up Foucault's work is used to great effect in Fraser (1989), Dean (1991), King (1991) and Dickens (1993). A different focus has been on the *patterns of institutionalisation or normalisation* to which developments in social policy and administration give rise. Cohen (1985) and Garland (1985) adopt this approach, examining the emergence of, and relationships between, particular sets of rules, sanctions and penalties in the criminal justice and social welfare systems. Finally, and closely related to this type of historical application, is an emphasis on unpacking the *political and social origins* of social policy fields – such as poverty, child abuse and protection, community health or family welfare, for example. Work by Donzelot (1980), Armstrong (1983) or Parton (1991) explores the historical shifts and the professional and political alliances that have given rise to the regulation of social 'problems' of these kinds. Below, we outline these applications in relation to the (re)iteration of identity and difference, needs discourses in social policy, and the control of the social.

Identity and difference

This aspect of the poststructuralist perspective draws attention to the (re)production or, more accurately, the (re)iteration of identity categories as a normative basis of social and political order. Contemporary institutions and discourses – of society, economy and polity – persist through the production of specific, differentiated identities and, further, exercise techniques of calibration, classification, codification and rationalisation in that production. Modern society is ingrained with the differentiation of identity, with the fabrication of socio-cultural differences and with the assignation of these differences to asymmetrical statuses and locations. Without this aspect of identity (re)iteration, the social orders in which modern economies and polities operate would be unworkable, even 'unthinkable'. Indeed, the entire edifice of the welfare system is simultaneously predicated upon and productive of this (re)iteration.

The concept of difference in poststructuralism refers not to natural, biological or individual variation, but to the generation of differential identities within particular régimes of power. Analysis of 'difference' has encouraged poststructuralist sociologists to highlight the ways that bodies, identities and cultures have been differentiated through political processes. As Gatens notes: 'The crux of the issue of difference as it is understood here is that difference does not have to do with biological "facts" so much as with the manner in which culture marks bodies and creates specific conditions in which they live and recreate themselves' (1992: 133).

The 'marking' of bodies with differentiated identities (of ethnicity, race, class, gender, sexuality, disability) is not a singular act of ascription: a human baby is not born, equipped with an identified body and locked forever in a social role. The 'marking' of bodies is a process of continuous (re)iteration and recurs through both symbolic and bureaucratic/administrative techniques in a matrix of what Butler (1993: 3) calls the 'regulation of identificatory practices'. Similarly, the work of Brah (1992a, 1992b), Hall (1992a, 1992b), Bhattacharyya (1994) and Roediger (1994) suggests that struggles over language and meaning are at the same time struggles over modes of identity. Thus, the 'Political Correctness' debate – which has generated some of the most vicious and vilificatory assaults on all forms of feminist, anti-racist and left-wing perspectives alike (Hughes, 1993; cf. Dunant, 1994) – itself represents the outcome of long struggles on the part of marginalised groups to have a voice in the institutions of learning, employment, welfare and the media. It has combined a struggle over the representation of marginalised peoples (i.e., a struggle over meaning) together with a struggle over the content of educational, employment and welfare opportunities (i.e., a struggle over access and participation). At the same time, it has drawn attention to the meanings and symbols that have been regularly used in the marginalisation of different identities.

Language and discourse are important in poststructuralism, then, because they are argued to be 'themselves productive of social relations, social and sexual inequalities, through the operations of identification, differentiation, and subject-positioning' (Hebdige, 1996: 181).

The focus on the fragmentation of political and intellectual authority, on the production of difference and 'positioning' in poststructuralism means that any centre of authority is effectively delegitimised, contested and undermined. The fragmentation of authority constitutes a crisis of representation in which 'in every image we must ask who speaks' (Hebdige, 1996: 180). Poststructuralism rejects the idea that the perspectives of racialised, gendered, differently abled and aged groups and individuals can be represented in universal discourses of need, identity or role. As Hall comments: 'The displacement of the "centred" discourses of the West entails putting in question its universalistic character and its transcendental claims to speak for everyone, while being itself everywhere and nowhere' (1992b: 257). Instead, poststructuralism points to the instabilities, gaps and silences in such discourses, and to the local struggles over need, identity or role that are continuously waged through them. Identities are not singular, fixed states within which individuals remain more or less in social equilibrium. Rather, they are multiple, fluid processes through which the social world is stabilised and destabilised: they are 'micro technologies' of power in which needs, statuses, rights and roles are configured into political relationships, social institutions and cultural representations. Individuals (and groups) shift between identities and often inhabit more than one identity location at the same time. Lemert (1995: 184) points to Anna Julia Cooper's (1892) experience of identity categories. As a black feminist writer travelling in segregated America she observed the signs outside the public facilities at a run-down railway station. Outside one 'dingy little room' hangs a sign 'FOR LADIES', outside the other hangs a sign 'FOR COLORED PEOPLE'. She was unsure how (or whether) these categories applied to her. Lemert explains:

> Cooper's Black Woman fits neither under 'LADIES' not 'COLOREDS' because she cannot be reduced to any conceivable universal subject. Neither her race nor her gender is sufficient to account for her social reality. She is not, therefore, any one subject because she is not subject to any one general category. (Lemert, 1995: 186)

Lemert's discussion of Cooper's analysis suggests that identity and its representations are, unevenly and contingently, socially and politically ordered in both the institutional and everyday contexts of the modern world. Poststructuralism focuses on such *instabilities* of identity representations in order to challenge dominant concepts of identity as an aspect of, or as belonging to, the self or subject. In construing identities as multiple, shifting, relational processes, poststructuralism also challenges the notion of 'subjectivity' itself. Whereas Enlightenment theories of Marxism and liberalism posited a universal subjectivity – a conscious, unitary individuality whose interests, desires and goals are realised in historical practice – poststructuralism posits a dynamic subjectivity – a fragmented, unconscious individuality whose interests, desires and goals are articulated through psychic and social identificatory practices.

Questions of subjectivity and identity lie at the heart of contemporary debates in social policy and social work, which constructs discrimination as arising on the basis of 'difference' – sexual, ethnic, bodily, age, regional, cognitive, gender, religious and so on. This understanding of difference and discrimination has become central to the agenda of social policy and social work. On the one hand is the claim that, despite the drive to universal citizenship and welfare provision, several groups in the population experience systematic discrimination and unequal access to resources, that is, work, benefits, etc., which impact on objective life-chances. On the other hand is the proposition that unequal status also has important subjective effects – lack of confidence, self-esteem, dignity and self-worth (Honneth, 1992; Ahmad, 1993; Dalrymple and Burke, 1995). These debates move uneasily between 'difference' and 'inequality', seeking to validate the former whilst overturning the latter. The strategy, however, begs the question of how 'difference' and 'inequality' come to be associated in concrete terms – whether, having solved the 'inequalities' rooted in sexuality, ethnicity, embodiment, age, region, cognition, gender and religion, the 'problem' of difference will be eliminated, or whether 'difference' is not reducible to such lists of ascribed or 'essential' identities.

In poststructuralist terms, as we noted above, 'differences' are marked, they have no essential existence in and of themselves, but are the products of power–knowledge relationships. Differences serve as the vehicles for the distribution of statuses, rights, entitlements, obligations, rewards and penalties: the social and political systems through which these distributions are routed constitute the inequalities that differences represent. They comprise the erection and policing of boundaries, borders, limits, inclusions and exclusions, demarcating access to and control over the cultural and social resources that define insider and outsider locations: who is heard and listened to, who defines, legitimates or validates struggles for opportunities and life-chances. Differences are always fully politicised; they are effects or dimensions of power relations, contesting in every particular arena of struggle for rights, benefits, etc., the 'universality' of individual needs and social identities.

Rejecting faith in universal history or geography (that is, rejecting the notion that identities are 'given' through the cultural evolution of traditions and norms or nations), Mohanty (1992) argues that the politics of difference provides a focus on locating subjective experiences in the context of extensive and interconnecting systems of oppression and struggles against them. Within and across societies the definitions and experiences of being female diverge radically through the cultural dimensions of race, class, status, sexuality and generation. Similarly, 'working class' identities are inflected by gender, race and so on. There is no universal, 'essential' subjectivity – no stable 'unit' of experience, desire, need and purpose – to which a social welfare discourse can appeal in order to explain inequality. Nor can the basic or common 'interests' of a differentiated society be used to mobilise universal policy programmes whose outcome will be the validation of difference at the same time as the redress of inequality. 'Difference' does not represent a binary state: 'black' and 'white', 'able-bodied' and 'disabled', 'straight' and 'gay', and so on, in which one represents the 'oppressor' and one the 'oppressed'. Rather, the production of difference is the criss-crossing and overlapping of struggles and resistances or, in other words, the outcome or manifestation of multiple relations of power.

As more and more groups struggle to politicise the identities through which their rights, entitlements and benefits are provided and to define identity as a matter of rights in itself – disability movements, anti-racist movements, gay, lesbian and bi- and trans-sexual movements, for example – so it becomes more apparent that social policies established to bestow, organise and regulate rights are embedded within political relations of identification. The process of defining, winning, imposing or resisting particular identities gives rise not to consensual or solidaristic projects of universal entitlement but to strategies of 'multiple discontinuous interpretation, by means of which our silent voices can be made to sound' (Cain, 1993: 86).

The normative bases of welfare entitlements, citizenship rights and social participation are rooted in prescriptive identity logics which sustain binary divisions between public and private, male and female, heterosexual and homosexual, resident and immigrant, able-bodied and disabled, even whilst these binary divisions are continuously and persistently challenged. Rules governing adoption, assessments of family income, access to benefits (such as the invalid care allowance), rates of pay for 'women's work' (and lack of pay for domestic labours), different taxation rules relating to heterosexual and homosexual co-habitees and the dependence of welfare services on gendered labour comprise a matrix of administrative régimes whose operations (re)iterate normative assumptions about and logics of family relations and community structures, sexuality and gender, cultural styles and social networks. The division and distribution of rights, access and entitlement, the marking of gendered, racialised, disabled and deviant bodies, the rationalised and calibrated matrix of differentiating inclusions and exclusions is the welfare system in practice: a cultural politics of representations and demarcations that centralises some forms of identity and marginalises others.

Needs discourses in social policy

These contestations and challenges are taken up by Fraser (1989), who develops a critical theory of welfare and needs through an application of Foucault's discourse analytic. She investigates 'needs-discourses' in order to show how definitions of needs are the products of political struggle over meaning. Concepts of 'need' enter into political debate, social research and welfare policies in complex and contradictory ways. Welfare policies on homelessness or disability, for example, are not straightforward responses

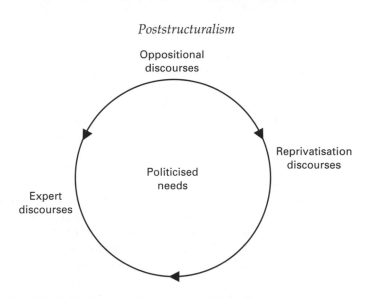

Figure 4.1 *Needs discourses in contemporary social policy*

to the plight of individuals without shelter or with specific classes of physical impairment. Rather, they are themselves the outcomes of struggles between 'power publics' (1989: 167) – or sections of the population with different degrees of relative power. Needs only become political – that is, subject to public action and contestation – when they are forced out of the arenas of private economic and domestic organisation, when community or domestic structures are deemed incapable of providing certain kinds of support and resources such that 'needs' become publicly visible and socially recognised. Fraser identifies three kinds of interacting needs discourse in late capitalist societies: expert discourses, oppositional discourses and reprivatisation discourses (Figure 4.1).

Expert needs discourses are associated with the major institutions of knowledge-production and application – including universities and think-tanks, professional associations and agencies of the social state (1989: 173). They serve most readily as vehicles for translating politicised needs into objects of state intervention by redefining them into categories of administrative service. This redefining process classically takes the form of translating a particular 'expressed' need into a 'case' of a more generalised social problem – unemployment, disability or homelessness, for example. The effect of the redefinition is to decontextualise the need from its class, gender and racial location and to depoliticise the conditions which gave rise to its expression in the first place.

Oppositional needs discourses are closely associated with active social movements and comprise an important feature of their self-definition. Here, private troubles and concerns are brought into the public arena by action on the part of disadvantaged or oppositional groupings. Fraser cites the political success of the women's movement in highlighting sexism, wife-battering, job-segregation and date-rape, among others. These, previously private, concerns are now the subject of intervention by various state and pseudo-state agencies – the police, social services and the Equal Opportunities Commission, for example – and are addressed in social legislation (such as the Equal Pay Act). Other examples would include the success of the disability movement in forcing problems of access, attitudes and resources on to the public agenda or the anti-racist struggle which has highlighted racial discrimination in areas as diverse as housing, employment and media representation.

Reprivatisation needs discourses challenge directly both expert and oppositional discourses by contesting the rationality, efficiency and morality of public responsibility for need. In essence, reprivatisation discourses seek to re-establish clear boundaries between public and private, political, domestic and economic interests and to shift responsibility for needs from the public to the private sphere. Reprivatisation discourses classically take the form of demands to 'roll back the state' or to make the individual or family responsible for their own welfare in order to counter 'dependency' on public provision. Contradictorily, as Fraser points out, by marginalising oppositional discourses and rejecting claims for public representation and action, reprivatisation discourses have the effect of further politicising the demands of oppositional social movements and strengthening their case for action.

Expert, oppositional and reprivatisation discourses coexist in programmes and policies for meeting need as contesting *logics of action* and are clearly visible in contemporary policy debates. For example, conflicting discourses on poverty create contradictory theories of and policy responses to inequalities of wealth and opportunity. The reprivatisation approach proposes that poverty and marginalisation result from the behaviour, norms and lifestyles of the poor themselves (see Rodger, 1992; Robinson and Gregson, 1992). It is a discourse that has made many different appearances in recent poverty literature – from the 'cycle of poverty' thesis in the 1960s and 1970s to current concern with the dependency culture of the 'underclass' (see Murray, 1994). Proposed 'solutions' to the poverty problem consist in developing a range of incentives, inducements and requirements for individuals to take personal responsibility for poverty which invariably stigmatise and intensify the experience of poverty. Thus, levels of social security benefit establish a wide margin between the unemployed, chronically sick and disabled and the average standard of living. At the same time, the private incomes of the poor are subjected to extensive scrutiny and are offset against public benefits. The contradictory consequence of this double strategy is to *increase* the distance between rich and poor and to deter any gradual exit from poverty through a strategy of building private income on top of public benefits.

Processes of social division and reprivatisation are countered by oppositional needs discourses which aim to reclassify poverty as a structural, rather than individual, problem. In this approach, features of the political economy (such as structural under-employment, social exclusion or cultural discrimination) are singled out as creating and supporting disparities in the distribution of wealth and income. Proposed responses focus on political intervention in existing economic, social and cultural institutions to combat exploitation and exclusion and the creation of new institutions in order to maintain the salience of poverty in the public eye. Oppositional discourses, it must be remembered, are precisely that: oppositional. They counter privatised and expert welfare programmes and policies and their successes are often contested by new groups formed to publicise failures and exclusions of existing oppositional discourses. Thus, feminism challenged liberal and Marxist discourses of poverty and was itself challenged by anti-racist movements. Oppositional discourses are forged out of the continuous cycle of absorption/exclusion and draw attention to the ways that policies create, rather than cure, economic and political inequality.

Expert needs discourses cross-cut reprivatisation and oppositional discourses and often seek a reconciliation between them. In so doing, Fraser (1989: 174) argues, they provide a formal bridge between social movements and the state, and, it might also be added, private economic interests. Expert needs discourses are dominated by technical disputes over categorisations of need – the extensive debate around concepts of 'relative' and 'absolute' poverty provide a case in point of the sorts of issues that are often central to expert needs discourses. The debate revolves around definitions of 'absolute' and 'relative' need in a modern society. One side of the debate proposes that people in modern societies are much better off in absolute terms than our parents and grandparents. This, it is proposed, can be seen in social indicators such as the increasing age structure of the population – more people live to an older age in modern societies than ever before; alternatively, measures of income and household expenditure seem to reveal that more money is spent on 'non-essential items' like cars, telephones, televisions, radios, tobacco, alcohol, clothes or pets than was the case historically. Using this sort of evidence, it is claimed that over time society as a whole has been growing healthier and wealthier and that the growth applies to all the different strata. The other side of the debate argues that historical comparisons of this kind are likening chalk with cheese and that, in absolute and relative terms, there are greater economic and social divisions between higher and lower strata than ever before. Modern societies, it is proposed, are highly mobile and depend upon sophisticated media of communication and information; leisure pursuits and other 'non-essential items' are now goods in a market rather than features of communal life: where our predecessors had access to land and common resources, these are now held in private hands and sold to consumers for cash. It is claimed that modern measures of poverty should take modern types of need into account and that doing so shows that there is greater inequality of access to both essential and non-essential items than was the case historically.

Analysing needs discourses in this way brings to light the fact that taken-for-granted concepts and categories in social policy are subject to persistent contestation and conflict. Discourses of need circulate around and through different societal groups and interests with the consequence that different social policy fields are criss-crossed by different construc-tions of the problem under analysis (cf. King, 1991). In turn, this obser-vation suggests that the very act of defining 'social problems' is itself an element in the political struggle over welfare. The political aspect emerges also, although in a different form, in the analysis of the 'penal-welfare' system (Cohen, 1985; Garland, 1985).

The control of the social

Cohen (1985) traces the career of the 'community corrections movement' from the 1960s onwards. Community corrections programmes were seen as alternatives to prison for non-serious offenders. They were developed most fully in the United States of America but elements of the community corrections philosophy were also influential in British programmes for dealing with juvenile crime – intermediate treatment, community service and the extensive use of supervised probation orders were introduced to divert offenders from the 'hard' end of criminal justice sanctions. These programmes drew into the criminal justice system a very wide range of social agencies whose humanistic aim was to redirect (predominantly young) offenders away from seemingly inappropriate penal sanctions. The philosophy stressed the importance of processes of 'normalisation' – including various forms of treatment and contracts between delinquent and supervisor – as a means of integrating offenders into lawful and socially useful patterns of behaviour. The movement was supported by groups from the left and the right of the political spectrum: it did not only originate as a state policy but was advocated and developed by alliances of voluntary organisations, professions, political organisations and counter-cultural groups, cutting across social categories and the pub-lic/private distinction. Two decades on, the effect has been as much to increase the scope and power of the criminal justice system as to divert offenders from custody – the entire system of sanctions has grown in absolute terms, containing a disproportionate number from marginalised groups whose lives are subject to increased surveillance and control. From social workers via probation officers and the police to community groups and charity organisations, the criminal justice net has absorbed more and more non-penal agencies into its administrative and disciplinary remit. So rapid and invidious was the growth of the system that some of the most ardent advocates of the community corrections philosophy came to ques-tion its development (see Lemert, 1981).

Cohen examines the logics of this transformation, charting the ways that disciplinary mechanisms of surveillance, control and punishment have become diffused and extended into ever more areas of social and personal life. In spite of observing that the community corrections movement did not originate as a state policy, none the less, Cohen suggests, the state

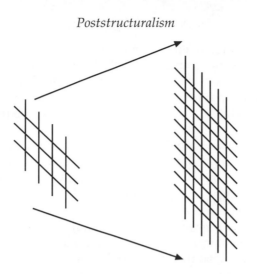

Figure 4.2   *The growth of the criminal justice 'net'*

emerged as the main beneficiary of these various struggles and conflicts that accompanied the movement's development. Thus, whilst the 1960s and 1970s did see a great deal of change in the institutions of social control and whilst there emerged numerous new initiatives for 'treating' deviants, these were not radical alternatives to the old system. Rather, argues Cohen, they comprised exercises in breaking down disciplinary methods, making them more flexible and circulating them around the institutional outposts of the social control network. The consequence was that, in contrast to the aims of the reformers, disciplinary methods became more rather than less important to the criminal justice system as more and more institutions adopted them. Cohen describes this process as an increase in the size of the criminal justice net and a decrease in the size of the criminal justice mesh (Figure 4.2).

The connections between welfare and penal institutions, in this case, become more firmly fixed in that there are increasing contacts between and increasing overlap of responsibilities within these different institutions. The meshing together of these institutions was, according to Garland (1985), part of a longer historical trend. The size of the system has increased – both in terms of institutions and personnel – but, importantly, the sanctions available for sentencing have also increased, drawing more and more interest groups into the overall system. Garland traces this development back to the turn of the twentieth century, showing its historical progress. Of particular interest to Garland is the emergence of finely detailed and extensive systems of classification of social problems. During the latter part of the nineteenth century and the early part of the twentieth century a great many new categories and labels were applied to social problems. New classifications of disease, deviance, social and psychological adaptation and family types provided more complex perspectives on the appropriate targets of social policy and on the ways that institutions should operate to 'normalise' the social and psychological characteristics of actually and potentially deviant populations. Garland's point is that the commitment to normalisation blurs the distinctions between 'welfare' and 'penal' systems and it is unclear precisely which parts of their operations are concerned with social or penal policy, for example.

In important respects, policies and programmes of 'normalisation' represent tensions between the institutions and the discourses of 'welfare' and 'law'. Whereas the latter is (ideal-typically) concerned with formal principles of justice and legality, applying the same codified system of abstract rules and procedures to all cases such that 'justice' will always be seen to be done, the former is (ideal-typically) concerned with the characteristics of each separate case, motivating and developing appropriate mixes of resources, treatments, provisions and supervisions so that welfare institutions and programmes will be able to respond to the diversity and individuality of needs to be found in society (King, 1991). In practice, however, as Donzelot (1980: 107, 150) and Garland and Young (1983: 15) observe, these distinctions are persistently challenged and redrawn as professional and special interest groups struggle to exert influence on and control over the institutions and organisations of the modern liberal-democratic state (cf. Dickens, 1993). The institutions and programmes that make up the state (including, in its penal-welfare dimensions, courts, government departments, detention or day centres, schools, social work, probation and psychiatric services, community homes and assessment centres, for example) comprise a multi-layered and complex network of practices, relationships, rights, duties and obligations, resources, rewards and sanctions. In turn, the control of this network constitutes control of the major forms of social, economic and political participation in modern society. Struggles between welfare and legal discourses, between social, psychiatric, criminal justice and medical interest groups are struggles over the institutional and political relationships which define and organise that participation.

Foucault uses the term 'power–knowledge' to explain the development of processes of 'normalisation', their techniques and the systems of classification that organise and define deviance and difference, referring to the relationship between the ways in which we have knowledge of things and the ways in which we organise them – the relationships between categories of thought and understanding and categories of experience and action. The disciplines of the human sciences – sociology, psychology, social work, economics and so on – are rooted in particular modes of thought and practice which serve to define and classify the characteristics of different dimensions of personal and social experience. For Foucault, the act of definition and classification is itself an exercise of power for two reasons. The very techniques of classifying and defining (through statistical, ethnographic or experimental analysis, for example) were developed within and currently persist through hierarchical and socially exclusive institutions – such as the universities and research institutes, hospitals, prisons or asylums, for example. Such institutions consist of social actors who have vested interests in codifying the methods for normalising deviance, constructing identity, regulating sexuality or the body, defining and controlling madness and so on.

The codification of norms, deviations, patterns of understanding and participation is a micro and macro political system entrenched in all modern institutional spheres. For example, the recent introduction of Quality procedures into the universities significantly affects both the administration and the definition of appropriate learning and knowledge production. The increasing monitoring and standardisation of student contact hours, relations with tutors, the process of grading, performance profiles, course development, progress statistics, publication and research output, publicity, image and much more establishes particular patterns of action and interaction between students, academics, administrators, counsellors, welfare officers and other social actors. The nature of the qualification, the expertises and skills acquired, and the interpretation of academic achievement are constructed within a monitoring and regulatory system that codifies the norms and produces the deviations. Certain types of knowledge, particular techniques, perspectives and evaluations are legitimised whilst others are excluded and/or marginalised.

Marginalisation/exclusion is inevitably accompanied by resistance and conflict which gives rise to political struggle over the meaning and experience of exclusion. For example, sections of the disability rights movement and the feminist movement challenge the dominant knowledges, procedures and practices of social institutions and their marginality to them (cf. Morris, 1991; Carabine, 1992; Taylor, 1993) and for as long as the institutional system of codification persists resistances and challenges will exist (Penna and O'Brien, 1996: 52–3). To the extent that institutional systems include and exclude, centralise and marginalise ways of seeing, knowing and acting they comprise a cultural politics that is pivotal in the legitimation/proscription of modes of self-understanding, self-expression and self-identity. It is in this sense that poststructuralism suggests that knowledge is an intrinsic feature of relations of subordination and domination.

Concluding remarks

Poststructuralist approaches to social welfare raise complex political questions around the origins of knowledge about social problems and the ways that knowledge is tied to power. They are direct and forceful challenges to conventional ways of interpreting the growth and development of the social institutions of welfare, pointing, in particular, to the political logics in which social policies are embedded. From Foucault's historical analyses of sexuality, madness and punishment to the explorations of welfare discourses, institutions and exclusions, grand visions of progress and reform are rejected in favour of much more detailed assessments of the conditions of emergence, maintenance and contestation of specific welfare programmes.

Like neo-liberalism, the poststructuralist challenge comprises a fundamental rejection of the Enlightenment ideals that have underpinned both the discipline of social policy and the vision of social welfare that it has helped to sustain. For all practical purposes poststructuralism dismisses as naive the search for normative standards against which to measure and assess the growth and progress of collective welfare. In place of this search, poststructuralists investigate the social and political alliances and conflicts through which such standards are formulated and carried through into concrete policy areas. In this sense they seek to show how the history of social policy and welfare is continually made and re-made through discursive and institutional struggles. Their analytical advantage lies in the commitment to grappling with the intersection of many different interests and organisations in the development of specific fields of welfare organisation. Foucault's studies themselves address scientific, philanthropic, religious and therapeutic models of human welfare in the investigation of penality, madness and sexuality and this complex strategy is taken up by those who apply his work to contemporary problems. The consequence of such complexity is to shift the agenda away from universal prescriptions for alleviating social distress and to emphasise the multiple agenda which any welfare programme generates. In this sense, the poststructuralist critique is central to the debate about the democratisation of welfare and the ways that changing patterns of organisation and delivery forge new lines of social inclusion and exclusion.

PART THREE
POST-ENLIGHTENMENT PROBLEMATICS

Preface

In this final part of the book we consider three contemporary perspectives that have been applied to the task of theorising welfare. These perspectives consist in new developments in political economy, the emergence of a political ecology of welfare, and postmodernism. Whilst these perspectives differ markedly from each other, none the less each is structured by a common series of theoretical problematics that comprise the 'modernity thesis' (cf. O'Brien, 1998). The modernity thesis construes the contemporary world as a world that differs radically from its past. In particular, the modern world is cut off from all of the customary, natural and metaphysical reference points by which traditional societies were regulated. Social action is no longer conditioned by place, tradition or religion. Instead, in the modern world, social action has become detraditionalised, globally diffused and rationalised. Human destiny lies in human, not divine, hands and the laws that govern the world are no longer 'natural' in the way that Enlightenment philosophy championed this term. If, for Rousseau and Smith, the task of philosophy and science was to understand the inherent order of things and help to construct a society which complied with this order, contemporary social science construes the order of society as a malleable product of human action which can take many different forms – none of which are inherently more or less compliant with how things really, naturally or 'lawfully' should be.

The 'modernity' of society lies in this malleability, in the possibility of transformation that underpins all the apparent fixities of habit and structure through which institutional and everyday life is co-ordinated and conducted. The 'promise' of Enlightenment – the rational, humane, progressive application of objective knowledge to people's needs and desires, the subjugation of history and nature to human purposes – has remained unfulfilled. Indeed, for some, the promise comprises a discourse which glosses over questions about whose purposes will be served (and how), whose rationalities will be applied and whose needs fulfilled (and how). The modernisation of society, legitimised and carried forward on the basis of Enlightenment principles, has resulted in the creation and maintenance of inequality, disadvantage and socio-political divisions.

In coming to terms with the distortions, ambiguities and inherent disadvantages that have continued to structure social life ever since the eighteenth century Enlightenment, contemporary social theory has been forced to abandon some of the central philosophical commitments that provided its ostensible coherence. Notable amongst these, and partly under the impact of the anti-Enlightenment philosophies that we outlined in Part Two, is the loss of faith in any form of positive historical continuity. Whereas liberalism and Marxism had initially projected a resolution of modern society's contradictions – either through evolution or revolution – contemporary social theory is much less eager to engage in such futuristic speculation. Indeed, in contrast to the perspectives in Parts One and Two it is hard to credit contemporary theories in political economy with the status of 'isms'. Postindustrialism, post-Fordism and disorganised capitalism do not themselves refer to theoretical perspectives. The first is the analytical object of a combination of liberal economics and critical sociology, the second a concept in a combination of structural Marxism and institutional economics, the third a category of a combined Austro-Marxism and Weberian sociology. One of the main reasons why we characterise the theories in Chapter 5 as 'post-Enlightenment' political economy is precisely because of their scepticism towards the possibility of a singular and unified theoretical system through which social change, both historically and in the contemporary world, can be explained.

A similar observation needs to be made of the political ecology referred to in Chapter 6. Theories of the relationships between ecological change and social welfare that we explore in this chapter are not versions of 'environmentalist' theory. By and large, they represent reconfigurations of already-existing theories but without the predictive confidence that characterised their past formulations. Gorz's thesis on the 'megamachine' of capitalist development represents an anarchist critique of his own earlier commitment to Marxism; Shiva's assessment of the uneven consequences of ecological degradation is a version of the feminist critique of modernisation theory; and Beck's perspective on the 'risk society' combines Weberian sociology with a systems theory inspired by Luhman. This is not to say that these perspectives are uninformative or unoriginal. On the contrary, they refocus social theory on previously marginalised questions about the relationships between power, wealth, science and ecological destruction. But they are not theories in the mould of Marxism, liberalism, poststructuralism or neo-liberalism. They do not overhaul central philosophical paradigms in order to generate new *logics* of interpretation or explanation.

In contrast, the perspectives we outline in Chapter 7 engage in precisely this sort of challenge. Collectively, they represent, at least potentially, a new 'ism' in the store of social theory, reinterpreting, reconceptualising and retheorising the relationships between identity, experience, action, structure, meaning, history and the present. We have called the chapter postmodern*ism* (as opposed to postmodern*ity* or *the* postmodern) because it is this process of *theorising* that we want to emphasise. Like Foucault's poststructuralism, however, postmodern theory often runs so against the grain of sociological scholarship that it is extremely difficult to situate the former in the context of the latter. In fact, so arduous has this challenge proved that few social theorists have declared their perspectives to be 'postmodern' at all. In consequence, the label 'postmodern' is currently applied to an eclectic range of perspectives on and beliefs about the contemporary world. Some argue that the postmodern represents a new historical era; others that the postmodern is a rupture in the modern era; others that the postmodern recovers traditions and knowledges hidden or subjugated by modernity. In this reassessment of modern life, the Enlightenment represents a philosophical plumb-line, defining and centring modern philosophy and politics. If there is a unifying commitment to the view from postmodernism it is that the plumb-line is not, and never has been, a reliable fixed point from which to measure social development and divergence.

5

Political Economy

As we saw in Chapter 2, classical Marxism begins from a view about the nature of human society founded on an analysis of the conditions, organisations and interests obtaining in industrial capitalist (class) societies. Marxist theories of class and revolution build on the 'social essence' of human identity and social arrangements are examined in terms of the extent to which this social essence is realised (or impeded) through the actions and interactions of organised groups of social agents, or classes. The base–superstructure distinction proposes that modern social development represents the unfolding of a higher-order historical logic driven by conflict between social classes. The emergence and development of social institutions and frameworks is understood as conforming to these embedded developmental logics. Differences between states, social institutions, political projects and ideologies are explained as variants of or deviations from the pattern implicit in the theory.

The break with this kind of theoretical argument – represented by a range of very different perspectives – signals a break with a view of social development and change as indicating 'normal' and 'abnormal' patterns. Contemporary political economy characteristically abandons the notion of an 'end' state of history, a final realisation or a utopian apex of civilisation. Rather than operating at the meta-theoretical level, the perspectives discussed in this chapter – postindustrialism, post-Fordism and the disorganisation thesis – are 'macro'-theoretical analyses of contemporary transformation, concerned with understanding the relationships between different elements of a changing, but persistent, capitalist economic structure. Through an emphasis on causal contingency, shifts in the organisation of capitalism and multiple frameworks or paradigms of societal development, 'post-Enlightenment' political economy represents a break with classical political economy, a modification of its premises, assumptions and theoretical categories. Three dimensions of this reformulated political economy are of particular significance in the analysis of social welfare. These are the focus on globalisation, the relationships between work and welfare and the emergence of new socio-political divisions. We will comment briefly on each of these before going on to outline the implications of the new political economies for theorising welfare.

Globalisation

Changes in global economic organisation represent a hugely complex phenomenon. These changes include the emergence of new centres of production and consumption, new technologies of production, transport and communication and new – or, rather, intensified – divisions of labour. *Globalisation* is not the same as, and can in fact be said to draw on, *internationalisation* – which refers to an increased geographical spread of economic activities across national boundaries. In effect, globalisation is 'a more advanced and complex form of internationalisation which implies a degree of functional integration between internationally dispersed economic activities' (Dicken, 1992: 1). The 'globalisation' perspective suggests that the production of goods during the growth of industrial capitalism took place within relatively discrete national economies. Since the 1950s, however, the national character of economies has become increasingly weakened with the emergence of a new global division of labour in which a significant bulk of the production process is fragmented and dispersed across numerous geopolitical regions. Thus, different components of a single product can be manufactured or assembled in different countries. The globalisation of production is paralleled by a new twenty-four-hour, global financial system whose transactions are concentrated in three major financial centres – New York, Tokyo and London (Dicken, 1992; Lash and Urry, 1994). The upheavals in the world economy and the social, industrial and political systems of both developed and developing economies occasioned by, and accompanying, such changes are a major focus of 'post' political economic theories.

Work and welfare

The various changes in global economies have important implications for the welfare state and its development. As Dicken (1992: 422) emphasises, the key to an individual's or a family's material well-being is income which, for many, is derived from paid work and its associated benefits. This relationship between work and welfare has been at the heart of social policy in the West since the nineteenth century (Offe, 1984, 1991; Esping-Andersen 1990, 1991). The earliest national-social welfare structures – the European social security systems – arose as a response to the 'social question' of visible, mass poverty which developed in the wake of industrial capitalism. The employment-centred nature of these systems has been their distinguishing feature, concerned, as they are, with regulating entry and exit from labour markets (Offe, 1984), maintaining work incentives and ascribing status within the system as a function of continuous full-time employment (or 'deviation' from it) (Macarov, 1980; Esping-Andersen, 1990; Offe, 1991). The Keynesian Welfare State of the postwar era was constructed on the basis of two important assumptions: the first was that the national state could manage a national economy and in so doing maintain full, male, life-long employment. The second was that the traditional nuclear family with its entrenched sexual division of labour would remain the social norm. In these senses, the Keynesian Welfare State has been implicated in the construction of a formally separated (male) public sphere of paid work and a (female) private sphere of unpaid domestic and caring work. The maintenance of these separate spheres and the assumptions underpinning them are called into question by the post-political economy perspectives, which suggest shifting patterns of social and economic divisions that undermine the administrative principles of the Keynesian Welfare State. Moreover, these shifting patterns do not reflect a universal historical logic that determines the 'convergence' of all economies to a single formal model. Instead, different nation-states experience and respond to such shifts differently, revealing different and uneven developmental trends in the character of national welfare states.

New social divisions

Shifts in the organisation of the *global* economy, together with transformations in the economic and employment characteristics of individual *national* economies have raised questions of the emergence of new social divisions deriving from these changes and the consequent complication of political representation and mobilisation. This is important because it exposes the problems of national consensus over and coordination of welfare programmes and projects. The problem, simply put, is that contemporary political-economic changes appear to be generating, on the one hand, *global and national* social and political fragmentation and, on the other, *international* strategic alliances and coalitions. These effects can be seen in the growing intensity of the polarisation between rich and poor both within nation states and at the global level and in the growing importance of regional and international political-economic alliances. Mobilisation for policy goals is now criss-crossed by a bewildering array of 'global' (for example, environmental change), 'regional' (for example, the strengthening of trading blocs such as the EU and NAFTA) and national (for example, the marketisation of welfare services) political-economic frameworks. How these frameworks are to be coordinated to achieve even relatively clear-cut objectives, such as national employment policy or urban/regional development policy, is a question that has eluded any coherent, politically effective answer in all nations.

Postindustrial, capitalist disorganisation and post-Fordist perspectives propose that these three features of contemporary global organisation represent constituent features of the ongoing development of capitalism. Their aim is to provide theoretical resources for understanding the shifts in global, international and national economic structures and activities and each presents a specific view of their welfare consequences. Whilst Marxism provides an important analytic resource for many theorists discussed in this chapter, there is a rejection of classical Marxism's base–superstructure distinction, with its understanding of the mode of production as the causal factor in political and social organisation. Below we consider how each of these perspectives contributes to the task of theorising welfare in the contemporary 'new world order'.

Postindustrialism

The postindustrialism debate draws on two important traditions: American liberal economics (via Bell, 1973) and European critical sociology (via Touraine, 1974). Out of these early sources has developed an attempt to establish whether or not modern industrial economies are undergoing a fundamental, rather than incidental, transformation (see Allen, 1992), and whether new forms of employment (in service industries rather than manufacturing, for example), new technologies of information (the electronic media, for example) and the emergence of 'core' and 'peripheral' workforces represent a new socio-economic era or indicate a cyclical feature of modern capitalist societies. Trying to capture the various changes taking place in economic processes is difficult, and Allen (1992: 172) points out that to decide whether or not these changes are fundamental we need to establish whether they are interconnected and, if so, what kind of economy is taking shape. This exercise is complicated further by the different effects of processes of economic restructuring on individual nation-states.

There is a number of different accounts of the processes of postindustrialisation which emphasise different aspects of change and its dynamics. Bell (1973), for example, highlights a shift from manufacturing to service sector employment, accompanied by the increasing importance of knowledge and information in the organisation of economic activity; indeed, for Bell, theoretical, scientific knowledge and information form the key components of transformation in postindustrial societies (Bell, 1980). One of the consequences of these shifts, for Bell, is that the rise of science and information technologies creates a society increasingly organised through and dependent on service employment and professional-technical groups. Status and privilege stem from control of knowledge, rather than inherited power or wealth, with a decline in class divisions and more meritocratic opportunity structures alongside more pluralistic lifestyles. This relatively optimistic view is contested by some. Touraine (1974), for example, similarly identified new technologies as crucially important in driving contemporary economic change and saw information technologies as its principal mechanism but, unlike Bell, Touraine noted the social divisions likely to emerge as a result of these processes. He identified growing polarisations between technical and managerial staff with access to the informational economy and a range of social groups who are uneasily and unequally situated in relation to the 'technocratic' group, opening up the possibility of a new range of social conflicts. Gershuny and Miles (1983), in contrast, draw attention to the development of the 'self-service' economy where service sector occupations are partially undermined by self-provisioning (the use of washing machines and not launderettes, or cars and bicycles instead of public transport), and new technologies provide alternative forms of leisure and employment. Technology also creates the possibility of mass joblessness due to the reduction in the need for human labour caused by automation. Despite such differences in emphasis, most post-industrialist writers point to the role of knowledge and information technology as vital new forces in the organisation and development of economies, displacing manufacturing technologies and production (Touraine, 1974; Gorz, 1982, 1989). The suggestion is that we are experiencing an economic transformation akin to the industrial revolution – a 'microchip' revolution.

A large body of work has been inspired by accounts of postindustrial development. Reviewing debates in this field, Kumar (1995) and Allen (1992: 181) note that there are differences in emphasis among postindustrial writers, but a number of core empirical processes can be taken to suggest the arrival of postindustrialism. These include:

- a shift in the balance of the Western economies from a manufacturing to a service base;
- the development of a core workforce in relatively secure employment and a growing peripheral workforce of low-paid, casualised labour, socially segmented;
- an associated transformation in the organisation of work and occupations, generating a new structuring of social divisions and life-chances.

The consequences of postindustrialisation for the welfare state is an issue taken up by Esping-Andersen (1990) in his research into the comparative development of employment in Germany, Sweden and the United States. Esping-Andersen, as Offe (1984, 1991; see below), argues that state welfare provision is not a by-product of capitalist industrialisation, but is a central feature of the process of industrialisation, its management and development. In short, 'it is, in its own right, a system of stratification' and 'an active force in the ordering of social relations'. Specifically, state welfare amounts to a system of *citizenship* stratification that 'will compete with, even replace, one's class position' (Esping-Andersen, 1990: 23). In making this argument, Esping-Andersen draws attention to the relationships between social policy and labour markets and to the 'decommodification' of the status of individuals within that market. 'Decommodification' occurs 'when a service is rendered as a matter of right, and when a person can maintain a livelihood without reliance on the market' (1990: 24). Thus, subsistence through the organised provision of welfare services in both cash and kind represents an alternative to subsistence through income derived from selling one's labour for wages. The problem for capitalist societies dependent on the wage-labour mechanism, therefore, is how to organise the welfare system such that the necessary types and degree of stratification are sustained whilst at the same time preventing the total exit of wage labourers from the market. According to Esping-Andersen, capitalist societies resolve this problem in different ways, leading to the emergence of different 'welfare régimes' which latter correspond to distinct configurations of the state–market–family nexus.

The focus of Esping-Andersen's research is on postindustrial occupational change and the relationships between this change and the organisation of decommodified rights, benefits and entitlements. The concern here is to test some of the theories of postindustrial development discussed above, and to establish whether, for example, Bell's optimistic view or Gershuny's more pessimistic conclusions are more representative of emerging occupational structures. Two broad trends are identified in Esping-Andersen's work. The first is the *common* structural transformation on which we commented above – a decline in manufacturing and extractive industries in the West accompanied by a major increase in service sector occupations. The second is a *contingent* structural transformation where the national trajectory of employment trends is determined by the specific political and institutional frameworks of each country. By examining national variations in occupational structures and social welfare arrangements, Esping-Andersen identifies three welfare-capitalist 'régime types'. The first is the *liberal* welfare régime, found in the United States, Britain, Canada and Australia for example, where means-tested and residual provision for the poor is the dominant form of state provision, alongside some limited state insurance, and in which the state actively encourages market and occupational welfare provision as the preferred form. The second is the *corporatist* régime exemplified by Germany, Austria and France, for example, characterised by a strong state social insurance scheme for those in work, which replicates occupational status differentials within its benefit structure. This régime is shaped by conservative and religious influences so that there is also a strong emphasis on family benefits to encourage the provision of welfare services by women in the family. Finally, the *social democratic* régime of the Scandinavian countries is characterised by universalism, inclusive social rights and relatively high standards of provision. In this régime, welfare structures aim at 'levelling up' and socialising the costs of caring for children and infirm and elderly people (Esping-Andersen, 1990: 26–9).

Whilst Esping-Andersen acknowledges that none of these régimes exists as a 'pure' type – each contains some elements of others – the point is that each contains a different stratification effect, both in terms of class and gender. The liberal régime offloads most welfare functions to markets and private provision, leaving those who cannot afford to pay for these services or benefits dependent on stigmatising and poor state services and low benefit levels. The corporatist régime upholds class and status differentials and discourages women from working, whilst the social-democratic régime minimises class and status differentials and makes it easier for women to take paid employment, although the labour market remains severely gender-segregated.

To examine the impact of welfare state régimes on new forms of stratification, Esping-Andersen arrives at a rough three-fold classification of the change in service sector employment, identifying growth in: (a) *social services* such as health, education and welfare; (b) *personal services* such as consumption, catering, tourism, etc.; and (c) *producer services* such as real estate, insurance, financial and business services. Within these sectors jobs are classified according to whether they are (a) *professional and scientific*; (b) *semi-professional and technical*; or (c) *skilled* and *unskilled* (junk jobs) *personal services*. There are considerable national differences in the types and rate of development of these service sectors and the occupational structures they produce. Table 5.1 summarises some of the differences in service sector employment change identified by Esping-Andersen in three countries from the early 1960s to the mid 1980s (1990: 192–217).

These different trajectories to postindustrial employment are influenced by the fact that each country is embedded within its own specific dynamics of development. There are certain parallels – industrial employment is losing prominence in all of the countries in Esping-Andersen's sample and almost everywhere women's employment is increasing – but the variations overshadow convergence. Esping-Andersen's point, here, is that 'politics matter' (Esping-Andersen, 1991: 148; 1990). Politics mattered in the past, in that the formation of welfare régimes has been tied to the specific political characteristics of each separate nation, and politics matter in the present, in that the employment and welfare trajectories of the different countries are inflected by the liberal, corporatist or social democratic régime type characterising their industrial development (Esping-Andersen, 1990). In short, an emphasis on techno-economic forces alone cannot account for the different routes that are taken in response to common structural shifts.

One of the consequences of Esping-Andersen's thesis is that it becomes much more problematic to assess what forms political action will take as changes in occupational structures and patterns of stratification have generated new social divisions, new dimensions of conflict and new forms of collective action. As he notes, much of the postindustrialism literature is concerned with questions of class inequality because class theories were originally formulated precisely to explain the inequalities produced by the division of labour and what the political implications of this process might be (Esping-Andersen, 1991: 148–51). However, Esping-Andersen argues that variations in régime types are importantly structured by class coalitions rather than simply by the binary opposition between a ruling and a working class and the levels of inequality by which the opposition is marked. A number of political implications follows from this emphasis. Esping-Andersen (1991) argues that where there are considerable labour market 'insiders' and 'outsiders' those in employment who have secure jobs and occupational benefits may mobilise against the perceived burden of supporting those outside the labour market, eroding general support for the welfare state. In countries such as Germany whose service sectors depend on migrant labour, divisions based on ethnicity may structure the politics of labour markets and welfare provision as they do in the United States; where public/private gender segregation in employment exists, as in Sweden, with women concentrated in the public sector and men in the private sector, distributional conflicts ensue around the public–private

Table 5.1   *Employment trajectories in three welfare régimes*

Country	Régime type	Change in employment sectors	Social divisions
USA	Liberal	No absolute decline in industrial employment; growth in labour force	Black, female and hispanic workers overrepresented in 'junk jobs'
		Increase in professional and in low-paid occupations; increase in full-time and in part-time employment	Black youth and single parents disproportionately affected by unemployment
		Increase in women's low-paid employment, especially in private social and personal services	Some decline in gender and ethnicity-based occupational segregation
		Significant increase in service occupations: business, finance, insurance, social, and leisure and consumption services	Significant and increasing earnings inequality and labour market polarisation
Germany	Corporatist	Decline in industrial employment and in labour force	Stagnant employment participation rates for women; overrepresentation in 'junk jobs'
		Declining employment rates for men	Slow development of service base combined with decline in industrial employment leading to joblessness
		Some increase in social and producer service employment	Acutely gendered work–family nexus; some decline in gender-based occupational segregation
		Growth in part-time employment; part-time replacing full-time jobs	Earnings structure less polarised than USA
		Decline of women's employment in private sector	
Sweden	Social democratic	Decline in industrial employment but overall growth in labour force	Feminisation of public sector workforce
		Increase in producer and social services	Private sector employment male dominated
		Increase in women's employment in welfare state service sector; better rates of pay and conditions of employment than Germany or USA	Least polarised earnings structure; relatively good wages and job security
		Increase in part-time employment	
		82% of job growth accounted for by increase in women's employment	

axis and electoral coalitions are inflected by this gender dimension (Esping-Andersen, 1991: 155–9).

The emphasis on the stratification effects of different welfare state régimes and the political dimensions of change mark out Esping-Andersen's contribution as unique in relating postindustrial employment patterns to welfare state structures. In general, the research agenda in this field has focused on the manufacturing sector of Western economies because it is here that major global shifts have been most evident. As the manufacturing sector in the West has declined during the postwar period, its activities have become increasingly concentrated in a small number of developing countries that have emerged as world centres of production and trade (Dicken, 1992: 5). The enormous displacement of predominantly male workforces in Europe resulting from this process of deindustrialisation is partly the result of the use of new technologies in the production process (automation), as in the automobile industry for example, and partly of a search for low-wage and low-cost locations, as in the clothing, textile and electronic industries, for example, which are now possible as a result of the speed and flexibility of movement and communications around the world. The electronics industry, for example, employs large numbers of young female workers on low wages in the assembly stages of production, who are often subject to extremely poor working conditions. Whilst this and other industries, as well as the global changes charted by Dicken (1992), are highly complex and diverse, an emerging distinction is that between a core of highly trained, well-paid professional and technical workers and a periphery of low-skilled, poorly paid workers, both within and between countries (Kumar, 1995), suggesting growing economic and social polarisation in most countries.

The relocation of production to newly industrialising and developing economies in Asia and Africa – the globalisation of the economy – and the growth of core and peripheral workforces alongside increasingly casualised, short-term, part-time and gendered forms of work in the West pose enormous problems for all of the welfare régimes described by Esping-Andersen. Corporatist, liberal and social democratic régimes have developed income maintenance systems rooted in the assumption of full-time, life-long, adult, male employment. Taxation and social insurance contributions are presumed to foot the bill for all forms of social expenditure. At the same time, it has been assumed that the male worker will be able to draw on the unpaid labour of women to provide personal and caring services in the home. But these assumptions are increasingly rendered obsolete by the postindustrialisation of economic organisation and the consequent shifts in employment trends and income distribution. The shifts in the gender balance of formal employment, and the uneven structuring of wages and earnings attached to it, the deindustrialisation of European labour markets and the rise of service-based economies, the fragmentation of the production process and the increasing diversity of consumption practices have uneven consequences for stratification systems. The 'welfare régimes' of Europe are in a process of restratifying citizenship entitlements under pressures from postindustrialising economic change.

Disorganised capitalism

The upheavals in the world economy described as the operations of 'postindustrial' society by Bell and Esping-Andersen are characterised more specifically as a reorganisation of *capitalist* socio-economic relations rather than *industrial* production in theories of 'disorganised capitalism' or, more accurately, the disorganisation and reorganisation of capitalism (Offe, 1985; Lash and Urry, 1987). Examining economic change in the United States, Germany, Sweden, France and Britain, Lash and Urry adopt a neo-Marxist model of change which focuses on shifts in the circuits of capital over time (Lash and Urry, 1987: 8; 1994: 1–2). Theirs is a focus that does not subscribe to a historical logic of class transformation and revolution but, rather, examines changes in economic structure through a sociological account of the relationships between politics, capital formation and social experience. Lash and Urry, as Marx, produce a periodisation of economic change but their emphasis is on stages of capitalism – that is, on the persistence and continuation of the capitalist mode of production – rather than on historical stages of successive modes of production. Broadly, Lash and Urry distinguish the period of liberal or *laissez-faire* capitalism (mid eighteenth to mid nineteenth century); the period of organised capitalism (late nineteenth to mid twentieth century); and the period of disorganised capitalism (mid twentieth century to the present). These periodisations need to be treated with some caution because Lash and Urry propose that different capitalist countries became 'organised' and 'disorganised' at different times.

Capitalist organisation and social welfare

Liberal or *laissez-faire* capitalism was characterised by a lack of central political coordination. Individuals, communities and enterprises were socially distributed and sustained through the operations of irregular and undisciplined market processes. In the late eighteenth and early nineteenth century, new forms of capitalist manufacture developed in the context of a breakdown in the traditional social and cultural networks that had been prevalent in the agrarian society of the immediately preceding period. The new forms of manufacture were taken forward by competing small and medium-sized firms in the rapidly expanding urban centres of production. Urbanisation, in turn, was accompanied by the development of relatively autonomous working class communities with few ties to the social and cultural structures of the emergent industrial bourgeois entrepreneurs (Lash and Urry, 1987: 94–7).

The displacement of *laissez-faire* capitalism towards the end of the nineteenth century was characterised by, amongst other things: the concentration and centralisation of capital; the regulation of markets; a mass production economy organised within national boundaries; large numbers of workers employed in the extractive and manufacturing industries; corporatist industrial relations; class-inflected welfare states; the growth of the nation-state as an important site of national social and economic management and regulation; and the growth of a professional-technical middle class. Within this ideal-typical depiction it is necessary to distinguish between the organisation of capitalism 'at the top' – including the concentration of industry and increasing formal connections between banks, industry and the state, for example – and organisation 'at the bottom', including the emergence of national working class trade and political organisations and the welfare state (Lash and Urry, 1987: 3–4). As in the postindustrialist perspective, some of the processes of welfare state development are common to all countries whilst some are specific to their different developmental trajectories.

Industrial capitalism and the extension of the franchise combined to form a powerful impetus to the expansion of welfare provision, so that in many Western countries, in the early stages of organised capitalism, welfare legislation was initiated and supported by a diverse range of professional, labour and political alliances. Similarly, the concentration of workers in manufacturing production and urban centres created the conditions for working-class political mobilisation in trade unions or labour or socialist parties in individual countries. Lash and Urry (1987: 229) see the development of social insurance-based benefit provision as belonging to this early stage of organised capitalism. An important political goal of labour parties was the use of state power to develop welfare state provision as protection from the vagaries of the market for workers and their families. Thus, 'organisation' represents a period in capitalist development where social and economic institutions quite literally become highly ordered along several distinct axes, including the organisation and regulation of industrial and financial capitals, coordination of the relationships between economic institutions and the state, the organisation of workers in trade unions and labourist political parties, and the administration of the national population through the welfare state. At this stage there are tightly bounded national economies, with the nation state holding responsibility for economic management and extensive social provision. The immediate postwar period represents the height of organised capitalism, the universalism of the Keynesian Welfare State representing a degree of 'unity between class and nation' through the incorporation of the working class into the structures of social citizenship (Lash and Urry, 1987: 229).

However, the process of capitalist organisation does not represent a straightforward developmental line but, rather, an uneven series of steps that are traversed differently in different countries. Germany, for example, represents an 'ideal type' of organised capitalism in that it became organised both at the top and at the bottom very early. Its heavy industries – steel, coal and chemicals, for example – were highly concentrated and highly integrated before the Great War, by which time a stable social insurance scheme was also already in place. Similarly, German welfare state legislation was instigated from above by powerful political and economic interests as part of a drive to undermine the appeal and influence of socialist parties – indeed, early welfare state legislation was introduced in tandem with legislation outlawing socialist parties. Britain, in contrast, achieved a relatively high degree of organisation at the bottom – including the formation of working class political organisations and systems of welfare provision before the First World War – but was only very weakly organised at the top until the interwar years. Towards the end of the nineteenth century, British working class organisations were pressuring for national legislation for welfare benefits to alleviate the burden of unemployment and retirement and it was this political activity, rather than the strategic foresight of the capitalist class that was the major driving force behind the new-century social insurance legislation. It was only as the Second World War approached, however, that government by 'national' administration – linking financial, industrial and working class organisations – began seriously to coordinate economic management 'at the top'.

Capitalist disorganisation and social welfare

Disorganised capitalism, in the postwar period, is characterised by a breakdown of the institutional relations governing organised capitalism. Among its most important elements are: the deindustrialisation of economies; the decline of national markets and nationally based corporations; a decline in the absolute and relative size of the industrial working class; a decline in national collective bargaining and the growth of company- and plant-level wage bargaining; 'flexible' forms of production and working practices; a considerable weakening of the power of the nation-state to manage a national economy; a decline in industrial cities; the expansion of the service class; a decline in class politics and the growth of new social movement politics; and an increase in cultural diversity and fragmentation (Lash and Urry, 1987: 5–6).

Since, according to Lash and Urry, the different capitalist countries of the West organised 'at the top' and 'at the bottom' at different times and rates and to different degrees, so their postwar disorganisation has followed different trajectories. In consequence, the contemporary character of European welfare states can be described as a function of the stages and processes of disorganisation of their capitalist economies.

The decline of organised capitalism from the 1950s onwards is occasioned partly by structural shifts in capital accumulation and partly by the structures of organised capitalism itself. The widespread changes, however, are not understood by Lash and Urry to result simply from the logic of capitalist economic relations, but from a number of contingent, multi-causal factors, in which the spatial organisation characteristic of organised capitalism – of capital, labour, communities and so on – undergo a process of *deconcentration, disaggregation* and *dispersal*. This disorganisation of capitalism's institutional elements is marked by the distribution of manufacturing activities across the globe, and in particular to the newly industrialising economies, the growth of 'flexible' production and working practices and an increase in the importance of the service sector. As the economic base of the industrial cities declines, so do the communities and social and political patterns which grew up around the latter. Thus, disorganised capitalism represents substantial changes in economic, social and political life.

The effects of economic change display considerable spatial and social diversity. Acknowledging Esping-Andersen's three régime types, Lash and Urry (1994) investigate the effects of occupational change in the United States and Europe, finding a concentration of poverty and jobless-ness in the deindustrialised cities. In the United States, such poverty concentration is intensely racialised, disproportionately affecting the non-WASP population. Whilst young black people have significantly im-proved their educational qualifications across the past two decades this has not translated into employment opportunities. This is not to say that whites are not also poor, but that they are not concentrated into ghettos of poverty to anything like the same degree. The development of an 'under-class' is seen to be connected not to cultural practices and behaviours, as in New Right perspectives, but to the fact that significant numbers of black people in the United States live in 'rustbelt' cities, once industrialised but now emptied of work.

Concentration of poverty persists also in Europe, as does its racialisa-tion. Lash and Urry document the complex spatial and social dimensions of disadvantage, arguing that everywhere there has been a polarisation of income and wealth. This growing polarisation is the outcome of both structural change and political strategy – that is, the production of wealth is inextricably linked to the production of poverty – in disorganised capitalism. As in the United States, one feature of importance is the way that densely populated manufacturing cities in Europe have been 'emptied' of important social and political institutions: labour markets, commodity markets, welfare state organisations, trade unions, and people with sufficient resources, move out to other locations, leaving behind a deficit of economic and social regulation (Lash and Urry, 1994: 160), leading to the development of 'ungovernable spaces'.

These developments highlight an important dimension of disorganised capitalist societies, namely, a change in the systems of governance through which labour is regulated. The systems of governance of migrant and marginalised labour include families, states and corporate bodies, where complex national and cross-national networks generate different combi-nations of governance systems. Thus the nation-state and the organised economic actors of organised capitalism have given way to more complex and fractured regulatory mechanisms, with racialisation, sexualisation and marginalisation of labour being configured differently in different contexts, sometimes through the market, sometimes through other social institutions.

This change in governance systems is partly the result of structural change but, importantly, partly the result of disorganisation wrought by the institutions of organised capitalism. For example, the development of the welfare state in organised capitalism generated substantial public sector employment and an important political division has emerged between those working in private and public sector services. The issues and interests of each diverge considerably, with public sector employees being much more likely to support social democratic political programmes and the maintenance and expansion of the public sector. This political division also highlights consumption-based divisions between, on the one hand, those who benefit from the welfare state as claimants and/or as employees and, on the other, those who benefit from reduced taxation through cuts in public sector expenditure (Lash and Urry, 1987: 229).

Class fragmentation and political culture

The division between welfare supporters and detractors forms the basis of Offe's (1991) account of the politics of welfare provision in Germany, an account that has implications for all European welfare systems. Since 1975, Germany has adopted a policy of adapting to new economic conditions through austerity measures aimed at preserving the institutional foundations of the welfare state. This has involved a pattern of 'targeting' benefits at selected groups, increasing or introducing fees for services, reducing services and benefits and off-loading responsibility, where possible (1991: 136–7). The piecemeal and gradualist nature of this strategy has generated a differentiated and fragmented system of entitlement, resulting in 'the emergence and consolidation of a class divided society in which each class is defined by its relation not to the means of production but to the state organised resources of welfare, and therefore by the differing degree to which it is vulnerable to being deprived of its share' (p. 144).

The fragmentation of classes through welfare state structures generates four winner and loser groups. The first is a privileged group of highly paid workers who enjoy job security and excellent occupational benefits; the second, largest, grouping is also in stable employment, maintains traditional family structures and benefits from the state insurance system; the third group consists of those out of work for various reasons but still eligible in the state scheme, who have less political clout than the others and whose benefits are more vulnerable to cuts; the fourth group – divided into two subsets – consists of, on the one hand, a disparate category of persons, reliant on means-tested and residual state provision, and, on the other, a group of refugees, immigrant workers, illegal entrants and asylum seekers who are the most vulnerable of all, mainly excluded from welfare provision altogether (p. 144). This fragmentation generates a number of political divisions and axes of conflict, so that the main lines of conflict are not capital versus labour but organised workers against unorganised workers, women, children and families against male-dominated and employment-centred corporate bodies, employed against unemployed, and so on (p. 145).

In a situation of economic decline, rising unemployment, casualised labour markets, growing and new forms of poverty and the 'two-thirds' society, where one-third of the population is excluded from growth and economic rewards, the 'social question' which generated reform in the nineteenth and twentieth centuries loses its significance. This is partly because of the fragmentation of interests and partly because of a political redefinition of social problems (such as poverty) as moral problems. An important effect of the casualisation of labour markets is the difficulty of collective worker representation, whilst welfare claimants whose entitlements do not derive from employment contributions represent a range of needs and interests which have never been part of the labourist agenda anyway. At the same time, party-political strategy in Germany since the mid 1970s has been concerned to redefine social problems as problems of moral order, national identity, the family and so on (p. 141). The consequence is a fragmentation of social groups and their associated political goals, which:

> become manifest in the rise of issues and demands having to do with regional interests, age categories, gender categories, health and agriculture, among numerous others; this centrifugal and 'disorderly' pattern of political issues dominating domestic politics over the last decade was not suitable for integration into a coherent and potentially hegemonic program of social reform . . . (p. 146)

The fracturing of social groups and their relationships to welfare state structures is an important feature of the disorganisation of capitalist social relations across all European states. Lash and Urry (1987) point to a further feature of this fragmentation arising from the growth in public sector employment. The high rates of women's employment in the public sector, combined with its high levels of unionisation, has had significant effects on the labour movement's agenda. The public sector service class is credited with providing a powerful contribution to the development of new social movements – feminism, environmentalism, anti-racism, for example – which have had some success, in the West, in shifting policy and political agenda. These social movements arise in the context of a decline in the industrial working class and traditional class politics. The decline in working class jobs in steel, coal, shipbuilding and other heavy industries has resulted in a reduction in the traditional social base of masculinistic working class political parties. At the same time, there has been a process of de-alignment in class voting, with class influence on voting behaviour weakening significantly, pointing towards changes in support for, and identification with, the mass parties of right and left. Of importance for 'left' parties has been an apparent decline in support for nationalisation, extending the welfare state and maintaining links with trade unions. For the 'right' in the UK, for example, the problem is a decline in respect for the authority of traditional icons of monarchy, House of Lords and so on, with which they are closely associated (Lash and Urry, 1987: 214–15).

These changes encourage the erosion of the modernist cultural tradition and the sense of culture as a 'lived unity of experience' – in particular, social class experience – as new technologies and patterns of mobility extend and make more accessible forms of popular culture, consumerism and diverse lifestyles. Together with new social movement politics, there is a considerable shift in the political arena, one which cuts across traditional political divides, directed at issues such as the environment, feminism, European integration, and so on. These political questions pose difficulties for mainstream parties at the same time that the latter show themselves unable to respond effectively to more traditional concerns, such as unemployment. Welfare state institutions find it increasingly difficult to respond to both the broader political agenda and the alienating, ineffective and oppressive effects of traditional bureaucratic and paternalistic welfare state structures. Thus, disorganised capitalism suggests a considerable shift in emphasis from class politics and issues of resource and income distribution to a politics based on what have been termed 'post-materialist' questions of life quality, equality, participation, self-determination and human rights (Lash and Urry, 1987: 215–19).

Disorganised capitalism leads to changes not only in economic institutions but also in political and cultural institutions. Here, the welfare state is held to be, on the one hand, an effect of organised capitalism and, on the other, an important cause of its subsequent disorganisation and recomposition. The characteristics of disorganised capitalism's economic structures – smaller and more dispersed production units, more irregular and insecure forms of work which do not generate the solidarity of the assembly-line or industrial workplace, the expansion of the service sector, spurring the influx of large numbers of women into the official workforce, growing socio-economic polarisation, the concentration and intensification of poverty and mass unemployment – means not only a collapse in the economic conditions which underpinned the welfare states of organised capitalism, but also the rise of new conflicts, divisions and political issues to which welfare states must respond.

Post-Fordism

The post-Fordism perspective draws on the managerialist, institutionalist and regulation schools of political economy (see Bagguley, 1991) and neo-Marxist state theory. The label 'post' in this usage suggests a crisis in Fordist organisation, with 'Fordism' corresponding to the period of industrialism. Conceiving of Fordism in ideal-typical terms, its main characteristics are a mass manufacturing base, mass consumption patterns and state organisation of national social and economic maintenance through Keynesian budgetary techniques and the Keynesian Welfare State. Post-Fordism represents a 'strategic reorientation' of state and economy aimed at resolving the crisis and consolidating a new accumulation régime in which production is organised around more 'flexible' practices and consumption is diversified. The rise of service industries, the emergence of a less secure workforce, the importance of knowledge and information – all of these are acknowledged but are represented as shifts in the location and form of industrial society rather than signals of its transformation into a 'post-industrial' society. Taking these changes together, in some uses (Burrows and Loader, 1994; Jessop, 1994a, 1994b) the terms Fordism and post-Fordism refer to broader patterns of social organisation, to particular kinds of social formation. Here, the post-Fordist debate centres on two related sets of phenomena: the interconnectedness of changes in different political-economic sectors and the transformation in the social relations of production and consumption. Burrows and Loader (1994: 1) summarise the central elements of post-Fordism:

> [If] Fordism is represented by a homology between mass production, mass consumption, modernist cultural forms and the mass public provision of welfare then post-Fordism is characterised by an emerging coalition between flexible production, differentiated and segmented consumption patterns, postmodernist cultural forms and a restructured welfare state.

As in the capitalist disorganisation thesis, on-going welfare state restructuring is understood as intrinsically connected with other patterns of socio-economic change, but there is a much greater emphasis on the forms and functions of the state. Economic restructuring is paralleled by the restructuring of other significant social and political institutions. The welfare state is understood not so much as a set of social service institutions but rather as an instrument of governance of the state (see below). The most developed attempt at theorising these sets of relationships is contained in Jessop's (1994b, 1995) state-theoretical analysis of the 'Schumpeterian Workfare State'. According to Jessop, the Schumpeterian Workfare State comprises a response to four sets of changes in international political-economic relations. These are:

- the rise of new technologies;
- growing internationalisation;
- a paradigm shift from Fordism to post-Fordism;
- the regionalisation of global and national economies.

Taken together, these four pressures provide the context for a 'hollowing out' of the nation-state, especially in relation to social policy, by which Jessop means that the power and autonomy of the state to set national policy objectives and programmes is deflected by the rise of new political organisations and relations. 'Hollowing out' is one of three sets of changes occurring in states in the context of a Fordist crisis and potential transition to post-Fordism. The three are: (a) de-nationalisation of statehood; (b) de-statisation of politics, or the rise of governance mechanisms alongside the state; and (c) the internationalisation of policy, that is, the increased significance of the international context for domestic policy. All three represent significant changes in the form of the state. Hence we now see: (a) social policy associated with the European Union (EU) or in some cases EU-sponsored transnational local networks, as well as regional or local states; (b) the rise of partnership mechanisms to deliver welfare; and (c) the increased significance of international competitiveness, labour market flexibility and the social wage for costs in the production process.

Thus, supra-national bodies such as the European Commission and powerful economic competitors in Europe and Asia, for example, and the emergence of powerful regional economies, simultaneously undermine the power of the state to control a national economy and stimulate the state's increasing involvement in managing the process of international-isation. This involves subordinating social policy to the push for economic innovation and competitiveness, negotiating agreements on trade and technology and political action aimed not at the functional requirements of a *national economy* but at the latter's insertion into the fragmented demand structure of an *international economic system*.

Jessop's analysis of these economic and political changes draws on regulationist concepts and neo-Marxist state theory. The concept of 'regulation' is the subject of complex debates developed in the analytical problematics of evolutionary and institutional economics. The regulation approach is concerned to understand periods of growth and decline in the 'advanced' economies through the use of two key ideas – a régime of accumulation and a mode of regulation.

The concept of a régime of accumulation refers to the relationships between production and consumption which exist during periods of economic growth – hence Fordism as a régime of accumulation is characterised by the congruence between mass production and consumption, for example (see Allen, 1992: 186–8). A mode of regulation provides a framework that supports the particular growth period, or régime of accumulation. It regulates a range of socio-economic actions – in the Fordist period, for example, expectations of life-long, full-time male employment and the social wage (extensive welfare provision) made up a major plank of the mode of regulation (Allen, 1992: 187), which functioned to provide the social conditions and stability deemed necessary for the operation of the accumulation process. How these processes of regulation interact is a complex question debated by those working in this field, covering the relationship between economic, political and cultural processes. It is clear that the interaction differs from country to country, as both régimes of accumulation and modes of regulation are historically constituted within their specific geopolitical and cultural contexts. For example, modes of regulation which developed in European welfare states in the wake of industrialisation varied considerably in the formation of both social policies and supporting institutional frameworks (Ashford, 1986). Similarly, like Esping-Andersen (1990) and Lash and Urry (1987), Jessop argues that nation-states are responding differently to economic change (Jessop, 1994a: 256–8). This observation is important because modes of regulation developed within a nation-state serve more than one political-economic purpose. The instruments of regulation – including social and economic policies – respond to both internal requirements for social order and international competition for markets and investment. National policy frameworks address both of these requirements simultaneously in order to offset economic crisis and stabilise conditions for growth.

Economic crisis in the regulation approach is regarded as intrinsic to the capitalist economy, and periodic shifts in the structure of the global economy can generate the breakdown of a régime of accumulation, prompting the eventual development of a new régime and with it a new mode of regulation. The departure from classical Marxism is particularly apparent here for, whilst maintaining an emphasis on economic logics in the organisation and development of industrial society, these are viewed as co-determinants of the institutions and structures of contemporary capitalism. Capitalism is, in effect, driven by a double dynamic comprising simultaneously, but independently, a techno-economic paradigm (Elam, 1994: 46, *et passim*) and a 'societal' paradigm (Lipietz, 1994: 338, *et passim*) or institutionalised 'way of life' (Boyer, 1990). The regulation approach develops a 'middle range' theory to account for specific relationships between these two paradigms, rather than a macro-theory that explains their emergence. Boyer (1990) characterises the regulation approach as a contingent analysis of specific social formations, whilst Jessop (1995: 1623) denies that it could provide 'a total theoretical solution to any conceivable problem in political economy'. The focus on contingency is maintained within the research agenda of the regulation approach. Jessop explains that 'the RA [regulation approach] is more concerned with the emergence over time of reproducible structural coherence in accumulation régimes in and through regulation than it is with the genesis of specific policy measures and their implementation in specific institutional or organisational sites' (1995: 1623).

The regulation approach thus rejects mono-causal explanations of social change based on direct determination by the mode of production, investigating instead the continuation and elaboration of capitalist social and economic relations. Working within this framework, Jessop argues that contemporary capitalism is in a transition to a post-Fordist era, in which the shifting axis of the world economy has generated a breakdown in the Fordist régime in Western economies. Taking the different elements of change, Jessop (1994b) states that their interconnectedness can be understood at four points or levels: at the level of the labour process (the ways that work is organised and socially and technically supported); at the level of the accumulation régime (the way in which economic production and growth are secured); at the level of the social mode of economic regulation (the way in which behaviour, expectations and norms are sustained); and at the level of societalisation (the ways that institutions operate to integrate and cohere social life around a dominant accumulation régime) (Jessop, 1994b: 14).

In the labour process, for example, post-Fordism can be said to represent a move from (Fordist) assembly-line, mass production techniques to flexible production in specialised industries geared towards niche markets. Industrial flexibility in the provision of goods and services is, some claim, accompanied by workforce flexibility in both employment patterns and skills and a consequent realignment of labour organisations (the emergence of workplace rather than workforce unions and the demise of the closed shop, for example). New types of machinery and vastly augmented communication networks enable industries to internationalise both the production and consumption of their goods and services. The development of a flexible workforce requires legal and social provision and new forms of bureaucracy and administration (the widespread introduction of contract working, decentralisation of operational control and just-in-time systems of industrial throughput, for example). In this way, post-Fordist processes impact across the entire spectrum of the labour process – from the tasks and activities performed in the workplace to the legal and institutional frameworks upholding specific ways of organising labour.

Post-Fordist analyses point to a similar interconnectedness in the organisation of social welfare, observing changes in working practices, employment patterns, decentralised operational control and the introduction of 'marketisation' in welfare institutions (see Burrows and Loader, 1994). 'Flexibility' is held to be a key characteristic of post-Fordism. Shifts in economic patterns result in different national transitions to post-Fordism, depending on political and discursive framings of the crisis of Fordism. In Jessop's (1994b) argument the response of the British state to the transition to post-Fordism has been to subordinate welfare policy to the demands of labour market flexibility. There is a general reorientation of economic and social policy to the perceived needs of the private sectors, and a wide range of measures to remodel social institutions along the lines of commercial enterprises.

A number of changes is held to be indicative of a post-Fordist régime of accumulation, mode of societalisation and social mode of economic regulation. In relation to the latter, there is a number of areas which the British government has targeted for change (Jessop, 1994b: 30–1), some of which we represent in Table 5.2.

Increasingly, Jessop argues, principles developed in the post-Fordist economy – flexibility, deregulation, market orientation – are applied to welfare institutions and services. A progressive shift has been under way which transforms the Keynesian Welfare State into a Schumpeterian

Table 5.2 *Neo-liberal regulation of public and private sectors*

Public sector	Private sector
Privatisation and liberalisation	Deregulation
Introduction of commercial criteria	Enterprise zones and private sector-led development; enterprise culture
Social security to support and subsidise low wages	'Flexible' working and wages
'Targeting' of welfare and restricted eligibility	Increasing social management role for private business through the growth of quangos
Dismantling of national collective bargaining; attempted introduction of performance-related pay and local pay deals	Support for workplace unions
Jobs and pay reduced and increased insecurity	Promotion of 'hire and fire' policy

Workfare State in which social policy is subordinated to the demands for competitiveness in the global economy. The particular post-Fordist path taken in Britain through Thatcherism has been a neo-liberal strategy (1994b: 23).

This strategy has been driven by the perceived need to create an enterprise culture in order to promote international competitiveness, a theme which drove reforms of the social security system in the 1980s, in which the need for reform was explicitly connected to requirements for change in labour markets and 'attitudes' to entrepreneurialism (Department of Employment, 1986, para 1.2; 1987, 1988; Department of Health and Social Security, 1985a, para. 1.12; 1985b, 1985c). The rationale legitimating such changes is that the regeneration of the economy requires work incentives, lower wages, 'flexibility' and low direct taxation rates with a consequently reduced public sector and expenditure. In other words, the creation of an enterprise economy involves deregulating labour markets in order to promote flexibility, weakening the strength of organised labour and maintaining a punitive benefits régime for those unemployed (Peck and Jones, 1995). This process has effected a redistribution of income from the poorest, who lost £11 billion from the social security system between 1979 and 1987, to the richest who gained virtually the same amount through tax reductions and concessions (Byrne, 1987; Hills, 1988). Thus, the neo-liberal strategy has resulted in greater polarisation of incomes. The labour market strategy, and the increasingly residualised benefits system which has accompanied it, has encouraged the growth of low-paid employment and pushed many people, both in and out of work, and their children, into greater poverty. In Esping-Andersen's (1990) terms, the welfare and employment strategy can be said to represent a *recommodification* of workers, with their power decreased and that of employers increased.

Following these measures, a further programme of compulsory competitive tendering was applied to NHS and local authority services, requiring that agencies put out to tender certain aspects of service provision (Cochrane and Clarke, 1993; Goodwin, 1995), as well as the creation of quasi-markets and internal markets with a separation of purchasers and providers overseen by a new managerialism and the introduction of private sector performance and monitoring criteria. All these changes took place in the context of a reduction of the full-time workforce and an increase in the use of part-time and temporary staff together with extensions in the tasks and roles of some workers (Pinch, 1994).

Similarly, contracting out of services and competitive tendering have become normal characteristics of welfare organisations and have led to a decrease in job security. The introduction of new technologies in the workplace has changed the nature of the work undertaken by core welfare workers, intensifying the information-gathering function at the expense of the care function. Welfare organisations are no longer seen as comprehensive care-providers but as client- and community-centred enterprises, specialising according to demand for particular types of service. The 'enabling' Local Authority has absorbed the language and principles of private sector management both at the level of labour relations and at the level of organisational goal-setting with a consequent blurring of the boundaries between private and public sector priorities. The consequence has been an institutional realignment with a multiplicity of service providers sometimes in competition and sometimes in alliance with statutory services (see Cochrane, 1994).

These various changes denote the changing role of the state from a provider of services to a market or quasi-market relationship between suppliers and 'customers' in a decentralised and fragmented system. Thus, recent changes in British social policy priorities – the introduction of hospital trusts and internal markets, purchaser–provider divisions, multiple service contracts, community care and the encouragement of private sector involvement in welfare provision – are understood as part of a process in which the welfare state is restructured to support a new phase of capital accumulation. State social service provision is rationed and 'targeted' (read residualised), cash-limited through financial regulations governing community care, and considerable proportions of services have to be purchased from the private and voluntary sectors. The total effect of these changes is the fragmentation and transferral of welfare functions to the 'community', voluntary organisations, charities, family and private sector. The new mode of welfare governance comprises a transfer of responsibility for delivering the services combined with a centralisation of state power over their organisation and distribution.

This neo-liberal strategy constitutes a reorientation of the Keynesian Welfare State towards a particular form of post-Fordist state – the Schumpeterian Workfare State. In contrast to the Keynesian Welfare State – based on the principles of demand-led growth, mass consumption and full employment within a national economy – Jessop (1994b) argues that the Schumpeterian Workfare State is geared towards enhancing competitiveness within the context of an internationalised economic framework, subordinating social policy to the demands of the market and supporting labour and product flexibility rather than stability and security. From the theoretical position developed by Jessop, the activities of the state in regard to social policy are not concerned with meeting need, ameliorating hardship or rational humanistic planning, but geared towards creating the conditions which are considered to promote economic competitiveness within the international economic order. Thus, no amount of objective social scientific research on social problems will set the policy agenda at the level of the state, for social policy is seen as strategically implicated in the social regulation of the new growth régime.

Concluding remarks

The perspectives discussed in this chapter raise a series of issues about both the organisation and the politics of social welfare, although each views the welfare state somewhat differently. Postindustrialist theories highlight changing forms of production and work, focusing on the ways that technological changes impact on the production process and the consequent effects on the occupational structure. Assessing welfare states in the postindustrial scenario, Esping-Andersen draws attention to the systems of stratification entrenched in the different régimes of welfare characterising European countries. The disorganisation thesis views the welfare state as an institutional arrangement of organised capitalism and draws attention to the roles of different institutional actors (at the 'top' and at the 'bottom') in coordinating the economic, cultural and political features of capitalist societies. At the same time, Lash and Urry, and Offe also point out that the very institutions of organised capitalism, including the welfare state, are themselves at least partly responsible for its eventual disorganisation. Similarly, Jessop's regulation approach views the welfare state as a crucial instrument of the mode of economic regulation that supplies stability and a social pattern to a specific accumulation régime. In short, the transition from a Fordist to a post-Fordist régime is characterised by a displacement of the Keynesian Welfare State by the Schumpeterian Workfare State, which latter is itself necessary to achieve a congruence between roles, norms and expectations and the means by which capital accumulation is secured in the new régime.

The rapid growth of service sector occupations, paralleled by rapid growth in service sector industries – which include financial and insurance industries in competition with state insurance schemes – is accompanied by growing social polarisation and economic insecurity. The growth of these industries signals, in part, a shift in consumption from public to private forms of insurance but also changes in the balance between public and private sector financing of risk. In turn, these shifts set boundaries around and build bridges to new types of inclusion and exclusion – based on access to information, consumption, child support, equal opportunities, geographical mobility and communications technologies, for example, which suggest a need for new social policy priorities (see Cahill, 1994). Both inclusions and exclusions are, as we have noted, spatially and socially diverse. Polarisation between 'work rich' and 'work poor' households is unevenly distributed across both geographical and social spaces. Thus, one of the main characteristics of contemporary societies is that the lines of division and disadvantage cross-cut class, gender, ethnic and other social identities leading to a correspondingly more complex and fragmented set of political dynamics. Whilst the different political-economic approaches we have outlined in this chapter provide pointers to some of these complexities, they represent variations on class- and state-theoretic perspectives on welfare.

6

Political Ecology

The relationship between social activities – of production, consumption, migration, technological development and pollution – and environmental change – global warming, resource depletion, diversity loss and increased eco-toxicity – is a topic high on the agenda of many public and private, local and transnational organisations. Almost every aspect of economic and social policy is inflected by environmental considerations, including policies on taxation, social planning, performance monitoring, waste management, local economic development and international trade relations. The incorporation of 'environmental' issues into policy and practice has given rise to a wide range of multi-faceted social and political conflicts. Disputes over fish quotas in depleted seas, the health hazards of urban pollution, the consequences and control of infectious (human and animal) diseases, or liability (and responsibility) for ecological disasters (oil spills, acid rain, nuclear discharges, etc.), for example, turn on the distribution of rights, duties, costs and benefits involved in inhabiting an increasingly poisoned and degraded global environment. Some of these disputes are openly economic, centring on gains and losses of income and wealth resulting from environmental change; others place ethics and morals at the forefront of policy and practice, emphasising both human dependence on and obligation towards a sustainable environment. The meanings and the consequences of, and responsibilities for, environmental change are the subject of intense and widespread negotiation and conflict (Burningham and O'Brien, 1994). Furthermore, they apply both to the direct and unmediated consequences of environmental exploitation and to the indirect, knock-on effects of particular ways of organising systems of production, distribution and consumption.

In terms of direct, unmediated impacts, for example, we note that, currently, a billion of the world's people live in 'absolute' poverty (that is, they have insufficient means to meet basic needs for shelter and sustenance) with a further 600 million on the verge of starvation. The developed countries of Europe and America share some 23 per cent of the global population but 85 per cent of the world's GNP. Per capita, this 23 per cent consumes over 90 per cent of the world's paper, steel and energy resources, whilst the remaining 77 per cent in the developing economies consume less than 10 per cent of these resources. To 'sustain' these patterns of wealth and poverty requires a production and distribution system geared towards maximising output and concentrating the benefits of agricultural and industrial activity on to specific beneficiaries. Robertson (1989: 2) points out that:

By the year 2000, if present trends continue, one third of the world's productive land will be turned to dust, one million species will be extinct, and the world's climate will be irreparably changed. The terrible famines in Africa are just the most striking among many symptoms of the growing sickness of people and the Earth, the devastating long-term effects of which are just beginning to become apparent.

The maximisation and concentration results in the creation of an increasingly poisonous and degraded global environment together with huge disparities in the relative qualities of different local environments and rapidly growing inequalities between the wealthy and the under-resourced populations within and across the world's political-economic regions. In global terms, millions of tonnes of pesticides are used annually – at a cost of approximately $16 billion per annum – in order to ensure that harvests are not destroyed by pests. The scale of the pest problem is itself a result of massified, monoculture agribusiness – several thousand acres of a single crop species represents a rich banquet for insects and parasites alike. Yet, it is estimated by the US Academy of Sciences and the UK Royal Society that only 0.1 per cent of all pesticides applied to croplands actually reaches the target species; 99.9 per cent of the chemical product is left to ebb and flow around (and ultimately beyond) the ecosystems in which the crops are located. To put this in quantitative terms, for every one *million* tonnes of pesticide used only one *thousand* tonnes actually reaches and destroys the target pest: *nine hundred and ninety-nine thousand* tonnes of toxins interact with other parts of the ecosystem. As a direct consequence of this scattergun approach to pest control there are over half a million accidental poisonings and some ten thousand deaths annually arising out of pesticide use (Rose, 1993: 5). It is a sobering thought to acknowledge that every year $15,984,000,000 (that is, a figure in excess of the GNP of a number of Southern nations combined) is expended on ensuring that ecosystems are poisoned by the coordinated actions of states, agribusiness and the pesticides industry alone!

In local terms, Phoon (1993) points out, for example, that the Asia–Pacific region – stretching from Indonesia to India – is the fastest growing region in the world in economic terms and is, as a consequence, experiencing significant changes in regional health problems – especially in a switch from communicable to non-communicable diseases – and significant environmental degradation. For example, air quality in Asian cities is almost without exception worse than in US or European counterparts; three of the world's top five sulphur dioxide-polluted cities are in Asia and these are also top of the list for pollution by suspended particulate matter; population concentration (required to feed industrial economic growth) has generated severe waste management problems such that Asian rivers are increasingly infested with faecal coliform bacteria; finally, levels of pesticide concentration in the body have risen dramatically across the region during the past three decades as agricultural systems have switched from locally based production of diverse foodstuffs to mass production of high-yield and cash crops.

In terms of indirect, mediated impacts, we note that intensified processing of environmental resources leads to a change in both the pattern and quality of life for different groups of people. For example, water is a multidimensional resource, used for many different purposes: people drink and cook with it, bathe and wash with it, swim or paddle in it, enjoy looking at it or migrate by sailing on it. Water is potentially used in a lot of different ways and all of these ways can contribute to our individual and collective welfare – by keeping us healthy and clean, providing enjoyment or a means of geographical mobility, and so on. However, when some of these dimensions of water-as-resource are concentrated and intensified other dimensions deteriorate. For example, the use of water resources as a cleaning agent and waste-sink increases the risks associated with using non-treated water and depletes the total resource that water represents – some of the uses to which water may be put are threatened or degraded by the intensity with which other uses are pursued. A striking example of this unwanted trade-off is all too visible around Britain's shoreline: parts of the coastline are polluted by domestic and industrial waste, making even the slightest of contacts with the water or the beach both a health hazard and a very unpleasant aesthetic experience. The intensification process is partly driven by increasing industrial productivity and partly by increasing privatised consumption. On the former, whilst rationalised and slimmed-down manufacturing industries like the car industry may need less labour and may be able to make more cars using less energy and metal there are no comparable total savings in the water required to heat, clean and cool plants and machinery or in the water required to run the paint shops. In relation to consumption, the credit and consumer booms of the 1980s have led to increases in the private ownership of consumer durables such as washing machines and showers which are themselves water polluters as well as water users.

Environmental impacts resulting from the indirect, mediated consequences of socio-economic activities are not 'side-effects' but are, rather, an intrinsic feature of the organisation of contemporary societies. Indeed, the detritus from these societies, and the ways that it is mediated and channelled through social and economic networks, constitutes an increasingly dangerous environmental risk. A good example of these mediated impacts in Britain is a hazard whose regulation lies at the intersection between different institutions: clinical waste. The entry of clinical waste into wider systems of *environmental* hazard management can be traced to the loss of Crown Immunity for NHS hospitals in the late 1980s. At this point, medical waste disposal facilities became subject to the same pollution and environmental health regulations as private and public waste disposal facilities. The maintenance of high-grade, efficient incinerators was beyond the capacity of many hospitals and clinical waste entered private and public waste management systems. More recently, the NHS and Community Care Act combined with efficiency drives in the NHS has resulted in large increases in community nursing and consequent large increases in the quantities of clinical waste circulating within communities. The British Medical Association (1994) expressed concern over the growing quantities of and uncertainties surrounding clinical waste resulting from organisational changes in the NHS. Since the Environmental Protection Act (1990, section 34), nurses are subject to the Duty of Care compliance regulation and are accountable for clinical wastes. The organisation of clinical waste collection services has not developed in parallel with the patterns of hospital discharge and home care. In short, a number of policy and organisational changes has resulted in both overlaps and potential conflicts between the responsibilities of different people in their roles as professional, political and economic groups in environmental planning and management around the hazard of clinical waste. These people include home carers, residential staff, chiropodists, pharmacists, community and school nurses, health centre administrators, caretakers, waste incinerator companies and waste disposal contractors as well as members of the general public.

Clinical wastes, particularly low-grade clinical wastes, are acquired and routed into the municipal waste stream by a very wide range and a very large number of individuals and groups, some of whom we have noted above, with the consequence that the distributive framework for these materials is fractured into many different networks. Whilst there are specific arrangements relating to clinical waste and the pharmacy, nursing homes and hospitals, health centres and other health service-controlled establishments, the applicability of these arrangements to private (or public) residential homes, supermarket pharmacy franchises, home carers, and so on has not been studied. The circulation of clinical wastes through these latter networks means that different people are defining 'clinical' wastes in different ways, are claiming and disclaiming responsibilities for these wastes and are – knowingly or otherwise – passing on both the hazard itself and its management to different sectors of the community (Collins, 1991; Phillipp, 1993; O'Brien et al., 1996).

These examples are presented in order to illustrate that all interactions between people and environments – even understood in very simplistic terms as use of water, air, soil and so on – are linked both directly and indirectly to health and welfare. We are not suggesting that this awareness is new: the public health reforms of the nineteenth century, the Clean Air Acts of the twentieth century, the formation of environmental action groups across the past hundred years – from the RSPB to the Ramblers' Association – suggest that these direct and indirect relationships have long been a part of the political consciousness of industrialised civil societies. There is a large number of organisations dedicated to ameliorating the negative effects of human actions on the external environment and, conversely, of the impact of that produced environment on people. But these organisations and this level of political action – whether voluntary or formal – has represented a system of expurgation, an effort at cleaning up after the fact, or a system of 'reservation', an effort at shielding species and environments from the effects of human action. In short, it has comprised a politics of protection: that is, a way of maintaining economic expansion and a societal status quo whilst also maintaining or restoring certain desired qualities in or rights to the environment – such as breathable air or drinkable water, a stock of whales, dolphins, or ospreys, for example.

But things have changed, and what has changed most drastically of all is the recognition that the generation of wealth, the maximisation of agricultural and industrial output, the production of consumer commodities and the organisation of mass social services like health care are *intrinsically* environmentally degrading. They lead to environmental hazards through the ways that they are carried out and controlled and through the ways that their benefits and burdens are socially and geographically distributed and administered. Modern societies are undeclared environmental disaster areas, awash with toxins, hazards and life-threatening technologies. Some groups of people have a solid, short-term interest in keeping things this way; other groups have an interest in seizing ownership and control of the technological and social systems that maintain the disaster; others again have an interest in a radical transformation of the system in order to foster 'sustainable' relationships between socio-economic activity and environmental resources. Conflicts between these groups represent disputes about social and economic development: about how resources are to be acquired, distributed and applied and, beyond this, about who will define what constitutes 'appropriate' use of those resources and who will control and benefit from them. In focusing on these issues, political ecologies of welfare are situated squarely in the problematic of socio-economic development and promote both a critique of contemporary society as a whole and a series of more detailed assessments of the welfare consequences of modern institutional arrangements.

Development and environment

> In contemporary India, conflicts over nature, just as much as the more conventional agrarian and industrial conflicts, raise important questions about distributive justice and economic efficiency. The distinguishing feature of this ... form of socio-economic conflict is that it simultaneously raises issues of environmental sustainability. In so far as the natural resources in question are vital to the agrarian and industrial sectors, the fate of these conflicts is intimately connected to the development process as a whole. (Gadgil and Guha, 1994: 103)

Gadgil and Guha here observe that conflicts over the use and degradation of natural resources – water, air, land, forestry, and so on – represent an additional series of divisions and disputes to those normally studied by social scientists (that is, peasant conflict over cultivated land and its produce, and proletarian conflict around industrial production and its rewards). These conflicts revolve around competing definitions and understandings of, and competing claims to and rights over, particular environments. At the same time, Gadgil and Guha also highlight some of the systematic and institutionally entrenched inequalities that underpin contemporary approaches to environment and development and the ways that such approaches are products of transnational socio-economic pressures and forces. In an independent report for the World Bank, the impacts of these pressures are summarised abruptly:

> In a mad rush to export to shrinking Northern markets, the nations of the South, aided by official lenders and Northern investors, have been raping their forests, polluting their rivers, poisoning their soil. . . . Biodiversity is being lost and land ownership further skewed in the attempt to modernise and maximise agricultural export production. Little time is given to a consideration of the quality and environmental impact of these projects and investments and even less to the views of the local population. (The Bank Information Centre, 1991: 1; cited in Seager, 1993: 133)

These brief comments on the industrialisation of the South are important for a number of reasons. First, they draw attention clearly and immediately to the local environmental devastation wrought by global economic modernisation: 'development', defined as intensification and maximisation of resource exploitation, degenerates the available stocks of environmental resources. Second, they draw attention to the global consequences of such local devastation, especially in relation to biodiversity: the extinction of species that inhabit one locality is their extinction everywhere, the loss of forest cover in Southern regions affects the climate and the atmosphere of the world as a whole, the poisoning of Southern rivers and landscapes adds to the world average levels of marine and soil toxicity or, in other words, increases the total toxicity of the biosphere inhabited by all species. Third, they acknowledge that forms of environmental exploitation are linked to particular interests – of multinational investors, on the one hand, and of 'local populations' on the other. They thus confirm that environmental change is a site of social struggle between different political ecologies, that is, between different organisations of rights, benefits and opportunities in the exploitation and/or maintenance of specific environmental qualities.

But the struggle is not conducted between forces of equal power. Rather, environmental change exposes uneven power relationships between different groups and interests and unequal statuses accorded to the definitions and understandings of, and responses to, such change. This unevenness can be seen in two different ways. First, it can be seen in the way that dominant European social institutions (the institutions of science, politics and commercial enterprise, for example) perform a displacement function on ecological relationships – that is, on environmental values, expertises and practices. Vandana Shiva's (1989) investigations of the relationships between women, ecology and development in developing countries suggests that indigenous practices of environmental

sustainability and eco-balance have been abandoned, modified or reinterpreted in order to fit into Western, rational, science-based and 'progressive' technological systems. The displacement is visible in the 'green
revolutions' in Asia, where indigenous agricultures were transformed
from community-based support systems into rationalised exploitations of
resources for profit. Under the world-saving banner of the 'green revolution' of the 1970s, Shiva writes:

> The very meaning of agriculture was transformed with the introduction of the
> western green revolution paradigm. It was no longer an activity that worked
> towards a careful maintenance of nature's capital in fertile soils and provided
> society with food and nutrition. It became an activity aimed primarily at the
> production of agricultural commodities for profit. With the shift in the nature of
> the activity came a shift in the nature of the actors; nature, women and peasants
> were no longer seen as the primary producers of food . . . The emergence of a
> new breed of agricultural 'experts' with fragmented knowledge of individual
> components of the farm system, and with a total knowledge of the market
> system, led to the displacement of the traditional agricultural experts – women
> and peasants. (1989: 103–4)

Shiva calls the ideas and ecological principles exported from Northern
to Southern nations examples of 'self-referential' modes of thinking. They
are self-referential in terms of the logics they embody – of which long-term
viability (or 'sustainability') is a good example: Indian agriculture has
been viable in the long term for thousands of years. What is meant by this
idea is viability in the sense of being able continually to profit from
environmental resources, a logic of greatest return for least effort. They are
also self-referential in terms of their reference to Western concepts of self-
hood. Patterns of environmental interaction are much more than mere
systems for extracting resources: they also serve to define social and
cultural identities, roles, responsibilities, rights of access and a host of
other socially and culturally generated statuses that alien, imported
systems destroy or transform. The consequence is that previously stable
agricultures become unstable as people's relationships with their environments alter. Joekes et al. (1994), for example, examine the gendered consequences of environmental change in Malaysia, Kenya and Mexico.
Acknowledging that women are in the 'front line' of exposure to environmental change, Joekes et al. propose that economic (i.e., commercial)
development of environmental resources has a number of consequences.
It alters the patterns of male and female labour, leads to a weakening of
women's livelihood base, and increases the environmental hazards that
local communities face. Often, it is these types of disruption to local political ecologies, as much as any 'natural threat' to an ecosystem, that underpin spiralling environmental degradation (Leach and Mearns, 1992).

A second element of self-referentiality is the process of overlaying
indigenous concepts and understandings with institutionalised, scientific
terminologies. Shiva points out that indigenous cultures all over the world
have their own concepts of sustainability (one of the Indian versions is

prakriti: the living force which supports life) and it is only when these are transmogrified into pigeon-holed, rationalised, measured, evaluated, scientific sets of statements and practices that sustainability becomes a problem to be solved rather than a normal condition to be experienced. Shiva observes that:

> Sustainability is a term that became significant in development discourse in the 1980s because four decades of the development experience had established that 'development' and its synonym 'economic growth' ... were unsustainable. Development was unsustainable because it undermined ecological stability, and it destroyed people's livelihoods. 'Growth with equity' and 'growth with sustainability' were attempts to legitimise and perpetuate economic growth in a period of doubt. (1992: 187)

Once established as a policy goal, a scientised 'sustainability', oriented towards maintaining the broad outlines of the status quo in international political and economic relations, requires the specification of costs and benefits, gains and losses, more and less 'efficient' usage of resources, and the entire range of micro and macro measurements that intergovernmental panels, research initiatives and bureaucracies demand. Whilst such knowledge processes appear, unreflectively, as neutral, objective or value-free assessments of cause and effect in well-defined environments, conducted according to the rigours of well-policed disciplines and professions, such modes of knowledge acquisition and application are rooted in specific cultural histories. They are continually diffracted by traditional and symbolic, religious and 'nostalgic' forces that uphold or promote very particular cultural priorities and convictions. According to Vattimo (1992: 42), it is precisely these cultural 'supplements' that give to scientific concepts of progress and development their concrete meanings. Thus, the export of environmental understandings and sciences is not simply the beneficent transfer of better, cleaner or more efficient technologies but also the transfer of particular sets of myths about morality, progress and equity: about better and worse ways of encountering environments, about aims and goals in environmental interactions and about rights and duties in relation to environmental resources.

The terms 'development' and, especially, 'economic development' have become synonymous in popular, and much academic, discourse with 'Third World' development. They have come to refer to the process whereby nations and regions that do not organise their economies and societies on the pattern of Western capitalism engage in the process of transforming into mutated clones of that capitalism. However, this popular conception is entirely misleading since it obscures the fact that 'Western capitalism' is itself a shorthand term for a way of developing social, economic, cultural and political resources, their organisation, distribution, use and control. 'Capitalism' is not a condition, a structure-in-stasis that envelops peoples' relationships with their environments, it is a dynamic process that drives those relationships in particular directions. 'Development', in the context of grossly uneven shares of resources and wealth, is in reality the management, government or supervision of that unevenness and inequality.

Although stated more elaborately, this idea of capitalism as a dynamic process underpins Gorz's (1980, 1989, 1994) critique of economic reason. According to Gorz, capitalist development represents a fundamental contradiction, even on its own terms. It combines an ethic of productivity and efficiency in each production unit with societal-wide parasitism on and waste of environmental resources (1980: 141); it increases the productive capacity of the total system whilst throwing potential consumers of its products on the economic and social scrap heap and by their impoverishment makes them less able to consume what capitalist enterprise produces (1994: 47–50). The logic of intensifying the industrial process ultimately destroys more than it produces, resulting in *'absolute and insurmountable* scarcities' of precious environmental resources (1980: 15–16). The economic rationality of capitalism emphasises growth at any cost, its goal is for the economy to grow bigger and bigger, faster and faster, and investment decisions are fixed on achieving that goal above all else. Whilst government ministers talk of 'heating up' or 'cooling down' the economic engine – of increasing or decreasing the rate of growth – in order to manage monetary inflation in one country, capitalist companies and cartels wander the globe seeking out the best investment opportunities, moving their capital around 'hot' economies and 'hot' sectors. When states impose conditions on capitalist financial transactions, such as fixing currency exchange rates, capitalists gleefully work on the anomalies between currency values, vacuuming up vast quantities of national incomes until the exchange policies lie in tatters (Yearley, 1996).

Following Illich (1973), Gorz's (1980: 17) assessment of contemporary capitalism presents a stark choice between two, and only two, alternatives: 'conviviality or technofascism'. To the extent that the means for sustaining, managing and controlling life are vested in bureaucracies, scientific-technical-expert 'élites' and the private financial and industrial monopolies – to the extent that the solutions to industrially and technologically generated environmental destruction are placed in the hands of the industrial and technological establishment – the logic of 'technofascism' will continue to determine economic development. 'Technofascism', in Gorz's formulation, comprises a system of production, consumption, professionalism and bureaucracy whose function is to reproduce individuals who will accept the roles of worker, consumer, client and subject that are assigned to them in the system. It represents a 'megamachine' (1994: 41), enslaving people to its purposes and whose self-development is an inbuilt goal of its operation. It is, as Shiva remarked of Western science, 'self-referential': the social, political and cultural desires and goals that circulate in the everyday worlds of peoples across the globe are subsumed under the instrumental 'need' for economic expansion.

Gorz contrasts the principle of technofascism with the principle of 'conviviality' – the development of tools which 'guarantee [people's] right to work with high, independent efficiency, thus simultaneously eliminating the need for either slaves or masters and enhancing each person's range of freedom' (Illich, 1973: 23, cited in Gorz, 1980: 51). Indirectly, Gorz elaborates on the notion of a *range* of freedom in his critique of capitalist work organisation and the way that work has come to be seen as the central vehicle for forming social identities. He points out (1989, 1994) that paid work is in reality only one of many social locations where people's identities are developed and maintained and that an increasing number of people are either excluded from work (and thus the identities it bestows) or are refusing to identify themselves with the work role. It is one thing for a skilled worker, belonging to large trade union and/or other organisations to see in the experience of work a commonality with co-workers and rest an important part of their self-understanding on that commonality. It is quite another matter for a member of the unemployed, occasionally employed, short-term or part-time workforce to invest a significant portion of their self-identity, self-awareness, self-esteem and political consciousness in the paid work relation. Instead, the struggle for 'freedom' is increasingly a matter of struggle across locations, where different identities are expressed and different needs are felt (1994: 72–3). Although Gorz can see no way out of capitalist economic rationalities, none the less it is possible to shift the priority of capitalism in the context of a broader range of societal and political interests. If state socialism has shown itself to be a catastrophic failure, this does not imply that there can be no socialism at all:

> A social project of the left should start out from the fact that there are activities which deserve to be done on their own account – activities on which the meaning and quality of life, and individual development and sovereignty, depend, but to which, as a result of the dominance of economic rationality, time and recognition have never been granted. (1989: 35)

For Gorz, a type of 'eco-socialism', that relegates capitalist production and, with it, the centrality of paid work, to a role secondary to that of personal and social development, can still be imagined and pursued. It is possible, in short, to transform the 'megamachine' into a system that is at least more convivial to the diversity of human needs and desires, at least more convivial to the qualities that make for a diversity of life experiences. By valuing this diversity it may then also be possible to overturn the logic in which all 'time is money' and all personal and environmental resources are commodities.

Our discussion of the development–environment relationship has emphasised several issues. These are, first, that we cannot address the relationships between 'environment' and 'welfare' without situating those relationships in the forms of social and economic development that are transforming the world's ecosystems. Second, although the quality of particular local environments differs markedly across the world's regions, none the less changes in those qualities are intimately connected to the

health and welfare conditions and resources of the world as a whole.
Third, people's relationships with their local (and translocal) environments comprise political ecologies – that is, they embody rights and
duties, rules of access, benefits, costs, opportunities and identities which
provide frameworks for environmental exploitation and maintenance.
Fourth, 'development' is not something done by the 'Third World' in order
to look more like the 'First World'. Capitalist industrial development
represents a dynamic that directs and governs the relationships between
people and between people and their environments. A political ecology
perspective that acknowledges the development–environment connection
focuses attention on the relationships between environment and welfare
conceived in their broadest senses.

Political ecologies of welfare

There is a strand of the environmentalist critique that retains a degree of
faith in the capacity of human rational and technological ingenuity to
solve environmental problems. This faith has persisted for as long as the
social and physical sciences have existed. It consists in the belief that
through the combination of scientific know-how and rational planning, it
is possible to control and regulate the sum total of socio-economic activity
so that 'nature' will not be destroyed and the earth will be able to sustain
our own and future generations. The faith is visible in commitments to
manipulating, managing and designing 'nature' so that, over time, its
resources will remain bountiful. Compare, below, the rhetoric of Moos and
Brownstein (1977) with that of Maser (1991):

> We must merge our capacity to imagine and innovate with our ability to compre-
> hend and *manipulate* natural and social forces. (Moos and Brownstein, 1977: 3–4;
> emphasis added)

> . . . we must look beyond the sustainability of forests as isolated entities in time
> and space to the long-term sustainability of forests as contextual components of
> landscapes, which *must be designed to be adaptable* to changing environmental
> conditions over time. (Maser, 1991: 55; cited in Adam, 1994: 103; emphasis
> added)

However, some commentators argue that it is precisely the belief that
human beings are sufficiently knowledgeable, capable and 'rational'
(especially once they have been armed with Western science and technology) to design and manipulate nature that has generated the environmental catastrophe in the first place. Obscuring the reality of
planetary devastation is an 'organised irresponsibility' in which the
scientific, legal and political systems deflect attention away from the
causes and consequences of environmental change, allowing eco-poison-
ing to continue apace under the safeguard of 'maximum permissible
levels' of toxic releases (Beck, 1995: 94–5, 134). The 'organised irresponsibility' (or 'non-liability') ensures that, on the one hand, continued

environmental degradation remains a source of inordinate profit but, on the other hand, it also comprises a challenge to mainstream political theory and practice. The growth of this irresponsibility can be explored through a contrast between the (industrial) 'insurance' society and the (industrial) 'risk' society (Beck, 1992a, 1992b, 1995).

Economic growth and social insurance

The neo-classical economic paradigm represents the environment as an open system which acts, simultaneously, as a source of natural goods and as a waste-processing sink that removes 'residuals' (i.e., muck and garbage) from the economy. The environment is considered an 'open system' to the extent that the limits to its capacity either to supply goods or to assimilate wastes are assumed to be infinite. The open system perspective is based on the 'free gifts' and 'free disposal' assumptions of conventional economics (Perrings, 1987) and leads to what Boulding (1966) has called a 'cowboy economy' view of the economic system. In this view, economic processes are understood as being linear, self-contained, rational, utility-generating and essentially disconnected from nature. Wealth is produced through the power of the economy to transform raw materials into saleable goods: the greater the transformative capacity of the economy, the greater the rate and quantity of wealth production. In turn, this rate of growth and level of total wealth production (usually measured in terms of GNP and GDP) is seen as the key to social welfare, understood as the sum of 'utilities' or 'satisfactions' available to individuals in society (Pearce et al., 1989).

In keeping with this 'open system' perspective, both Beveridge's Social Insurance plan for welfare, and the Keynesian economic framework on which the plan is based, propose that a competitive, expanding economy can be politically regulated by a national state in order to distribute wealth and welfare gains among the population. The explicit logic of this proposal is that as an efficient economy expands so do the goods and services (the 'utilities' and 'satisfactions') available for distribution or, in other words, economic growth leads to growth in absolute welfare. Because the sum total of welfare increases, it is possible to ameliorate the conditions of those disadvantaged through illness or misfortune by allocating a fraction of the resources from the economic system to targeted groups. The social insurance plan, as we discussed in Chapter 1, is a distribution framework but it is not a *redistribution* framework: it does not conceive a *finite* economy whose benefits must be *equalised* among the population. Instead, the plan conceives a *dynamic* economy whose benefits are *regulated and organised* to socially manage the population's welfare according to selective criteria of need (in Beveridge's terms: want, idleness, squalor, ignorance and disease).

Economic dynamism thus lies at the heart of the social insurance scheme: so long as the dynamism is maintained, absolute social welfare is sustained. There are two implications of this process, one internal to the distributive system and one external, relating to the generation of usable resources – both of which have contradictory effects. Internally, an economy produces resources which are used up in the form of non-productive goods and services (that is, they are consumed by people rather than utilised by them to produce more goods and services). Whilst the economy generates sufficient quantities of goods and services there will be sufficient capacity to meet the needs of the less well-off: the litmus test of welfare efficiency then turns on the absolute distribution of *non-productive* goods and on the degree of access to these goods – which is why welfare state comparisons typically take the form of measures of expenditure and consumption as a percentage of GDP (Pierson, 1991: 111). Within such a scheme it is possible to increase the total (or 'absolute') welfare of a population whilst at the same time supporting inequalities of resource distribution within it. The reason for this is that the social insurance plan for welfare consists in both a form of protection against individual misfortune and a form of institutional support for the social distribution of rights and opportunities. Demands for increased welfare provision take the form of demands for increased non-productivity or, in other words, increased access to consumption opportunities. So long as 'welfare' is understood in terms of access to non-productive goods and services, and so long as the welfare system depends on increasing the quantities of these 'satisfactions' as a means of enhancing individual well-being, the economy will be locked into an ever-increasing rate of environmental exploitation with no guarantees of long-term sustainability.

Externally, the concept of 'non-productive goods' is applied also to certain dimensions of the environment itself; in particular, the waste-processing capacity of ecosystems is treated not as a finite resource which needs careful management but as an unlimited dustbin into which the detritus of the economy can be thrown. One consequence of this assumption is that depletions in the environment's waste-processing capacity come to affect human welfare – in the spread of illness and disease, such as asthma, poisonings from pollutants, cancers from holes in the ozone layer or malnourishment caused by depleted output from poisoned or degraded land-stocks, for example. Under such circumstances, a portion of the products of economic activity must be devoted to compensating for the latter's own effects. As the waste sink becomes more and more overloaded, more resources must be expended in compensating for the consequences, leading to a further intensification of materials processing in a cycle of increasing environmental depletion. Environmental economists point to the cycle of diminishing returns accompanying 'open system' economic policies: more resources must be expended at a faster rate in order to achieve the same level of welfare (Ross and Usher, 1986; Jacobs, 1991). Thus, the very measure of 'growth' – as a quantitative expression of expenditures and consumption – may actually obscure what is the real nature of the wealth produced and gloss over the fact that, over time, more intense exploitation is required in order to generate each unit of welfare.

To the extent that postwar social policies – rooted in Keynesian economics and administered through the legacy of Beveridge's social insurance plan – depend upon a dynamic economy in an open environmental system, they give rise to two political frameworks of dispute over social welfare policy.

On the one hand, struggles over welfare revolve around the degree to which different social groups gain a share of the ever-expanding economic cake and are visible, for example, in the disputes over definitions of poverty that surface regularly in the social policy and administration literature. If, year on year, GNP continues to grow – that is, if the total volume of wealth in society continues to rise – it appears both unjust and illogical to champion an income maintenance (and low-wage) system for the poor that persistently provides little more (and often less) than the bare essentials required to keep body and soul together. It seems unjust because a very large section of the population is denied the life-chances afforded to their (increasingly) richer counterparts and illogical since it undermines the value of pursuing economic growth in the first place. What is the point of society getting absolutely wealthier if its poorest sections can barely keep their heads above the poverty level? A divided society in which the haves always increase their share of the cake whilst the have-nots always share smaller portions of it is not readily associated with social stability and cohesion. Nor is it understood to motivate people to participate in those very social institutions and cultural traditions that maintain the growing disparities between rich and poor.

On the other hand, the welfare system is based in large measure on protection from and security against unforeseen (such as illness or accident), unpredictable (redundancy or 'de-jobbing') or 'exceptional' (childbirth or widow/erhood) (that is, exceptional in relation to presumed and essentially discriminatory patterns of 'normal' working and earnings) circumstances. Such circumstances, of course, are only unpredictable, unforeseen or exceptional from the point of view of the individual. From the point of view of the insurance system (whether publicly or privately organised) they are entirely predictable, statistical probabilities to which rules of compensation can be applied (Beck, 1992b: 99). Thus, struggles over welfare are, in equally large measure, compensatory struggles. They revolve around the justness, equability or practicality of specific compensatory packages, or 'entitlements' to certain types and quantities of 'non-productive goods': specific social, welfare and health services, levels of insurance payment or income guarantee, the inclusion or exclusion of specific circumstances in the protective framework – compensation for RSI (repetitive strain injury) or deaths from diseases related to BSE (bovine spongiform encephalopathy); entitlements to medical services for drug-takers.

In both of these cases – disputes over shares of the cake and disputes over its ingredients – the politics of welfare promote a fully socialised conception of entitlement. They ignore the production and distribution of environmental hazards, applying the rules of allocation and compensation only to the human consequences of industrial society. In addition, their focus is on the regulation and organisation of measures that are aimed at specific social groups. They do not specify the regulation of ecological relationships as means for delivering or achieving welfare, even though such regulation is in practice a cornerstone of the entire welfare system.

Environment, welfare and the risk society

> Where the world has become perilous, the world population is becoming a consumer of hazard prevention. The more menacing, encompassing and ineluctable the hazard, the more inexhaustible is the market for 'fighting' it. (Beck, 1995: 138)

A welfare system operating within a compensatory framework, in which the central struggles revolve around shares of the cake (who gets how much) and grounds of entitlement to portions of it (why do they get it), makes sense only if the 'cake' is itself a desirable good, that is, if the acquisition of shares does indeed enhance individual and collective welfare. What happens, however, if the cake is intrinsically poisonous, if its production is the cause of individual and collective sickness and illness and if possession of its portions is life-threatening, rather than life-enhancing (Beck, 1995: 128)? What if the socio-economic system which ostensibly 'guarantees' welfare, is a system for the production and distribution of hazards and risks, rather than a system for the production and distribution of wealth and welfare? Under these circumstances, Beck (1992b) argues, the insurance principle through which the welfare state purports to provide social security for all becomes redundant, 'with protection paradoxically diminishing as the danger grows' (1992b: 101).

Beck's assessment of contemporary science, politics and society suggests, as does McKibben (1990), that every particle of planetary life is now shot through with human-induced impacts: from ozone holes to genetically modified organisms, from 'artificial' reproduction to 'synthetic' landscapes, there is no place either in 'internal' (i.e., organismic) or 'external' (i.e., ecosystemic) nature that does not bear the marks of human intervention. Increasingly, economic activity is oriented not towards infinite expansion or acquisitive exploitation in an open, natural-environmental system, but towards the intensified reprocessing, reconfiguration and reconstruction of a closed, socio-environmental system. In this situation, 'economic growth' proceeds on the twin bases of despoiling and degrading ecosystems whilst simultaneously offering protective goods and services to counter the consequences of the degradation. Contemporary society is a 'risk society' to the extent that the production, displacement and mediation of ecological hazards increasingly drives technological innovation, market development, political regulation and capital investment as well as cultural perception and social organisation (Beck, 1995: 152, *et passim*).

We can note, here, that whilst the state remains an important axis in struggles around welfare, there is an increasing tendency to bypass the state in direct confrontations between ecological degraders and groups and individuals affected by environmental change. Indeed, there is a sense in which the state is caught in the contradictions opened up by the lines of direct and indirect conflict around the social distribution of ecological hazards. Whether in terms of public order legislation that criminalises alternative lifestyles (such as travellers or squatters), environmental legislation that aims to be 'business friendly' (such as the stipulation in the Environmental Protection Act that industry should adopt the 'Best Available Technology Not Entailing Excessive Cost') or transnational negotiations over transport and waste regulation (such as the Trans-European Networks for transport, or the Polluter Pays Principle), contemporary states persistently confront policy dilemmas that have emerged through conflicts over environmental change. Each of these cases represents a short-term response to the problem of ecological incorporation or assimilation: they regulate the burdens and benefits that flow to the winner and loser groups exposed by the process of ecological change.

On the basis of Beck's (1995) analysis, short-termism is inevitable because neither the political state nor the legions of scientific experts employed to measure the effects of ecological degradation can ever be confident about the consequences of technological developments and applications. Beck points out that contemporary science has been forced to reverse its own rules of conduct in order to gauge the impacts of new technologies. The individual, social and ecological effects of a nuclear meltdown, for example, cannot be known until there has been a nuclear meltdown; the impacts of releasing genetically modified organisms into the environment cannot be known until they have been released; the transgenerational significance of steady increases in environmental toxicity cannot be known until those transgenerational effects have occurred. Rather than 'proving' technological efficacy and safety in the laboratory and then applying the technology to real-world situations, contemporary science provides only statistical probabilities for selected dangers from new technologies and is forced to wait and see what real-world devastations flow from their insertion into socio-economic systems. The paradoxical consequence of this scientific and technological progress is that the safest place to be in the modern world is inside the laboratories where 'cutting-edge', dangerous technologies are developed! Everywhere else is potentially (and actually) poisonous.

To what extent is the welfare state 'liable' for the gradual accumulation of hazards, poisons and risks that are part of the 'normal' functioning of modern socio-economic activities? In the insurance society, a social compact between state, capital and labour serves to maintain the capitalist economic system through a series of welfare state 'liabilities' – social policy measures designed to provide required knowledge and skills, care for the young or infirm, arrangements for the transition between work and non-work, and so on – that remove from individual capitalists or labourers the political responsibility to organise compensation and entitlement. A collective 'welfare fund' is established (i.e., portions of GNP) which, whilst in no way equalising the costs and benefits of the system, none the less provides for classes of need emerging within it. The fund, as we noted above, is sustained through continued economic expansion, and administered and regulated according to specified criteria of entitlement to enable sufficient quantities of benefits to be distributed throughout the society.

However, the risk society sees a reversal of this logic, in so far as the social compact allows (indeed, encourages) the economic system as a whole to continue poisoning the environment in the name of economic development, leaving companies and communities to fight over who is liable for what ecological degradation: who is 'causing' ground-level ozone accumulation or stratospheric ozone depletion, who is responsible and liable for pesticide or nitrate accumulation in the water stocks, who is causing the spread of synthetic carcinogens in everything from foodstuffs to traffic fumes? Is it the industrialists, whose plants and products pump out the pollution, or is it the consumers, whose insatiable demand for goods and services 'forces' the industrialist to pollute in order to survive? The ready answer, of course, is that 'everyone' is responsible: industrialists, consumers, politicians and scientists alike all share in the 'blame' for this state of the affairs. The consequence of this generalised fault on the part of humanity-as-a-whole is that no one is at fault. The risk society comprises a system of organised 'non-liability': since every individual, group, company or organisation is 'responsible' for the ecological catastrophe, then no one is 'liable' for it. In order to substantiate the claim, Beck points out that in Germany in 1985 five thousand legal actions were brought to court under Germany's environmental legislation, yet only twenty-seven resulted in convictions involving prison sentences and, of these, twenty-four were held over pending appeal: 'The remaining cases – just under 100 per cent, that is – were abandoned in spite of the flood of legislation, in spite of the public objections of ever more zealous and well-equipped inspectorates invested with police powers' (1995: 134).

Both the 'insurance' society, bureaucratically embedded in postwar welfare systems, and the 'risk' society which grew alongside it, represent political ecologies of welfare. They represent entrenched political logics in the operations of legal and social institutions, the organisation and distribution of classes of benefit and burden among winner and loser groups, and the definition, control and administration (or lack thereof) of responsibilities and liabilities for the welfare outcomes of socio-economic activities. In so far as the insurance society and the risk society comprise political ecologies of welfare, they reveal specific questions about citizenship and the citizen's role in the process of environmental change and regulation.

Citizenship, welfare and ecology

There is a political current in contemporary societies that can be summed up as the 'crisis of citizenship'. Lash and Urry's (1987) *End of Organized Capitalism* and Claus Offe's (1985) *Disorganized Capitalism*, for example, both suggest that increasing political and economic fragmentation – resulting from changes in cultural technologies, the internationalisation of capital and the commodification of social goods, together with associated shifts in labour organisation and community structures – effectively undermines prevailing concepts of 'static' social citizenship (see Chapter 5 above). A static notion of citizenship is one in which citizenship is seen as a state or condition to be achieved by acquiring specific rights and resources for participation in civil life. This notion has come under attack theoretically and practically from a number of sources.

Both the New Right and the New Left have attacked the assumption that a centralised state can (or does) distribute the rights and benefits of citizenship effectively. Feminists have attacked the masculinist paradigm underpinning modern citizenship concepts – based on a restrictive public sphere and a discriminatory process of social boundary-setting. Post-imperialists have attacked the basic humanism behind contemporary concepts of citizenship, arguing that this humanism represents an imperialist occlusion of the social systems and social identities of colonised peoples: even the notion of a 'nation-state' on which the idea of citizenship has depended is a recent invention that has been imposed on many peoples as a result of imperialist expansion. Recently, also, the position and practice of labour organisations has changed whilst new social movements have taken up the political mantle in areas ranging from environment to sexuality. Each of these movements brings political matters into the public arena in a different way, focusing on different targets and offering different solutions. Yet they share a change of emphasis in their concept of citizenship. That change involves rejecting the idea that citizenship is coterminous with the acquisition of rights and proposing that it also involves the fulfilment of duties and responsibilities.

In British politics, the concept of 'active' or 'participatory' citizenship surfaced in the mid 1980s to describe a form of social contract based on the responsibility of each individual to contribute to the communities in which they lived. It underpinned the notorious 'poll tax' legislation introduced by Margaret Thatcher's Conservative government, was promoted by the Liberal Democrat leader Paddy Ashdown in his book *Citizen's Britain*, and provided an important element of the Charter 88 Movement for constitutional reform (Plant, 1991: 50). The emergence of the 'active', 'participatory' prefix can be traced to a number of different sources: participation and community control were central themes of the World

Health Organisation's health empowerment philosophy of the 1970s and 1980s and were important organising principles underlying the United Nations Community Development Projects across the same period (Morley et al., 1987; Martin and McQueen, 1989). Variations on the 'active' citizenship theme have also been important in environmentalist perspectives, in terms of both 'green' social theory and in terms of constructing green social and economic alternatives (Ward and Dubois, 1972; Ward, 1979; Bookchin, 1982; Bahro, 1986; Tokar, 1987).

According to Steward (1991), ecological citizenship implies that people have an ethic of care for nature and all of its contents. This means that ecological citizens must accept that both human beings and other species have fundamental rights but, at the same time, that these are only one side of the ethic of ecological care. This 'planetary ethic' (Jonas, 1984) implies that people have a duty and a responsibility to build ecologically sustainable social and economic arrangements that fulfil not only immediate human needs, but also the needs of other species and genera as well as providing for the needs of future generations. The ethical argument for an ecological citizenship encounters a number of theoretical problems. For example, if 'citizenship' implies both rights and duties, and if 'rights' are to be extended to non-human species, what 'duties' will zooplankton be expected to perform? (See also Martell, 1994, Chapter 3, on some of the philosophical dilemmas of attaching value to non-human entities.) Similarly, Steward (1991: 71) suggests that citizens will have to accept more social regulation and businesses will have to accept more control by government. However, there is no evidence to suggest that, having vested such power in governments, the social controls and business regulations will deliver any more caring or ethical outcomes than currently. In spite of these problems the concept of 'ecological citizenship' helps to clarify some important dimensions of contemporary environmental struggles.

For example, environmental conflicts are regularly characterised by definitional disputes: whether or not a substance is harmful, whether a patch of land is beautiful, valuable, rich in wildlife, or provides scarce amenity values; whether a development plan addresses all of the environmental, social, psychological and economic impacts that are likely to arise following its implementation; and so on. Such conflicts characteristically expose, and often lead to the validation of, the broader environmental benefits that people accrue from a given resource (see Burningham and O'Brien, 1994). The consequence of this process is that, for example, local environmental struggles over roads, nuclear plants and chemical industries bring into public-political arena issues around quality of life, moral discourses about both human rights and the wider implications of specific plans and policies for environmental quality, and much else beyond their technical or economic characteristics.

Similarly, many such conflicts also raise precisely those issues of 'responsibility' and 'duty' emphasised in green ethics, although in a somewhat different form. In particular, there is a regular demand that those who actually do benefit from the impact bear a responsibility for carrying its costs (see Cable and Benson, 1993). The demand is often not simply that polluters should have financial liability, but that they should also bear the environmental and associated health and welfare costs, rather than distributing these among victim communities.

Finally, as Beck (see above) observed, an important feature of environmental struggles is that, increasingly, they bypass the state and pit community against corporation directly, often leading to a politicisation of the community's members. Hannigan (1995) notes several examples of community politicisation resulting from the attempted local imposition of waste-management schemes and polluting discharges. He notes how community members quickly became experts in gathering and presenting evidence, interpreting laws and motivating support to oppose both corporations and state institutions. Seager (1993) recounts the exploits of the New York activist Lois Gibbs in the late 1970s, whose initial politicisation and subsequent rise to environmental activist and organiser began when the Hooker Chemical Company tried to discredit her evidence of the impacts of the Love Canal toxic waste dump on the neighbourhood built on top of it. Without the support of the state or, initially, any expert or legal organisations, Gibbs and other community members tirelessly exposed both the dangers of the dump and the devious tactics of Hooker Chemicals in trying to evade their responsibility for the health damage caused by their waste. Other striking examples of direct action by communities against multinational corporations include the 'Chipko' movement in India (Shiva, 1989; Joekes et al., 1994), and the African women's groups involved in the Women, Environment and Development Network (Kettel, 1995).

These examples, especially of the process of community politicisation, point to an important feature of environmental activism, namely, that it is conducted overwhelmingly by women. Not only do women make up the bulk of the membership of environmental organisations – especially grassroots organisations – but they are also in the front line of environmental change as global economic restructuring robs communities of their own resources and 'formalises' their labour, drawing more and more women into unhealthy, discriminatory and environmentally despoiling patterns of work (Moghadam, 1995). Seager proposes that:

> It is the linkage of 'women's work' to the environments of lived ordinariness that explains why, globally, it is women who are usually the first to become environmental activists in their community. Everywhere in the world, women are responsible for making sure that their families are fed, housed, and kept healthy. . . . In environmental management terms, we could say that women make the primary consumer and resource-use decisions for their families and their communities – that women in all countries serve as managers of fixed resources. (1993: 270)

As the degradation of the environment makes access to primary resources more difficult, more competitive and more costly, so contemporary industrialised societies move more and more towards the extraction of 'used' resources from the mountains of waste that they produce. Increasingly, 'waste' becomes not an end-product of industrial activity, but the first stage in industrial production. In the UK, in 1996, a County Council (Berkshire) examined bids from a hundred companies from all over the world to begin 'mining' a full landfill site in search of valuable plastics, glass and metals. These valuable items are the accumulated wealth of fifteen years of the dumping of household and commercial waste into a hole previously left by sand and gravel quarrying. The valuables could be sorted on site and the remaining semi-rotted materials reburied (Schoon, 1996) – with the possibility that someone else will come along in fifteen years and discover that other components are also 'valuable' enough for further 'mining'.

The increasing value attached to waste is not unconnected to the issues of gender that we discussed above. As 'waste' is redefined as a resource comprising valuable commodity materials, so new of types of labour and labour relations emerge in order to facilitate its exploitation. The increasing cost of raw materials, and the concomitant increase in the value of wastes, has spurred the development of a range of social and political regulations designed to manage and supervise the economic channels through which waste objects pass. The connection between women, labour and waste in the new regulatory system has been reported by Schultz (1993).

Schultz's analysis refers to the German system of collecting, sorting and recycling waste, but has implications for the approach to labour and labour relations in all nations. She observes that in Germany, as in other industrial economies, materials and resources have tended to flow along a linear track: from the extraction of raw materials through product manufacture, distribution and consumption to disposal. Contemporary industrial systems place more emphasis on the recycling or re-use of materials throughout an economy; they tend towards a circular economy where secondary (waste or residue) materials – rather than primary, raw materials – become the first stage in the process of manufacture. Over the past two decades, but especially since the mid 1980s, rates of household recycling, sorting and re-supplying have increased markedly, with a disproportionate share of the labour falling on women. Also, the elimination of household wastes – by planning a minimum-waste cooking régime, for example, repairing and re-using items – as well as their recycling is labour for which householders are not paid. Schultz argues that the focus of 'environmental education' and local recycling schemes has been on convincing women in the home to take responsibility for wastes whilst the major industrial waste manufacturers profit from their unpaid sorting and recycling labours.

A number of implications follows from Schultz's analysis. For example, the (economic and environmental) benefits or burdens of a circular system will be affected significantly by the costs of gaining access to the commodity materials in the waste stream – just as the benefits and burdens of mining, drilling, quarrying or chemically synthesising 'primary' materials affect the costs of a linear system. Access can be gained by 'mining' wastes after disposal (as in the Berkshire example, above) or by sorting and routing the materials prior to disposal. The first system connects with the socially organised labour of men in traditional male industries. The second system connects with the domestically organised labour of women in traditional female unpaid roles. Note that the change in gendered relationships around extractive labour occurs not by incorporating women into men's occupations and associated benefits (or vice versa), but by resiting or relocating the focus of materials extraction on to traditionally defined women's labours. Thus, the circular economy signals a reiteration of the gendered division of labour in the extractive industries: men exploit depleting resources, women exchange fixed resources. In this way, the new organisation breaks down entrenched distinctions between production and consumption, 'official' work (paid work in the public sphere) and 'unofficial' work (unpaid work in the private or domestic sphere), whilst reaffirming the gendered division of labour in resource exploitation.

The new organisation also signals a challenge to concepts of 'productive' and 'reproductive' labour, a challenge to the rules governing social insurance and welfare entitlements and, in consequence, a challenge to the organisational bases of 'citizenship' entitlements and obligations. The basis of citizenship in modern societies is participation in a public sphere and in socially regulated productive labour – labour that contributes to social wealth and thus generates an income and rights. In this model, the private sphere of domestically regulated reproductive labour does not contribute to social wealth and thus does not generate an income or rights. If, however, a greater portion of wealth-contributing labour takes place in the private sphere it will have two obvious consequences. First, there will be proportionally less availability of publicly 'productive' labour and the rights and benefits of such production will apply to fewer and fewer people. Second, there will be either a new public welfare system based on the productivity of private labour, or the distinction between private and public labour will intensify the inequalities that accompany the paradigm shift from linear to circular industrial systems. Thus, environmental changes affect the economics of industrial organisation and the basis and distribution of citizenship rights and entitlements simultaneously.

The idea of and the struggles around 'ecological citizenship' display a number of the characteristics that Beck identified as the elements of the risk society. They promote and pursue conflicts over definitions and understandings, challenging the authority of scientific 'expertise' and corporate power alike; they bring to the foreground the question of who is responsible for what human and environmental damage, and thereby who has the 'duty' to respond to it; and they pit communities against corporations directly, bringing the politics of what was once understood as the 'private' sphere of household and community to the centre stage of public political conflict. The political transformations that coordinate 'sustainable' or 'eco-friendly' industrial and economic systems, however – establishing gendered relations of production and divisions of labour, together with boundaries between public and private spheres of life – also challenge the basis of contemporary citizenship rights and benefits. A political ecology perspective thereby proposes that environmental change and the bases of social citizenship are inextricably intertwined. Environmental struggle and the ecological citizen's action is likely to have effects on contemporary economies at least as profound as, and possibly more so than, those of their nineteenth and twentieth century industrial counterparts. Let us hope so: the domination of the environmental agenda by the interests of big business is currently stifling the creative political alternatives promoted through alternative political ecologies of modern society.

Concluding remarks

The politics of ecology comprises an important new element in theorising social welfare for a number of reasons. These include the way that ecological critiques draw attention to the association between environment and development and the struggle over resources represented by that association; the critique of the logic of growth on which postwar, industrialised welfare systems have been constructed; and the reformulation of concepts of citizenship and participation through which social policies have attempted to legitimate the institutions of the welfare state.

In this chapter we have shown how social action, economic development and environmental damage interact in political ecologies of welfare, that is, in the organisation of rights and responsibilities in, and benefits and costs of, environmental change. The environmentalist critique of modern society is a 'reflexive' critique in the sense that it addresses the connections between the socio-political characteristics of industrial societies and the technologies and scientific knowledges that they develop. Indeed, in many ways, environmentalist critiques turn science against itself, contesting, on the basis of scientific assessment, the capacity of science to deliver sustainable or environmentally friendly technological solutions to ecological degradation. In environmentalist perspectives, science is not the great hope of civilisation, it is a tool of exploitation and conflict: 'nature' cannot be subdued or controlled – by human ingenuity and objective method – in the service of global welfare. All ecological relationships, that is all relationships between human activity and particular environments, bring costs as well as benefits, costs that someone, somewhere, somehow must pay. The more that human beings transform all local and global environments, the more they impact on nature globally, immediately and totally, the more the costs that must be borne become immediately apparent. As societies industrialise, capitalise and modernise, as they place ever greater faith in technological provisions for human existence, the more the environment becomes a human-induced hazard. From holes in the ozone layer to fish that disappear from the oceans to mass-produced meat that kills, human welfare is systematically undermined by the technological systems that promise its delivery.

As in all forms of political action, the 'costs' of environmental degradation are unevenly distributed. The health consequences of pesticide use, the malnutrition stemming from desertification and the over-production of cash crops in place of food crops, the human impacts of poisoned seas, rivers and lakes, do not kill or injure in some strict mathematical ratio. There is not an 'environment' or 'nature' existing somewhere beyond the bounds of human life that has 'effects' or 'impacts' on people's experiences. The degradation of environments – of particular places (such as rainforest regions or coastal deltas), particular qualities (such as breathable air or clean water), particular resources (such as mineral or food stocks) – is a political-ecological process: it is tied in to the means of organising and profiting from environmental exploitation. Those with a greater capacity to exert power and influence over the lives of others suffer least from the hazards generated by industrial technologies and economic systems. So long as contemporary environmental exploitation is characterised by a system of ' irresponsibility', the uneven distribution of costs and benefits and the continued despoliation of the world is assured.

7

Postmodernism

The postwar welfare state comprises a configuration of powers, controls, opportunities, rights, inclusions, exclusions and memberships. Its foundation held out the promise of abolishing the iniquitous, dispassionate and grossly impoverishing operations of an unfettered market capitalism by democratising and humanising the social conditions under which national prosperity was organised and its growth directed. Yet the promise had a hollow ring that has echoed down the decades since its declaration. Only some inequalities and impoverishments were attacked by Beveridge's proposals and subsequent British welfare policy:

> When Beveridge announced his attack on the five giants – Want, Squalor, Ignorance, Idleness and Disease – he hid the giants of Racism and Sexism, and the fights against them, behind statues to the Nation and the White Family. (Williams, 1989: 162)

As Williams points out, the gendered and racialised political outlines of Beveridge's scheme were sharply criticised when the proposals were published and have been the source of unrelenting dispute and struggle ever since.

Theoretically, however, for any given welfare system, the specific configuration of powers, rights, etc., to which we referred above, can be understood in two contrasting ways. First, it may be understood as the *contingent* outcome of a more or less well-designed or consciously manipulated system whose ongoing reform might lead to a yet-more-democratic or yet-more-humanitarian organisation of welfare. Second, it may be understood as an *intrinsically* divisive pattern of social coordination whose continued existence is rooted in and dependent upon processes of exclusion and marginalisation. These two theoretical perspectives have radically opposing political consequences. In the first perspective, which historically has been and remains dominant in the disciplines of sociology, social policy and administration and political science, struggle about with, in normative philosophical principles of 'justice', 'rights' and 'needs' is seen as a rational response to problems of the maldistribution of resources or to the dysfunctional operations of social welfare institutions. In the second perspective the practice of imposing such normative principles on to institutional arrangements leads inevitably to exclusion, marginalisation and discrimination.

This division in perspectives, which we have simplified here, is a tension that lies at the heart of social theory. Commonly, in social policy and social welfare analysis it leads to the substitution of social theory by political philosophy – that is, such analyses revolve around what should or should not be supported, is or is not right or just, rather than around how and why decades of reform and reconstruction persistently reiterate political asymmetries and social and cultural exclusions in the social welfare system. But the important questions to keep in mind concern how the asymmetries and exclusions are sustained and how they might be connected with welfare policy and practice. These questions have been posed with increasing insistence across the past three decades. As the Keynesian postwar compact between capital, labour and the state showed itself not to resolve social divisions and inequalities but to be complicit with their generation and solidification, so the resulting excluded groups and marginalised social statuses came to represent more and more radical constituencies in struggles over political change. The more the political landscape was reconfigured, the more vigorous became the challenges from groups outside the Keynesian compact. The increasing visibility of these struggles – enhanced by the migrations of people between the ex-colonies and ex-empires, the spread of rapid electronic communications technologies and networks, the shifting patterns of production, consumption and employment, and the incapacity of scientific-technical and governmental-bureaucratic organisations to develop effective solutions to political, economic and environmental problems – effectively undermined the ideological-mythic closure that the political centre could and would hold together the diverse constituencies around which social welfare policies and practices revolved.

In this context, the debate about welfare came over time to encounter questions of social, political and cultural differences in status, identity, personal and social autonomy as well as questions of opportunities, rights and needs. Feminist, anti-racist, disability, ecology, and gay and lesbian movements confronted both the centralised monoliths of state welfare organisation and control and the traditional oppositional and reformist organisations whose agenda had excluded and marginalised the former's claims since the postwar settlement. For brevity, here, we can say that such movements forced on to the political agenda the social and cultural *differences* through which welfare (and other) programmes were structured and experienced and, further, focused attention on the exclusionary processes upon which the centralised state welfare system had been constructed. The 'politics of difference' (West, 1990) are commonly represented as a form of 'postmodern' politics in their own right (McLaren, 1995). However, it is more useful to assert that they opened up the way to a 'revisioning' of the political sphere and to the development of new perspectives on the cultural and political processes by which the policy and practice of welfare sustains asymmetrical differences in the organisation of social life. It is at this level – at the level of 'revisioning the political' (Yeatman, 1994) – that what have been called the 'new social movements' have been instrumental in forcing a series of new political engagements with the structures and experiences of social life.

In previous chapters of this book we have documented the reorientations that have characterised theories of social welfare across the postwar period. Beginning with two major traditions in welfare theory – Marxism and liberalism – we showed how such traditions have been subject to both internal revisions and external challenges. The neo-liberal critique charged the welfare state and its 'socialist' proponents with the creation of a dependency culture and with undermining the civil and communal institutions which organise everyday life. Poststructuralism unpacked the surveillance and disciplinary characteristics of purportedly humane reforms in psychiatry, penology and medicine. Post-Fordism, postindustrialism and the disorganisation thesis focused on the persistence or development of capitalism, rather than its demise. Political ecology has contested the productivist logic embedded in political economy and drawn attention to the interactions between both capitalist and state socialist régimes and environmental degradation. Each challenge illuminates different facets of the social organisation of welfare and each establishes different grounds for reflection and action on welfare. Yet, however much they differ, each also addresses whether the processes, conditions and characteristics they identify are incidental and contingent or essential and foundational. In other words, they are part of a theoretical and empirical debate about social change, its causes and consequences: does the emergence of new social movements, global social connections, new computer technologies, new states or economic blocs signal the end of the modern era and the dawn of a new one, or an intensification of the dynamics of modernity? At the same time, they are part of a related debate about the validity and legitimacy of different ways of theorising the social world and its change.

One of the most influential and well-publicised versions of this debate recently has been that around modernism and postmodernism. Of all the perspectives and critiques that we have examined in this book none is more confused or more elaborate than the question of the postmodern. In order to show how and why this question is significant we begin by defining the different terms in the debate before going on to discuss postmodern theory and welfare.

The 'modern' and the 'postmodern'

The terms 'modern' and 'postmodern' are now commonplace in contemporary social science but there is no agreement over their respective meanings and implications. As we have noted already, the modern–postmodern dyad is shorthand for an extensive series of debates about central concepts and perspectives in social theory more widely. The debates range across concepts of structure and agency, history, culture, subjectivity, public and private identity, ethics and science, and many more. They also signal disputes around epistemological problems in social science: the techniques and status of interpretation in social theory and research, the nature of cultural movements and institutions and their role in generating social change or maintaining social stasis, the capacity of established canons of theory and research to advance or obstruct political awareness, and the adequacy and validity of 'local' knowledges and experiences as grounds for sociological accounts of social life, for example.

We do not have the space, here, to explore all of the subtle intricacies that distinguish among and between 'modern' and 'postmodern' perspectives (cf. Butler, 1994; Lemert, 1994). We also acknowledge that our grouping of modern and postmodern characteristics glosses over many of the theoretical and philosophical problems that stimulate and sustain the debates around them. Our aim is to outline some of the important theoretical features of modern and postmodern perspectives as they apply to theorising social welfare. In order to do this we outline the 'modernity thesis' and some of the important postmodern challenges to it. Our main concern is to address postmodern theories of welfare, so most of what follows deals with this perspective. We begin our exposition, however, with a brief introduction to the modernity thesis in order to show, later, how the 'post' relates to the 'modern'.

The modernity thesis

There is a number of theoretical perspectives which share the view that contemporary society is either continuous with or an evolution of established historical patterns in Western societies. Whilst some argue that there has been a 'break' – from industrialism to postindustrialism, or from Fordism to post-Fordism, for example – the logic of the transformation is seen to reiterate the social dynamics of 'modern' society.

Simply put, the modernity thesis considers the major lines of development and change in the contemporary world as being consistent with, or as a historical product of, an unfolding pattern of events inaugurated by the social, political and epistemological revolutions of the Enlightenment. The era immediately following the Enlightenment appeared to produce both the technological and organisational capacity to feed, clothe and care for everyone and also liberate people from the injustices and arbitrary power imposed by monarchs, lords and other organised powers (notably, the established church). But these capacities might be put to ends that are 'good' or to ends that are 'bad'. Thus, this historical era saw also the production of the technological and organisational capacity for repression, domination and destruction. However, at the same time, Enlightenment philosophy and its subsequent elaboration in scientific, legal and moral discourses established universal principles of conduct, reason and justice against which to measure the efficacy, goodness or desirability of particular applications of these capacities. In short, Enlightenment provided standards of conduct and thought through which all 'rational' humans could, in principle, agree on the objective benefits and burdens of scientific, economic and social development and how these should be organised and controlled. The fact that all humans do not actually agree on the benefits and burdens and the fact that quite a lot of humans have been and are excluded from even taking part in the process of reaching agreement is explained as the *contingent* outcome of structural and ideological forces. These forces, embedded in capitalist, militarist and bureaucratic modernisation, have transformed the rational promise of the Enlightenment into an ambivalent and distorted system of coercions and controls over public and private life. The struggle between the rational promise of Enlightenment and the contingent exclusion of the masses from it is often explained through three interlocking logics peculiar to the modernisation of society – differentiation, detraditionalisation and rationalisation.

Differentiation consists in the process of classifying and categorising the manifold experiences in, and forms of, life and segregating them into distinct, autonomous spheres that are separately coordinated and socially ordered. Thus, modernisation leads to the separation of church and state, law and politics, art and science, the public and the private, economy and society, work and leisure, rationality and irrationality, fact and fiction, the citizen and the alien, and so on. The distinctions are both philosophical – in the sense that they serve to organise how the complexity of modern life is understood – and practical – in that they uphold different rules of evaluation, norms and expectations, institutional arrangements and forms of control. In these respects, modernisation is the elaboration of systems for instituting and managing differences, for establishing differences between individual and group experience and coordinating these within the modern order by allocating to them an appropriate location in the total social system.

Detraditionalisation consists in the displacement of established customs, habits, institutions and beliefs and their substitution by seemingly impersonalised and objective systems of social coordination. Whereas in premodern societies, communal traditions are the major vehicles through which individuals develop their self-identities, norms and moral codes, in modern societies such identities and morals are increasingly organised outside of these communal traditions by new institutions governing collective life – including the modern communications media, educational and financial institutions – and the interconnections between them. Localised traditions are supplanted by seemingly universal precepts tied to complex, bureaucratic institutions operating in the public sphere. Over time, the public sphere comes to represent the site where rights, statuses, identities, collective morals and norms are validated and regulated. In these respects, modernisation is the relocation or reorganisation – the making public – of authority over the development of moral codes, patterns of self-understanding, economic, cultural and social development.

Rationalisation is closely tied to this latter process and consists in the substitution of objective criteria and standards for subjective preferences and desires. Increasingly, social action and social institutions are organised on the basis of efficiency calculations, that is, on the basis of the extent to which they represent the most logical, effective and instrumental means to realise a given end. Rationalisation comprises the emergence of systems of assessment, judgement and interpretation that do not depend on the identity of the person doing the judging and interpreting. In short, the 'truth' or veracity of an interpretation is understood to derive from its adherence to formal principles rather than from the power or status of the interpreter. The displacement of preference, desire and identity by abstract rules and codes requires the development of extensive systems of (bureaucratic) administration which, over time, come to adjudicate over and process more and more of individual and collective life. The development of abstract rules and codes becomes an end in itself, such that modern life is overseen by a soulless administrative machinery disconnected from individual and collective purposes, hopes and aspirations.

In a series of recent books, Giddens (1990, 1991, 1994) has attempted a synthesis of the different layers of the thesis to theorise what he calls 'reflexive modernization'. Giddens uses this term to define processes of globalisation, social reflexivity and the emergence of a post-traditional (which he prefers to 'postmodern') social order. Giddens counterposes the 'simple modernization' of earlier social development with the 'reflexive modernization' of the postwar period, each stage of development characterised by a specific form of risk: external risk belonging to simple modernisation and manufactured risk to the current stage of reflexive modernisation. Contemporary political institutions face the problem of managing uncertainty and risk generated by human intervention in the social and natural worlds (1994: 4). This 'manufactured uncertainty' is amplified by the process of globalisation, detraditionalisation and social reflexivity. The political and social welfare institutions which responded to external risk and promoted social solidarity under conditions of simple modernisation are no longer adequate responses to contemporary life. The world is now a 'plastic', malleable entity: both the social and natural worlds being *subject to* constant intervention and the *subject of* disputes over the causes and consequences of such interventions.

Giddens suggests that the changes afflicting contemporary everyday and institutional life represent a framework of risks and opportunities for personal and social development. The framework is mediated by both flexible or mobile structures – including structures of accumulation, surveillance, political regulation and communication – and by the actions and choices of individuals. People's behaviours, expectations and personal styles are influenced by global forces and, in turn, those behaviours, expectations and styles have effects on the lives of others far distant. For example, buying an item of clothing, notes Giddens (1994: 5), has consequences for the international division of labour and planetary ecology.

At the institutional level, reflexive modernisation generates 'global risk environments' of four high-consequence risks: *capitalism* generates economic and social polarisation, both within and between nations; *industrialism* threatens the world's ecosystems; *surveillance* is linked to widespread repression and abuse of human rights; whilst the *means of violence* encompasses, a spectrum of brutal phenomena ranging from nuclear confrontations to male assaults on women (1994: 81, 88–90, 97–100). According to Giddens, these ills of contemporary life cannot be resolved through the politics of either left or right: both neo-liberalism and socialism represent exhausted and discredited philosophical systems that are unable to provide guidelines for political action. Socialism, once the basis for hopes of a radical transformative project, degenerates into a 'defensive conservatism' which defends existing welfare state institutions even though they are no longer capable of responding to manufactured uncertainty. Neo-liberalism, having eclipsed Conservative philosophy to become the radical force behind a destructive, untrammelled capitalism (1994: 2–4), has proved morally destructive, undermining the collective fabric of social life in pursuit of efficient accumulation. Late modernity betrays the incapacity of left–right thinking to address the complex uncertainties of contemporary society. For Giddens, it is necessary to move *Beyond Left and Right*, to a transformative project of the 'social self', a project rooted in a critical theory for contemporary times: 'utopian realism' (1994: 101–3).

The outlook of utopian realism recognises that history is contingent and risk-pervasive. 'Realism' suggests that a radical politics has to be based on 'actual social processes' to generate effective strategies. 'Utopian' refers to the possibility that, in a 'social universe more and more pervaded by social reflexivity', alternative visions and models of the future can actively shape the present (1994: 249–50). Giddens argues that utopian realism provides a framework for a programme of political action aimed at transforming late modern societies. It envisages four alternative socio-political forms counterposed to the risk environments of late modernity. First, counterposed to the ecological and economic dysfunctions of capitalist accumulation is a post-scarcity economy which rejects economic growth as the overriding objective of modern life and in which combating poverty is a central objective. Second, counterposed to environmentally destructive industrialism is the humanisation of nature which comprises a strategy of conservation but also a new ecology which values the interdependence of humans and nature. Third, counterposed to the politics of violence is the politics of negotiated power aimed at reducing all forms of violence and diminishing arbitrary power. Fourth, counterposed to the surveillance and control systems of states and institutions is a tendency towards 'dialogic democracy' which comprises a politics of trust and integrity.

In this context, for Giddens, the major task facing a welfare state in the late modern era is to develop forms of insurance, protection and support that comply with 'life values' – the desire to live a 'happy and satisfying life' (Giddens, 1994: 174). The provision and organisation of welfare guided by life-values requires that the productivist logic of the welfare state be displaced and substituted by a generative 'affluent/poor lifestyle pact' (1994: 196) in which environmental protection, local traditions and networks and flexible working patterns are supported for the contribution they make to personal well-being. Such measures correspond to an 'ethics of a globalizing, post-traditional society' which recognises 'the sanctity of human life and the universal right to happiness and self-actualization – coupled to the obligation to promote cosmopolitan solidarity and an attitude of respect towards non-human agencies and beings, present and future' (p. 253).

This brief outline of Giddens' argument brings into focus the importance of a 'normative paradigm' in social welfare theory. Such a paradigm, as we have discussed elsewhere (O'Brien and Penna, 1998), construes social welfare policy and practice as a mediation between public and private experiences and actions. It is a paradigm in which social welfare and social policy comprise vehicles for realising and organising the benefits of social citizenship. The acquisition of rights (and obligations), access to entitlements and benefits (such as welfare payments and services), is a public validation of societal membership. To the extent that more private needs can be accommodated within social policy's arsenal of entitlements and rights, so it is possible to counter disadvantage and discrimination by an enlargement of the public sphere. Similarly, to the extent that the enlargement incorporates more claims for rights and entitlements, it is consonant with a policy for social justice; since more people (as well as 'non-human agencies') and their needs are recognised and included in the rights/entitlements framework, then more people are treated 'justly'.

Theoretically, however, this perspective on the relationships between social policy, the public sphere and social justice begs the question of whether the *process* of conferring modern citizenship rights and entitlements is itself a process of marginalisation. In other words: are the divisions and exclusions of modern societies resolved through public incorporation? Or: is public incorporation itself a means of organising divisions and exclusions? In postmodern terms, as we explain below, the process of public incorporation is not an evolutionary expansion of social membership. It is, rather, inconsistent and unstable. Social struggles around inclusion, exclusion and solidarity are divisive and fragmenting but they also comprise a dynamic that continually challenges the operations of the public sphere over time. Postmodern approaches to social welfare can be used to theorise the dynamism through which membership and inclusion are socially effected: *how* are they realised in institutional and everyday life and in what does their 'publicity' (their socially sanctioned public expression) consist? Below, we explore the different dimensions of this question in postmodern theory and discuss some of the insights they provide into social welfare policy and practice.

Postmodern perspectives

The term 'postmodern' has come to symbolise a vigorous dispute in social science about personal and social change in the contemporary world. The debate, as we noted in our introductory comments, addresses both empirical and theoretical matters. Some commentators treat the postmodern as a distinct form of society or a historical period. Others assert that the 'post' is a part of the modern. Others again treat the postmodern as an epistemological or theoretical rupture which signals a change both in social experience and in the cultural categories in which such experience is explained and understood. In many instances, these different layers of meaning – historical, sociological and philosophical – are tangled together and lead to confusion about whether the debate refers to evidence of a transition to a postmodern era or to a clash of perspectives through which to theorise the modern era. Thus, the flexibility debate, which forms a central focus of political-economic accounts of contemporary change, is commonly treated as symptomatic of postmodernity, as evidence of a historical transformation. On the other hand, the term 'postmodern' is used also to depict a change in *modern* consciousness: a new way of relating to or theorising the persistence of modernity. The confusion of these two referents leads to ambivalence and often hostility towards postmodern intellectual and political questions – they are seen as distractions from urgent questions of personal needs and social rights. There are several types of postmodern social theory which we have discussed elsewhere (O'Brien and Penna, 1998). Each is an attempt to disentagle the theoretical and empirical dimensions of the postmodern question. Here, for reasons of space and brevity, we group the different perspectives into two categories: 'the postmodernisation thesis' and 'social postmodernism'.

The postmodernisation thesis

The postmodernisation thesis defines the postmodern as an excessive or 'hyper-' manifestation of the modern: the characteristics of modern society (rationalisation, differentiation, detraditionalisation) are seen to be intensified and doubled back upon themselves. Parton (1994: 10) puts this view clearly, depicting postmodernity as 'a world which has become disorientated, disturbed and subject to doubt . . . [Post]modernity is characterised by the fragmentation of modernity into forms of institutional pluralism, marked by variety, difference, contingency, relativism and ambivalence – all of which modernity sought to overcome.' The postmodernisation thesis proposes that all of the world's societies are undergoing a process of profound and foundational social change or, as Crook et al. (1992: 1), put it: 'Although the matter should be approached with considerable caution, the conclusion that radical change is occurring is inescapable. This is because change is now so widespread in its penetration of various social and cultural realms and because it reverses so many of the normal patterns of modernity.'

The idea that contemporary social institutions, relationships and structures serve to reverse or invert modern patterns of everyday and institutional life is central to the argument that the postmodern represents a historical break with the modern. This does not mean, however, that the postmodern returns to traditions or values of the past. Rather, in Crook et al.'s formulation, the inversion of modern social life is visible in the 'hyper-differentiation' of scientific/technical knowledges and cultural values, in the 'hyper-rationalisation' of political-economic authority and in the 'hyper-commodification' of lifestyles. The core of the thesis is that it is possible to detect in the contemporary world patterns of social organisation, control and experience that differ both quantitatively and qualitatively from those of the recent past. There is, again, inordinate confusion about the dates and places when and where these changes can be said to have begun and, commonly, it is argued that postmodernisation represents a transitional stage between an existing modern social order and a new (postmodern) order that has not yet fully emerged. The patterns of change are understood as conforming to emergent trends through which every dimension of social life is being reconfigured. Of particular note are trends towards political-economic decentralisation, localisation, fragmentation and desocialisation. We deal with each in turn.

Decentralisation refers to the tendency of large-scale organisations and blocs to diffuse authority over production and administration processes to subsidiary institutions and sites. Although decentralisation is not understood strategically – as the conscious activity of capitalist or class actors, for example – none the less, it is claimed, all economic, political and cultural relations are affected by it. Decentralisation comprises a revision of social life as a whole, reconstructing the institutions and networks through which power is exercised. Crook et al. distinguish between 'horizontal' and 'vertical' decentralisation. Horizontal decentralisation consists in a transfer of power from centralised executive bodies – such as government departments – to specialised quasi-autonomous organisations (quangos). Vertical decentralisation comprises a form of devolution in which power shifts downwards to smaller and more specialised units. In each case, the specialised organisations operate as forms of government and develop governmental procedures to manage the specialised powers they have come to coordinate. Parton (1994: 93) provides a graphic example of this argument in his observation that social work and social services generally have shifted from an ethos and practice of genericism to one of administrative specialism. Whereas, until recently, social work had been conceived as a generic activity, operating in a unified organisational structure and focused on case *work*, contemporary social work practice is dominated by assessment, monitoring, inter-agency coordination, multiple service provision and case *management*. Decentralisation does not necessarily imply a democratic form of power-sharing and, indeed, is a trend that intersects with privatisation and deregulation where public services are commodified for profit – as in the private insurance or care industries – and removed from democratic accountability – classically in the case of the quango.

Closely connected to the decentralisation trend is the emergence of new connections between local and global contexts. Instantaneous communications technologies, together with patterns of mass migration and world trade, are said to increase awareness of and dependence between localities far distant from each other. As Giddens (see above) noted, the choices and actions of consumers in one locality can have effects on the international division of labour and planetary ecology. At the same time, global corporations, military alliances and economic blocs exert influences over the choices and actions of people everywhere from Padiham to São Paulo. The postmodernisation thesis contends that the growth of local struggles over road-building, animal rights, ethnic or cultural identities, for example, indicate new forms of resistance politics. Whereas the mass demonstration and mass strike in support of rights, services or pay comprised a modernist politics, depending on mass political solidarity to achieve complex, corporatist demands, new social movements (NSMs) represent specific issues and often focus on local needs and conditions. The localisation of political struggle, as we noted in Chapter 6, often pits communities directly against global corporations but at the same time it distances local alliances and organisations from central coordination.

Localisation of political struggle is paralleled by a fragmentation of political culture in which party allegiances and class alliances give way to more fluid and informal networks of action. The networks are often staunchly anti-bureaucratic and anti-centralist, suspicious of large, organised formal institutional politics. In turn, the fragmentation of political culture is fuelled by the rise of identity politics in which modern logics of incorporation and representation are challenged on the twin bases of their rigidity and exclusiveness. For example, the British welfare state has been described, as we have noted earlier, as a means of coordinating and underpinning a system of entitlements and rights ostensibly applying equally and universally to all members of the British citizenry. Yet, the struggle for citizenship status has intensified, rather than subsided, during the postwar era. As the industrial working class has declined, so has its status as the political constituency through whom struggles for welfare entitlements and benefits are conducted. Instead, contemporary struggles around welfare and social development are undertaken through many competing and conflicting interest groups, expressing many different claims and critiques. In some cases, the struggles are fought on behalf of the welfare and the rights of animals or ecosystems as well as, and sometimes rather than, people. The postmodernisation of citizenship comprises the 'dealignment' of political identifications and the 'decomposition' of the political (class) networks of the modern citizenry. In their place, new social movements are said to refocus attention on values and to pose new ethical and cultural challenges to dominant political institutions.

Together with a number of related trends, decentralisation, localisation and fragmentation support a process of desocialisation or, more accurately, desocietalisation. An important strand of this argument is that a separation between 'nation' and 'state' is cutting through contemporary politics. In the modern global order, society has effectively been defined as the nation-state. The idea of a 'British' or 'Yugoslav' society, for example, has implied the territorial, cultural or political boundaries of the British or (former) Yugoslav nation-state. Postmodernisation undermines the strong connection between society and nation-state in two ways. First, the process of fragmentation, which we discussed above, leads to a dispersion of national and social identities. Europe, for example, contains more nations than nation-states and both the existence and the boundaries of those nation-states are unstable. Following the restructuring of the Soviet bloc several nation-states re-emerged in Europe, sometimes in somewhat different form (as in former Yugoslavia), but there are also several candidate nations whose status within the boundaries of European political states is the subject of intense and often fatal dispute – including Ireland, Kurdistan and the Basque region, amongst others. Second, global media of communication, trade and transport enable both corporations and communities to sustain international economic and social networks. Migrant communities exchange large quantities of income between and maintain social contacts across nation-state boundaries. Here, it is clear neither which society is the home of migrants nor which social and economic networks comprise the society where exchanges and contacts occur. In both of these ways, postmodernisation is said to disrupt existing societal patterns of norms and relationships.

As we noted above, the postmodernisation thesis focuses on a perceived transition between a modern society with well-mapped characteristics and tendencies and a yet-to-appear (postmodern) society whose contents and principles currently exist only as outline sketches. The sociology of postmodernisation seeks to identify empirically the important emergent trends of this transformation – the outlines of the new social order – in order to clarify and contribute to its development.

Social postmodernism

Theoretically, there is nothing specifically postmodern about the postmodernisation thesis. Its theory of social change is based on a concept of system self-transformation, the connection between whose parts is indicative of change in the larger whole. This construction is contested in postmodern social theory, or what we here call 'social postmodernism'. The latter is not a single academic or theoretical enterprise. In fact, in what follows, we group together a number of distinct postmodern theoretical schools in order to clarify in what ways, *as theories*, they can be construed as 'postmodern'. Elsewhere (O'Brien and Penna, 1998), following Hall (1996: 289), we have defined postmodernism as an 'elective affinity' which upholds certain cultural convergences of style and focus. These convergences comprise a frame of theoretical interpretation that differs from modernist paradigms such as systems theory.

There are some straightforward and easily recognisable differences between the two paradigms. For example, whilst the postmodernisation thesis draws on a mainstream sociological tradition invoking Durkheim, Weber, Merton and Habermas, social postmodernism draws on a different range of traditions including the poststructuralist influences of Nietzsche, Derrida, Kristeva and Lacan. The postmodernisation thesis, in Crook et al.'s exposition, posits a two-dimensional model of change: system change is the summation of changes along the axes of differentiation and organisation. In other words, the system betrays a logic or design that supersedes the intentions and actions of its component members. Social postmodernism understands change episodically – specific changes are theorised as 'condensed' or 'located' dynamics of struggle rather than as examples of emergent systemic patterns. Finally, the postmodernisation thesis is embedded in a humanistic pragmatism – where sociology serves to clarify the empirical facts of social change in order to assist rational decision-making. In this construction, the tools of sociological research can be applied to the discovery and collation of relevant facts in order to produce a model for use in social planning and management. Social post-modernism comprises a political counterpoint to this intellectual role, as would any theoretical programme informed by Nietzsche, who writes, for example, 'Against positivism, which halts at phenomena – "There are only facts" – I would say: No, facts are precisely what there is not, only interpretations. We cannot establish any fact "in itself"' (cited in Dickens and Fontana, 1994: 7).

We do not have the space here to discuss in detail the 'radical perspectivism' (Dickens and Fontana, 1994) exemplified in Nietzsche's claim. It implies, however, that since there is no factual ground on which to base theory and practice – in other words, since there are no factual grounds to distinguish true and false interpretations – then all knowledges of the world, including scientific and religious knowledges, are equally ungrounded interpretations of it. Poverty, disability, discrimination, it seems, are not facts but interpretations and combating them is the expression of a value based on interpretation rather than a theory based on fact. In other words, perspectivism is said to imply relativism. The point to note is not whether the *values* implied in the struggle against inequality are legitimate or worthy, but whether the social scientific *theory* can 'avoid being made part of what it attempts to comprehend' (Ashley, 1994: 56), or whether it is itself an element of the struggle.

The distinction draws attention to the poststructuralist roots of postmodern theory. As we saw in Chapter 4, Foucault's work has challenged the normative view of social science as the progressive accumulation of knowledge in the service of human values, suggesting that knowledge and power are inextricably linked. His work has been taken up in contemporary social policy. Parton (1996), for example, views social work as a technology of regulation, a form of micro or capillary power that supports a 'welfarist' complex. Social work, as a form of knowledge and practice, represents an instrument of management, development and control: a 'modernist' project in which the application of social scientific knowledge combined with the reformist values of a liberal public sector regulate, rather than alleviate, poverty and inequality. The link between knowledge and power in poststructuralism has shifted sociological perspectives on institutional domination and resistance and has had a major impact on postmodern writing (see also Hewitt, 1992, 1996). Foucault sums up the broader political outlook of this theoretical focus:

> Humanity does not gradually progress from combat to combat until it arrives at universal reciprocity, where the rule of law finally replaces warfare; humanity instills each of its violences in a system of rules and thus proceeds from domination to domination. (1977: 151)

A poststructuralist conception of power is central to postmodern sociologies: the theoretical focus on the socio-cultural, as well as political-economic, construction of exclusion and marginalisation, the political emphasis on domination and resistance and the analytic concentration on the institutional and everyday realisation of meanings and codes around difference and identity comprise social postmodernism's sociological field. In the study of social welfare the contours of this field include both historical and contemporary cultural and political struggles.

Culture and citizenship

The importance of such struggles is illustrated by McClintock's (1995) study of Western imperialism and its role in the formation of capitalism. According to McClintock, imperialism's social and cultural dynamism did not derive from the political economy of modern societies. Instead, this dynamism lies at the core of contemporary European modernity and its development. McClintock's (1995) study discusses the ways that European political and economic institutions have been constituted within cultural and symbolic processes that marked the encounter between the 'West' and 'the rest' during imperialism. Her cultural analysis focuses on how class, gender and race inequalities became incorporated into the institutions of Western modernity. European modernity grew in the soil of pre-existing hierarchies of power: class, gender and race dynamics spurred the development of imperial and colonial enterprises and their associated social institutions.

McClintock's examination of the cultural products and practices of the imperial era details how the development of markets and commodity production were shaped by dominant systems of cultural representation which rendered black people and their cultures as inferior: black men and women were positioned as barbaric, savage, bestial, promiscuous and unclean, requiring the wholesale attention of a European 'civilising mission'. One important element of McClintock's work is that she points to the ways that capitalist and imperialist political economies are based on specific social and cultural constructions of gendered, racialised and

stratified rights and duties. It is wrong to assume that the modern political economy itself is responsible for these constructions. On the contrary,
without them it could neither have emerged nor continue to exist: the
everyday racialisation and sexualisation of the social institutions of
modern society is the operationalisation, the realisation of a political
economy that is rooted in cultural relations. One important implication of
this is that a theory of social welfare needs to address the cultural processes by which its everyday gendering and race-ing occur.

The cultural rootedness of the imperial encounter underpins both the
'official' and the 'unofficial' dimensions of European social development.
Access to services, opportunities in labour markets, the distribution of
social and cultural statuses, divisions between private and public duties
and obligations draw their social power from the historic structuring of
racialised, gendered and stratified imperialisms and not from the abstract
universalisation of rational principles. The encounters between racialised,
gendered and stratified groups and labour markets, welfare services, legal
systems and communities are inherently complex and unstable. Indeed,
these institutions are intertwined with discriminatory cultural logics,
rooted in the values and assumptions of their members as well as in the
categories of entitlement and benefit that they make available. The persistence of such logics in contemporary social welfare sectors has been
commented on extensively in mainstream sociology and social policy.

For example, discrimination and marginalisation are firmly established
within the national labour markets of Britain and Europe. Roberts et al.
(1992) point to the everyday strategies that marginalise Asian Africans in
UK training and employment bureaux. The marginalisation draws on
linguistic, cultural and racist resources, reinforcing differential treatment
and unequal opportunities. Different communicative styles, cultural
assumptions, economic goals and support networks incite discriminatory
practices in relation to different ethnic groups. Brown (1992) documents a
disturbing catalogue of racial discriminations in UK employment, arguing
that the underlying stimulus for these processes is overt and covert racial
hostility.

In many senses, the interaction between formal and informal inequalities can be seen to contribute directly to discrimination. For example, the
consequences of migratory patterns are very different for men and
women. Muslim, Sikh and Hindu women migrants were (and are)
ensnared in a double exclusionary structure. On the one hand, they experience the ideology of domesticity which encourages the view that women
should tend the hearth and child only. On the other hand, Asian men, on
average, earn far less than their white counterparts such that employment
for Asian women in the low-paid, sweated sectors of the labour market is
often a financial necessity. The opportunities for employment for these
women are far more restricted than for their white counterparts precisely
because of the hostility observed by Brown (see above). These patterns of
discrimination are visible across Europe, in both social democratic and

liberal nation-states. In Scandinavia, for example, institutional racism is apparent in the instructions to border officials to watch out for 'non-Nordic' peoples at entry points and in the justification of rigid immigration controls on the basis that they enable 'underemployed national groups to have access to the labour market' (Ginsburg, 1992b: 46). These 'underemployed' groups are not Sweden's ethnic minorities who, instead, are subject to harassment and discrimination by landlords, public officials and the police (Larsson, 1991; Ginsburg, 1992b: 47).

Similarly, in the area of welfare policy, imperialist constructions of ethnicities, genders and entitlements can be seen in the contemporary organisation of services (Williams, 1989). Mama (1989, 1992) has drawn attention to the relationships between a white slavemaster mentality and the configuration of medical and social services around black women's sexuality and parenting. Myths about black sexual promiscuity and breeding intersect with notions of 'racial purity' and national identity to construct systematically exclusive models of entitlement and regulation. Similarly, the stereotypes and symbolic divisions of Europe's imperial history structure important everyday encounters between racialised groups and the labour and housing markets (Vos, 1995), and between resident and immigrant communities and between the latter and legal and cultural institutions (Solé, 1995). There are many examples of the endemic racism which enforces racial discrimination and marginalisation (Mercer, 1992; Taylor, 1993).

Ginsburg (1992b) argues that from the 1970s onwards social policies have contributed to widening existing inequalities based on race, gender and class. Even systems that are often described as 'models' such as the Federal Republic of Germany or the social democracies of Scandinavia, institutionalise inequalities and oppressions in their labour market and welfare policies. In Germany, the guest-worker scheme, rigid stratifications of welfare consumers and the privatisation of women's unpaid domestic labours, each contribute to the effective operation of the overall welfare system. In Denmark, twenty years of differential access to welfare benefits and the institutionalisation of racial and ethnic discrimination are culminating in the social segregation of ethnic minority groups and a growing demand for their more rigid regulation (Schierup, 1994).

Sibley (1995), argues that the organisation of public and private spaces – a cornerstone of national welfare policy in European states – comprises a political geography. Such spaces are regions of different exclusions – they are marked by social boundaries or 'secure borders' (Sibley, 1995: 183). Sibley's concept of 'geographies of exclusion' and the patterns of exclusivity, assumptions and rights that it bestows provides insights into the organisation of social welfare. 'Private' rights – relating to the family, for example – are encoded in public rules for the regulation of sexuality: gay and lesbian co-habiting couples, it can be noted, have unequal access to benefits in the areas of income support, pensions and taxation compared to those available to heterosexual couples. Similarly, they also face exclusion from adoption and are subject to a range of exclusions and intrusive regulations when fostering children (Taylor, 1993). Feminists have highlighted the contradictory nature of European welfare institutions for women (cf. Showstack Sassoon, 1987), including the differential access of men and women to benefits and services (Bryson, 1992) and the way in which the entire edifice of the welfare state is premised upon women's unpaid and low-paid labour in both public and private spaces (Finch and Groves, 1983; Graham, 1987; Williams, 1989). The Disability Rights movement has mounted a trenchant critique of the uneven patterns of access to public political-economic institutions and their benefits and of the uneven private intrusions of medical and social authorities into people's lives (cf. Oliver, 1990; Morris, 1993). In each of these cases, the relationship between public and private rights, duties or assumptions differs according to cultural categories of sexual, gender, ethnic and embodied identity.

This catalogue of division and exclusion suggests that there is at least a *prima facie* case for understanding the 'integrative' institutions of social welfare policy and practice as locked into processes of discrimination and marginalisation. Exclusion, it can be argued, is woven into the fabric of those institutions – the labour market, welfare system and cultural system – that are offered as both the route to citizenship and the means to resolve the problem of exclusion. From a postmodern perspective, the point is not to draw attention to the catalogue of divisions in itself. It is to emphasise the politically dynamic character of citizenship – the extent to which social membership is an ongoing struggle: a struggle within, as Foucault observed (see above), a system of violences encoded as cultural rules. However, it is not a *solidaristic* struggle. Rather, social membership is 'agonistic' (Lyotard, 1986) in the sense that it has to be reiterated, defended, advanced or realised in many different encounters, every day. Social membership is a precarious political status that changes across institutional contexts and cultural reference points: it goes much deeper than economic disadvantage or public-political recognition *per se*. It lies at the heart of political and cultural territorialisation, where communities are formed and re-formed, where beliefs, symbols, expectations and conventions are applied on a routine basis. Social membership, or the question of citizenship, consists simultaneously and equally in processes of economic distribution, equity and investment, and in the habitual, commonplace contours of daily life – with whom you can sit, or not; how you can worship, or not; what you can wear, or not; where you can shop, eat and drink, or not: *whether you can belong, or not* (cf. Hall and Held, 1989: 175; Bhabha, 1994).

These observations are important for the analysis of citizenship because they draw attention to the everyday world: the world where theory (and policy) occurs but which is not itself theorised (Smith, 1993: 242). The everyday world where the lived practicalities of both formal and informal rights, duties, identities, attachments, social and cultural boundaries are encountered and ordered is concealed in the administrative procedures

that arrange democratic citizenship. Rosaldo (1989) draws out the implication of this occlusion in the American case, pointing out that the acquisition of formal citizenship status requires individuals to undergo a
process of 'identity-stripping' – where their own cultural resources and
meanings are divested in order to become 'fully' American citizens. Copjec
(1991: 30) elaborates:

> If *all* our citizens can be said to be Americans, this is not because we share any
> positive characteristics, but rather because we have all been given the right to
> *shed* these characteristics, to present ourselves as disembodied before the law. I
> divest myself of my identity, therefore I am a citizen. This is the peculiar logic
> of democracy.

At the same time, the socio-economic and cultural networks of modern
democracies make this identity displacement, the precondition for full
citizenship, a practical impossibility. The globalised economic complex,
and its uneven local impacts, persistently exposes new inequalities, new
exploitative spaces, new divisions on which to feed such that, as Harvey
(1993) observes, the cheap availability of goods in one geographical
location depends upon the abuse of workers (and, one might add, environments) in another. The very structures of production, exchange and
consumption establish a complicity between the denial of rights and
opportunities in one social space and the provision of both basic and
luxury goods elsewhere. The exploited provide cheap commodities for
oppressors to consume whilst the oppressed provide a well of cultural and
social resources to exploit. The social and political divisions through
which these provisions, denials and exploitations are realised indicate,
however, that the cultural demarcations of social membership express
complex, not simple, relations of domination (O'Brien and Penna, 1996:
192–4).

Postmodern perspectives on citizenship (such as Fraser, 1995; Mouffe,
1995) view social membership not as a status to be bestowed or acquired
but as an ongoing struggle among gendered, sexualised, stratifed,
racialised and embodied publics. Rather than viewing citizenship as an
identity that equalises differences and provides a foundation for collective
welfare, postmodern theory understands citizenship as the figure of those
differences: as the fragmented and conflictual realisation of uneven social
membership. A postmodern theory of welfare draws attention to the socio-
political divisions that permeate the everyday encounters between people
and the institutions of the labour market and the welfare state as well as
the cultural and communal relationships through which those encounters
are meaningfully organised.

Postmodern publicity

Postmodern theory points to the 'decentring' of the social relations of
welfare. Whilst social policy traditionally has served to represent a process

of public incorporation and collective development, postmodernism points to the cultural fracturing of, and domination in, public and private life. Postmodernism shifts attention away from normative issues of defining universals, applying objective knowledge to planning and realising rational goals. Instead, it focuses on the multiple and uneven networks of power that sustain the fragmentation of political and institutional life and on how these networks support definitions of what is 'universal', 'rational' and 'objective'. In this regard, postmodern perspectives challenge the rationality of traditional policy discourses and practices and contest their logics, conventions and norms. The challenge, in postmodern terms, disturbs modern conceptions of rights and entitlements by exposing the inconsistency of 'publicity', that is, the fragmented and intrinsically confrontational ways that social membership or citizenship is organised through welfare projects (Fraser, 1994, 1995).

An ironic demonstration of the fragmented character of public rights and entitlements to social participation is visible clearly in the British state's policy towards wheelchair users. This policy has represented, and continues to reproduce, a glaring distinction between two groups of wheelchair user. On the one hand, successive British governments have invested massive amounts of money in providing special facilities for one group of wheelchair users. These facilities have included the construction of the most direct and practical routes between home, work and shops, and between towns and the countryside. They have included the construction of special stop-off points so that wheelchair users can break their journeys to prevent exhaustion. In order to make the use of these wheelchairs attractive, their manufacturers have spent billions of pounds on advertising how sexy, cool, convenient and sophisticated they are. In the postwar period, both the routes and the wheelchairs have also received incalculable public subsidies equivalent to hundreds of billions of pounds of taxpayers' money. These wheelchair users have benefited enormously from both state and commercial spending and support. However, another group of wheelchair users has been, and continues to be, marginalised, excluded, stigmatised and patronised. They are routinely denied access to public and private facilities, their journeys through town and country are made inconvenient and difficult by specially designed barriers, bumps, narrow entryways and steps. When they make any kind of visible public statement about the conditions imposed on them they are labelled as extremist and dismissed as a loony fringe. They receive a pittance in public subsidies and on the rare occasions they are represented in the media it is most commonly as sad cases for whom everyone else should feel pity.

The first group of wheelchair users are commonly referred to as motorists. They sit for hours on end in a chair on wheels powered by an internal combustion engine and have untrammelled access to the length and breadth of the country. The style of their wheelchairs is used to display aspects of their self-identities – sexy, cool, macho, suave, etc. – that are publicly endorsed through the media, school and local cultures. The second group of wheelchair user is subject to a host of negative and usually inaccurate labels, is disabled by the massive social priority accorded to certain types of mobility over others and by the design and construction of the sorts of facilities that the first group of wheelchair user takes for granted. Often, the style of their wheelchairs is also used to display aspects of their self-identities – suave, sexy, macho, etc. – but the styles are not publicly validated through the media, school or local cultures. Both groups of wheelchair users work through specialist organisations to issue claims and lobby government and industry, but although they share the characteristic of using types of wheelchair, their claims and interests rarely coincide and often conflict.

This example is offered to illustrate two related points. The first is that it indicates the problems with a unitary account of the public sphere. The second is that it exposes the inadequacy of a one-dimensional definition of identity. In relation to the first point, the public construction of facilities, routes, access points and cultural images is different in the case of the two types of wheelchair, as are the organisations through which claims, rights and entitlements are publicised and consolidated on behalf of their users. The struggles and resistances that characterise the everyday actions and experiences of the first group of wheelchair users transpire largely without any explicit reference or acknowledgement to the actions and experiences of the second group of wheelchair users. It might be contended that it is obvious that this is the case since the two groups share only a tenuous connection with each other based on accepting a partial definition of what their interests are. But that is the point. It is correct that, in their everyday political locations, they do indeed have only the most tenuous and partial connections with each other; they do not, for all practical purposes, share in a common public sphere of rights-granting and needs-satisfying activity. Thus, the fact that they both use a type of wheelchair is not sufficient to account for their public claims and memberships. Their societal membership is criss-crossed by too many competing claims, interests and experiences to reduce their public status to a common denominator. Yet, what seems *all too* obvious in the case of these two groups of wheelchair user has not *at all* been obvious in relation to other distinguishing features of wheelchair users. The proliferation of medical and administrative diagnoses of disability has been targeted at obscuring important social, cultural and political differences within the second group of wheelchair users and uniting them instead under professionally regulated systems of personal treatment and public entitlement. Since the early 1970s a range of disability movements has been challenging this pattern of definition, allocation and 'public access' to rights and entitlements. In so doing, the disability movements have themselves encountered the problem of differential claims, identities and interests. Differences within and between classes, genders, sexualities, ethnicities, ages, cultural locations, political affiliations, religions and nationalities cross-cut the agenda of the disability movements in the same way that other movements are similarly fragmented and diversified. There is not 'a' disability movement that is capable of articulating, in a preconstituted public sphere, the diversity of interests that are voiced by, for example, wheelchair users (Davis, 1993; Hasler, 1993).

In relation to the second point, what characterises the disability movements also characterises other cultural and social movements: they expose and reaffirm a 'politics of difference' in the heart of the modern public sphere which, in turn, raises two sets of important questions about struggles for welfare resources and services. The first is the question of central and marginal 'identities' in the mobilisation of political demands and claims; the second is the rationality and irrationality of norms, conventions and codes of authority and control.

An effective demonstration of the centralisation and marginalisation of identities in social struggles over welfare is political contestation around treatments and services for HIV-positive people. Thorogood (1995), presenting the findings of a survey on attitudes to HIV and dentistry, notes that the incalculability of the 'risk' of HIV infection underlies the 'anti-rational' discourses through which knowledges about HIV and AIDS circulate amongst population groups: 'Popular discourse around HIV and dentistry is a shining example of the fragility of rationality and of the co-existence of contemporary anti-rational alternative discourses' (Thorogood, 1995: 154). The 'anti-rationality' of such discourses should not be seen as rendering them less 'true' or 'valid' than scientific, legal or bureaucratic discourses around HIV and AIDS. Indeed, Thorogood's analysis suggests that such discourses are 'rational' in Weber's sense of 'affective' rationality: they draw on norms and conventions of 'feeling' and 'emotion' that are as consistent in their own terms as scientific rationalities, even though the conventions are different. The point about the 'anti-rationality' of such discourses is that they are part and parcel of how the 'normal' world works. In a footnote, Thorogood comments on the 'normality' of such discourses in reference to newspaper coverage of HIV and AIDS issues between 1993 and 1995:

> I was shocked and depressed to see the press cuttings related to HIV when researching this paper – two D-ring binder files of A4 paper collected since March 1993. Shocked at the volume and depressed at the salacious, sordid, homophobic and pejorative nature of the articles. I had not previously realised the extent to which HIV/AIDS and anti-lesbian and gay utterances were needed/produced/used as a tool through which to construct the 'normal' world. I had simply not realised it was that important. Perhaps this too underscores the fragility of the dominant rational discourse. (1995: 154)

Thorogood is not alone in failing to understand how dependent is the 'normal world' on the pejoration and alienation of identities that display differences from the myth of heterosexuality. Anyone who displays any kind of difference at all to what is (rationally adjudicated as) 'normal' is a rich source of pejoration and put-down: 'cripples', 'loonies', 'coons', 'slags', 'pakis', 'wimps', and an extensive list of synonyms for each of these terms, are all important linguistic and conceptual devices for classifying diversity as abnormality. Thorogood has observed that what is 'rational' about modern society is sustained by the 'irrational' scaffolding of marginalisation, exclusion, abuse and discrimination and that this scaffolding is a necessary and 'important' element of how that rationality is applied and experienced.

The rational–irrational connection is not a static condition but is instead a political dynamic through which marginalised and excluded people struggle to bring about change. Aronowitz (1995) explores the tactics and strategies of the leading AIDS activist movement in New York in the 1980s, 'ACT-UP', in order to outline the politics of resistance generated by the complicity between the 'irrational' and 'rational' elements of the contemporary ('normal') world. Aronowitz (1995: 366) notes, like Thorogood in the UK context, that the American political arena is 'suffused with homophobic responses to the urgency of the AIDS epidemic'. Whilst state legislatures and public institutions dragged their feet over procedures, rules, codes and régimes through which AIDS would be managed, ACT-UP focused on substantive issues of resources, access, drug-licensing, advice and information, as well as on the secrecy and closed-door policy of scientific institutions working on potentially profitable pills and potions for the treatment of HIV/AIDS. In engaging in a struggle over resources for health and well-being, ACT-UP simultaneously struggled over the homophobic rationalities that governed the institutions and organisations charged, ostensibly, with responding to HIV/AIDS as a 'public', as well as a 'private' health issue.

ACT-UP's struggles were, in part, struggles over publicity, that is, over how HIV/AIDS would enter and be located in public knowledge, action and management. They can be seen also as struggles over what is and is not 'rational' in the responses to HIV/AIDS: over how the rationalities of scientific and bureaucratic organisations impose irrational conventions and norms on access to information, resources and decision-making structures, and over who is to adjudicate what is and is not rational in the treatment and management of HIV/AIDS. ACT-UP's complex local struggles with bureaucratic systems, scientific rationalities, homophobic conventions and exclusionary public institutions indicate the locatedness of political conflict in the modern world. The struggle for information, access, resources, statuses – over what modern society defines as the conditions for individual and collective welfare – is conducted in and through different institutional locations, public arena and decision-making processes. No 'universal' rationality applies to all of these fields of dispute and conflict, claim and counter-claim. The processes of discrimination and disadvantage mark different conflicts differently: ACT-UP was involved in decentring the authority of science and the law – refusing to accept the procedural rationalities that kept experiments, and experimental treatments behind closed doors, for example – and bringing to the centre of the dispute the operation and embeddedness of homophobias and marginalisations that excluded gay knowledges and experiences from the control of the HIV/AIDS agenda.

The race-ing, embody-ing, gendering and sexing of welfare services, resources and systems cannot be explained by the 'failure' of a basically sound modern rationality – unless the failure is so spectacular as to render 'rational' decision-making pointless for ever more. Rather, these processes can only be understood if the distinction between the 'rational' and the 'irrational' is overturned: if it is acknowledged that the growth, consolidation and organisation of modern welfare systems is in part, at least, 'irrational': its procedural rationality embedded in substantive irrationality, its promise of social inclusion locked into processes of political exclusion.

In postmodern terms, the publicity of struggles such as those we have exemplified – the ways that they drive public regulations, projects, rights and entitlements – exposes the fractured cultural boundaries of social membership or citizenship. The categories of entitlement, the resources distributed and the logics of action are rooted in sexual and ethnic identifications, embodied experiences and irrational discourses. Social membership is itself a compaction or condensation of these cultural forces and it is through them that people engage with both the everyday and institutional contexts of their welfare.

Concluding remarks

We began this chapter by noting that in the foundations of the welfare state are to be found exclusions, discriminations and iniquities. Our purpose in doing this was not to signal an attack on the welfare state as such but to locate our theoretical survey of postmodernism in relation to critical questions about the political organisation of welfare. Understanding the connections between cultural, social and economic processes in the politics of welfare is a task of no small theoretical significance. Recent interest in questions of modernity and postmodernity designates a series of intellectual disputes about the adequacy and legitimacy of theoretical and analytical traditions in the social sciences. It also signals the continuing dynamism of cultural struggles across a wide range of social and political institutions. We have noted a number of responses to and positions in these disputes, showing that different theoretical constructs illuminate alternative experiences and discourses of welfare – including health, sexuality, citizenship and identity. This emphasis on cultural resources and identity within postmodern theory has exposed the inherently fragmented, divisive and contested character of social development. In so doing it has helped to challenge entrenched theoretical assumptions about an essential identity and a universal standard of truth that can be realised in both theory and practice. The ideal of a 'universal humanity', denuded of religion, locality, conflict, and contingency, for example, is considered an abiding myth of Enlightenment.

In conclusion, it is worthy of note that postmodern perspectives have provided fruitful philosophical and theoretical resources for the exploration of gender, race, embodiment and sexuality and a productive space where post-colonial, feminist, anti-racist and queer-theoretic discourses have encountered one another. This encounter has generated new sets of theoretical problems and new sets of responses to those problems that are characterised at least by the attempt to theorise without foreclosing on the divergent experiences of marginalised groups. In doing so, postmodernism has questioned critically the integrative ideology of social policy, indicating that the problem of social and political inclusion is not equivalent to the extent to which a public sphere bestows rights or entitlements on citizens as a means of mitigating their socio-economic disadvantage. Social membership is an ongoing, dynamic struggle that reconstructs the experience and the organisation of rights and entitlements in the everyday conduct of social life. By highlighting the categories and the logics of inclusionary/exclusionary welfare, postmodern theory refocuses the sociology of welfare on to critical connections between identity, agency and institutions in contemporary society.

CRITIQUES AND CONCLUSIONS

Definitions and concepts of welfare are embedded in extensive theoretical perspectives on the nature of the individual, on the operation of social institutions, on the interpretation of historical and contemporary phenomena. They comprise understandings of how people, and the institutions and relationships through which our lives are connected together, do or might operate. In this regard, theories of welfare are always both social and normative in the way that we defined these terms in the introduction to the book. They are not only disinterested reflections on the human condition but are also motivated by some idea of or commitment to a specific arrangement of social relations, and often by both together. Theories of welfare are inescapably political, in the sense that to adopt or promote a way of understanding social welfare is to adopt or promote a way of understanding the organisation of social life and its consequences. In assessing the contribution that different perspectives make to the task of theorising welfare, therefore, it is necessary to assess the contribution they make to the task of theorising the organisation of social life. In this concluding chapter we assess the potentials and problems of the seven different perspectives we have outlined in the book in these terms, although our emphasis primarily will be on the perspectives in Parts Two and Three.

Enlightenment and progress

The themes of freedom and emancipation that underpin liberalism and Marxism need to be situated in the context of the social, cultural and political struggles characteristic of nineteenth century Europe. Liberalism and Marxism provide specific understandings of what 'freedom' and 'emancipation' mean. They are concepts in a series of philosophical and theoretical discourses about the historical development and direction of societies.

Liberalism and Marxism

Nineteenth century liberals were not early prototypes of Beveridge. They did not seek to secure the freedom of all individuals from the 'giants' of want, ignorance, disease, idleness and squalor. As we saw in Chapter 1, the poverty of the masses was accepted largely as the condition on which social wealth could be generated. Although the liberal conscience frayed at the edges at the sight of mass penury, starvation and famine, the incentive to work – that is, the lack of sufficient resources to manage life independently of wage labour – was considered necessary to achieve economic growth. A liberal society was not one in which all enjoyed the same freedoms. It was a society in which it was necessary for some people to enjoy more freedoms than others – a stratified society. Stratification was, and is, central to liberal social theory, for stratification is the dynamic that ensures the economic progress of the whole. If people are freed from the necessity to work they will not work, profits will not accrue, economic activity will stagnate, progress will cease. Thus, a liberal approach to social policy requires that it supports economic stratification, that inequality is the means and the goal of that policy. In some of its earlier formulations, such as Spencer's, this principle was taken to the extreme, suggesting that the consequences of inequality – starvation, disease and death – might be seen as the positive outcomes of a social evolution in which the surviving social strata became ever more advanced representatives of the species. In some later formulations, such as Beveridge's, it is said to be possible to tinker at the edges of the unequal society, ensuring that, by and large, such inequality does not result in mass starvation, disease or premature death. Indeed, it is possible, over time, to use social policy as a tool to maintain 'relative' inequality whilst simultaneously abolishing 'absolute' poverty. The distinction between these two views encapsulates a division in liberal philosophy that was most obvious at the turn of the nineteenth century, between *laissez-faire* liberals and reformist liberals. The division between the two strands of liberal philosophy split liberalism into two mutually hostile political camps and effectively ended liberalism's association with direct political rule. Even in the second formulation, however, liberalism did not reject the proposition that some *races* might be more equal than others, that racial groupings, organised into societies, might represent different stages of social, rather than strictly biological, evolution. In this version, what was at stake was the fitness of the British (or other Western) nation to rule over an empire, rather than the fitness of one class to rule over another class.

There is a sense, as we saw in Chapter 2, that Marxist theory also understood inequality as an inevitable characteristic of economic and social progress, although the nature, causes and consequences of that inequality were not at all the same as they appeared in liberalism. In Marxist theory, material inequality was a feature of the organisation of production rather than an abiding characteristic of the human condition. Material inequality existed because the mode of production was based on an antagonism between classes such that whilst inequality was certainly the dynamic that maintained *capitalist* economic progress it was not at all inevitable that inequality should always and forever divide human societies. In Marx and Engels' early work such inequality would lead inexorably to the downfall of capitalism and its replacement by communism. Thus, progress was as assured in Marxism as it was in liberalism but involved the destruction of the existing system of wealth distribution rather than its elaboration. Marxism proposes that an incentive to work – that is, work for wages or starve to death – is necessary only where work is an exploitative activity. Where people's labour is exploited for another's gain, some mechanism for inducing or coercing people to work is absolutely required. However, it is not necessary for work to be exploitative: it is not necessary that people's labour and its products should always belong to someone else. This ownership of both labour and its products is itself a consequence of the class character of capitalist societies: if the exploitation of work is removed, there is no need to induce or coerce people to work, since what they work for belongs to themselves and what they create is their own self-development. A Marxist social policy, thus, is premised on the abolition of the ownership of labour and its products by people other than those who do the labouring. The means and the goal of Marxist social policy is the emancipation of labour from exploitation, the self-fulfilment of each individual and the whole society through creative and free labour.

In both liberalism and Marxism, then, there is an essential connection between labour, the welfare of each individual and the welfare of the whole society, although the connection is formulated in radically different ways. Liberal social theory proposes a view of social progress in which each individual and each social group fulfils a necessary role in maintaining the development of the whole. In turn, the most free and most efficient development of the whole promotes the fullest welfare of each individual. The development of the whole depends on enabling the most free and most efficiently coordinated access to the stratified socio-economic system. Liberal normative theory, by extension, proposes organising stratification systems so that both individual and social development are most effectively enabled. Marxist social theory, in contrast, proposes a view of social progress in which each individual is a material product of the social whole. It is the destiny of humanity to overcome the divisions and contradictions that underpin the exploitation of labour and uphold the private ownership of the means of production. The development of the whole depends on the historical abolition of class divisions around ownership of those means. In turn, the abolition of those divisions promotes the emancipation of each individual from exploitation and thereby promotes their fullest welfare. Marxist normative theory, by extension, proposes to destratify the socio-economic system so that individual and social development are most effectively enabled.

Both Marxism and liberalism theorise an underlying or essential unity to human affairs that gives coherence and direction to the apparently chaotic disorder of social life. The liberal focus on the invisible hand or the evolution of races and societies is contested by the Marxist focus on historical stages and species being. None the less, theoretically, both posit a direction to social change: societies progressively – either through evolution or revolution – become more advanced and the welfare of each individual is a function of the level or stage of development of the social whole. Liberal and Marxist perspectives thus interpret social policies in terms not only of their contribution to or impacts on individual welfare but also in terms of historical trajectories through which societies are seen to progress. The character of social policies and their consequences for social welfare are conceptualised through the lenses of individual property rights and *laissez-faire*, on the one hand, or class domination and struggle on the other. Liberal analyses of the family or religion, for example, stress their roles in personality stabilisation, socialisation or the transmission of morals and norms that enable social order to persist. Marxist analyses of these institutions make similar claims but stress their roles in enabling *capitalist* social order to persist. For Marxists, religion is an 'opiate' of the masses and the bourgeois family a system of repression which either maintains 'wives in common' or contributes to the reproduction of labour power. Liberal and Marxist theory are locked in a permanent contest, each asserting the primacy of competing principles of order and progress, each building conceptual schemes derived from opposing standpoints on the real, underlying essence of social life.

Anti-Enlightenment critiques

The proposition that, beneath the apparent chaos of social life, there persists a principle of order or progress through which human destiny is realised is a philosophical commitment, not an empirical fact: it is an element in a theoretical scheme through which both historical change and contemporary experience can be interpreted. In fact, such a proposition reiterates the philosophical frameworks of Enlightenment thought in that it upholds the search for the independent laws of the social (and natural) order. As such, it can be, and has been, challenged; perhaps the chaos of the world is all there really is, perhaps there is no historical 'telos', no human destiny and no fundamental meaning beneath the flux of social life. The 'view from chaos' has fundamental implications for the construction of social theory, including social theories of welfare. It implies the development of new concepts or the reinterpretation of existing concepts as well as a reformulation of the interpretive frameworks that make sense of observations about social life. As we saw in Part Two, neo-liberalism and poststructuralism attempt a reformulation of this magnitude and, in so doing, offer very different perspectives on the nature of social welfare and the effects of social policy. At the same time, the reformulations are not without problems; both neo-liberal and poststructuralist critiques of Enlightenment theory raise unanswered theoretical questions.

Neo-liberalism

The anti-Enlightenment philosophy and theory of Hayek, Friedman and their neo-liberal adherents comprises a rich discourse on the problems and prospects of the contemporary welfare state. Spanning consumer choice, the character of the state, the history of 'liberty', the concept of 'freedom', and the relationships between 'justice', 'welfare', 'rights', 'responsibility' and 'duty', neo-liberal political and economic philosophy purports to establish the basis upon which modern societies can best cater for the needs and wants of their members. The 'rational' or 'scientific' knowledge of the (French) Enlightenment is seen as leading to a fundamentally erroneous belief that societies can be successfully organised and directed by a technocratic state. In contrast, neo-liberalism holds that the market is the measure of efficiency, the standard against which our very under-standings of what should and should not be are judged. It achieves an efficient distribution of goods and services, it enables freely undertaken human intercourse and negotiation, it provides a forum in which skills can be exchanged and distributed and defines the values of commodities without reference to the power or status of their owners and controllers. In short, it enables the free pursuit of individual life unfettered by collec-tive obligation. Unlike classical liberalism, however, there is no 'invisible hand' guiding the totality of market transactions, guaranteeing a positive expansion and coordination of economic progress.

'Freedom', here, is reduced to free-individualism: the well-being of society is nothing other than the realisation by private individuals of their own interests within a framework of abstract legal rules. Freedom is equated with freedom-to-act without the constraints imposed by a collec-tively organised normative ethics. It is, on the surface, a purely formal concept. The guarantee that all individuals are at liberty to engage equally in any activity sanctioned by the abstract legal code is the limit-point and defining feature of the neo-liberal free society. The substantive fact that not all individuals can in reality equally engage in such actions – because of material barriers to participation such as insufficient individual resources or group-exclusionary strategies – does not, for neo-liberals, undermine the normative value of an approach based on formal equality. This is because inequality is seen as a 'natural' outcome of free activity: the market enables individuals freely to realise their unequal freedoms. Thus, the concept of freedom in neo-liberal thought is tied intrinsically to politi-cal principles. 'Freedom' requires a particular politics for its achievement. The absence of a politics of freedom – for neo-liberals an absence em-bodied in the social democratic structures of the welfare state – engenders an enslavement and serfdom of the whole society. Breaking out of this enslavement is equivalent to *repoliticising* the relations between indi-viduals by strengthening the power of the market against the welfare state.

Thus, the definition of 'freedom' and the characterisation of 'the market' are inextricably bound together. Indeed, it is the market which defines the freedom of society and the individuals within it: for 'free society' one should read 'free (market) society'. Whilst neo-liberals do not claim that the market can do everything – for example, there remains a role for the state in providing national security and minimal welfare and infrastructural services – it none the less functions, theoretically, as the organic structure of social organisation, meeting needs and fulfilling human instinctual drives. In this way, the market is held to comprise not only the most efficient, but also the only *natural* mechanism of social reproduction. There are two problems with this conception worthy of particular note, one relating to historiography, the other relating to anthropology.

At the heart of Hayek's system of ideas is his conception of the nature of knowledge and its place in a market system. However, this conception rests on an idiosyncratic use of philosophical argument and a one-dimensional account of historical and evolutionary change. According to Hayek, modern societies are too complex to be 'known' explicitly by any individual. In the very distant past, small-scale, 'primitive' societies were sufficiently simple for each individual to be able to grasp explicitly all the relevant information which s/he needed to know about its processes and conventions. Now, in contrast, societies are complex and – from the individual's point of view – apparently chaotic. Modern individuals have no hope of grasping, in its totality, the knowledge required to regulate society in a rational way. Indeed, no single collective body (including the state) could hope to do this either, since the knowledge required outstrips in its range and complexity any possibility of consciously organising social relationships. Thus, the most important type of knowledge in modern society is 'tacit' knowledge – knowledge of the rules of engagement. Because no individual can ever grasp explicitly all the knowledge about society's functioning there has to be a mechanism by which elements of such knowledge can be transmitted to individuals where and when necessary. This 'knowledge-transmission' function is fulfilled by the market and enables individuals to continue to act even in ignorance of the total effects of their actions.

However, this thesis is problematic in several respects. The sociology of knowledge has demonstrated that knowledge is not a 'thing' which can with impunity be sliced into two simple categories. There are not just two types of knowledge but a plethora of knowledges with their own special characteristics. Many of these knowledges are vested in and tied to specific social groups who patently *do not* enter them into the market for distribution. Knowledge is a category, not of culture-in-general, but of particular groups and organised interests who fight hard to retain control over it and avoid its 'free market' distribution. This has been the case historically and remains so in present-day society. The burning of women healers in post-medieval Europe with the dawn of a male-controlled medical profession testifies to the struggles in which different types of knowledge are locked. Social groups – and especially professions – develop exclusionary tactics precisely for the purpose of restricting access to knowledge in order to further their collective interests and material positions in society (Witz, 1992).

A second notable problem is that Hayek, and neo-liberal theory in general, has a very limited understanding of social anthropology. Hayek trained initially as a micro economist before turning his attention to political philosophy, so the limitation is perhaps not surprising in his case. What is surprising is the emphasis he places on the differences between 'primitive' and 'modern' societies. Hayek has no theoretical or substantive warrant for arguing that societies in prehistory operated as he says they did. His assumptions about smallness and lack of complexity, coupled with his assertions about the associated tacit nature of knowledge recall the prejudices of nineteenth century anthropologists in assuming there was some fundamental difference between the knowledge operations of 'primitive' and 'civilised' people. Anthropological work contemporaneous with Hayek's writing contested this myth with some force. Winch (1958) and Geertz (1975), for example, demonstrate that in what Hayek would consider a close approximation to a 'primitive' society both tacit and explicit forms of knowledge interrelate in highly complex and sophisticated ways.

It is reasonable to suppose that the same complexity should hold in contemporary societies. However, there is no way, in Hayek's work, to identify which is 'tacit' and which 'explicit' (reason) knowledge. Without a proper ontology of 'tacit' and 'explicit' knowledge it is impossible to identify in empirical investigation when and under what conditions either of these forms is being used. Additionally, if we cannot tell which is which then neither can we tell whether any given actor is drawing on the *same* tacit knowledge as any other given actor. Thus, it is just as legitimate to argue that an uncontrolled market *produces* chaos, disadvantage, discrimination, domination and exploitation by distributing totally inappropriate forms of information and resources, based on the uncoordinated tacit knowledges of individuals, as it is to argue that the uncontrolled market provides a valuable service by distilling such knowledge for distribution *out of* the chaos of human life. Hayek provides no basis upon which to assert which of these interpretations is warranted from his theory. By deriving everything that is good from market processes and deriving the market from nowhere except 'natural' human development, there remain no criteria and no guidelines that can be used to investigate the social relations through which markets are in reality built and maintained.

These two problems – of historical and anthropological inaccuracy – are carried into the work of other neo-liberals who base their arguments on Hayek's philosophical system. Green and Morgan, for example, accept at face value the state–bad/market–good dichotomy, an acceptance which leads to a problematic notion of cultural change. Green, for example, is concerned with the rise of a 'victim culture' and the 'therapeutic state'. Focusing on the decline in individual responsibility and duty that these developments are said to generate, Green argues for a *return* to ideals of duty and civic welfare delivered within an apolitical community. There are at least two major difficulties here. First, Green accepts the premise that markets are necessary to accommodate the wide range of values and wants existing in any modern society. The state cannot legislate for outcomes because there can be no consensus on social goals in the plurality of competing values. Yet, having accepted value-plurality as a characteristic of modern life, Green argues simultaneously for an apolitical civil society in which everyone shares common values and morals in relation to duty and responsibility for welfare. 'The community' can perform the role Green assigns to it only if moral codes are more or less shared among its members. This same tension runs throughout Hayek's work, where value-plurality is held up as a desirable feature to be protected by the market against the encroachments of the state but where, at the same time, families and other social institutions are held to be the transmitters of the traditional values that uphold market structures. Thus, on the one hand, there is a plurality of values but, on the other hand, there is a homogeneity of the 'successful' cultural values developed during the process of human evolution. Quite how these opposing conceptions of cultural values and practices can be held within the same theoretical framework is not explained.

The second problem is that Green accuses the cultural changes of the 1960s of undermining individual responsibility for self-maintenance, counterposing this development to the nineteenth century where duty prevailed. This represents an astonishing reading (or mis-reading) of historical change. The nineteenth century, as we saw in Part One, was a period of intense political struggle around political power and against poverty and injustice. The development of welfare states has been subject to a variety of pressures and forces often directed at offsetting the dire consequences of market-generated inequalities (such as starvation, disease, unfit working conditions, lack of basic resources such as housing and clean water and so on). In the nineteenth century, individuals organised in collective unions and pressure groups, fought long and hard, often facing extreme consequences such as execution, deportation or imprisonment, to force basic provisions for the poor and disadvantaged which the 'market' simply did not provide. Such struggles were fought on the basis of the unwillingness and absolute incapacity of market entrepreneurs to cater for basic human needs. The second half of the twentieth century is filled with examples of such struggles: black civil rights activism in America and Catholic activism in Ireland, for example, were aimed at forcing state intervention to offset material disadvantage and social discrimination. Struggles by women for sex equality in work and welfare benefits are a continuing feature of welfare reforms across the world. The history of welfare provision – and not just 'the sixties' – is littered with the struggles of oppressed peoples rendered politically and economically unfree by markets and market-based systems dominated by powerful economic interests. Neo-liberal theorists write histories and accounts of state interventions as if this element of struggle had no bearing upon the forms that both market and state provisions have taken. Such historical amnesia denies the significance of political struggle in wresting even minor benefits from economic systems that systematically and compre-hensively discriminate in favour of already-entrenched interests.

Furthermore, there is no evidence to support the neo-liberal mantra of declining responsibility for welfare provision. The social policy literature is filled with studies of informal and community care, pointing to the role of (predominantly, but not exclusively) women in providing the informal care that has underpinned and made possible the formal sector of care. From the care of elderly people, mentally and physically disabled people, young people, through to financial and other support for family and friends, women (and families) have been the bedrock of welfare services. Changes in the position of women and in family formations have not led to the abandonment of this role. Morgan decries the decline of the traditional family which she sees as a result of the impact of feminism. However, the 'decline thesis' has been reiterated for more than a century, with the consequence that it is difficult to grasp any longer what exactly is supposedly declining. More importantly, the view of the family contained in neo-liberal theory is simplistic and romanticised, seriously underestimating, and often completely neglecting, sexual and physical violence within families. This is not to say that contemporary neo-liberal writings do not address some important social issues: the point is that the simplistic dichotomies through which they are addressed – market–good/state–bad, traditional family–good/other family–bad – do nothing to further our understanding of the processes and conditions (unemployment, violence, illness, abuse, discrimination, and so on) within which many individuals, families and social groups struggle to survive. In these ways, neo-liberalism has as many affinities with roman-tic conservatism as it does with classical liberalism (Gray, 1996).

Poststructuralism

The charge of (neo-)conservatism has been levelled also against both post-structuralist and postmodern philosophy (Habermas, 1985), although, in our view, these two perspectives represent somewhat different ap-proaches to the activity of theorising. Poststructuralism has been accused of 'evaporating' power as a theoretical question, of undermining the criti-cal capacity of social theory to envisage an alternative 'culture of soli-darity' through which to contest exploitative political arrangements and of failing to recognise the experience and real conditions of victims of violence and abuse (Minson, 1980; Hewitt, 1992: 171, 201; McCannell and McCannell, 1993: 230). The rejection of poststructuralism in much main-stream social theory and social policy is rooted in a desire to maintain a unique rational standard around which the efficacy and acceptability of political projects can be assessed and measured. On this basis, the critique of poststructuralist theory centres on two closely related sets of questions: on the validity of poststructuralism's analytical categories (a conceptual-cum-methodological critique) and a critique of the standpoint (or lack thereof) from which poststructuralist theory views the world (a methodo-logical-cum-political critique).

In Chapter 4 we noted that Foucault's approach to historical research shifted from an *archaeological* to a *genealogical* strategy in response to methodological problems with the idea that the meaning of past events could be 'read' in the present in any straightforward way. The strategic shift, however, reveals more than a 'corrective' attempt to provide a 'truer' or 'more accurate' historical representation. It comprises a redefinition of terms and concepts in the theoretical framework that Foucault adopted to interpret the relationships between past and present and between the subjects and objects of knowledge. Both sets of relationships, according to Foucault, are constituted in 'discourses', conceptualised as power–know-ledge systems that establish both specific *ways of knowing* and simul-taneously specific forms of authority over the contents of knowledge, over *what is known*. For Foucault, it is a philosophical error to distinguish between 'thinking' and 'knowing', on the one hand, and 'acting' and 'doing', on the other. In this respect, Foucault's thesis has affinities with Wittgenstein's philosophy of language games – where languages and meanings are active elements of a community's way of living. For Wittgen-stein, meanings are not 'given' in a language and then 'used' in a way of life. On the contrary, the meanings that language provides are embedded in the actions and relationships through which everyday life is organised and carried out. Foucault's philosophy, however, attempts to radicalise this perspective further, suggesting that meanings are not neutral expres-sions of social relationships but are exercises of power, opening up and objectifying some of those relationships and closing off or repressing others. What is meant by 'deviance', 'need', 'illness', the 'normal' or the 'abnormal' is a product of a discursive closure that is both historical – in the sense that discourses emerge and consolidate over time – and eco-nomic – in that discourses comprise frameworks and rules by which meanings and concepts can be exchanged, valued and developed and through which the world can be 'invested' with sense and order. The order of the world is not reflected in knowledge about it; rather, the world is ordered through discourse (through power–knowledge). The medieval world of God and faith, evil and sin, of inexplicable disaster and catas-trophe is not a *false* world that has been superseded by the *true* world of particles and matter, rationality and science, of knowable laws, causes and effects. The two worlds represent different orders of discourse that invest different meanings and truths in experience and perception.

A clear problem with such a radicalised discourse theory is that it becomes at least very difficult, and potentially impossible, to know the meaning of anything. The problem applies to Foucault's own perspective as much as to the effort to theorise through Foucault's philosophy. If the meaning of the world is given in orders of discourse, the grounds on which meanings might be shared or communicated become very slippery – is it necessary to identify the discursive order before a meaning can be grasped? If so, what is the order of discourse in which Foucault's concepts and categories make sense? Foucault evaded this question by proposing that his works represented 'tools' or 'weapons' that could be used by groups in struggle to disturb and disrupt the conventions and taken-for-granted assumptions underpinning contemporary expert and professional knowledges. However, if the distinction between 'knowing' and 'doing' is erroneous, then it is difficult to understand (to 'know') what it is about Foucault's works that such groups might 'use' or what use they might make of them. To put this another way, are there 'orders of usage', like there are orders of discourse, that clarify the implications of Foucault's works for social and political projects, or are these works equally useful to a rampant New Right, hell-bent on dismantling any and all forms of social support and to marginalised groups challenging the dismantling process?

This question is one that applies also to Foucault's interpreters. Fraser, for example, developed Foucault's discourse analytic in her investigation of 'needs' discourses in social policy. Her division between 'expert', 'oppositional' and 'reprivatisation' discourses is a useful device for investigating struggles over needs. It begs the question, however, of how to distinguish between such discourses in empirical research: can an 'oppositional' movement expound a 'reprivatisation' discourse? Can an 'expert' representative of an official institution of knowledge-production expound an 'oppositional' discourse, and so on? Similar problems are encountered in relation to theories that treat professional knowledges (such as law or medicine, for example) as discourse in their own right. Whilst it may be the case that lawyers and doctors (and judges, social workers, psychologists, police officers, and others) may struggle over the control of social rights and obligations, this does not imply that there is an automatic correspondence between such struggles and the discourses in which medical and legal, and so on, knowledges are formulated and transmitted.

Similarly, the marking of bodies and identities with differences need not be understood as an abstract expression of culture, as Gatens proposes, nor simply as an effect of discursive relations. The mobilisation or manipulation of cultural symbols and signs that realise marked bodies and identities may equally be theorised as a social process of domination, classification or even resistance (or a combination of all three). Here, the relationships between signs, symbols and identificatory practices may be related to the interests, goals or projects of individuals and groups struggling over specific inequalities or oppressions. Such struggles, in turn, may relate to more extensive dimensions of social or economic exploitation of which the individuals and groups may themselves be unaware. The point, here, is not to argue that discourses or meanings are not in themselves contradictory or antagonistic. Rather, it is to note that there may be *non-discursive* reasons why this is the case or *non-discursive* causes of such contradictions and antagonisms. If the entirety of experience and perception is conceptualised as a feature of discourse, the question arises as to the standpoint from which such a claim can be issued. In what discourse is the claim that 'knowledge is discourse' situated?

Applying this sort of questioning to poststructuralist theorising leads into a series of circular arguments about the respective value of the view from within and the view from outside discourse. Underlying the circularity is a more fundamental issue that characterises both poststructuralist and neo-liberal theory, namely, the rejection of the claim that the social whole can be known in and of itself, that there is a type of knowledge or a way of knowing in and through which the real or essential basis of the social world can be grasped and reflected in the form of a theory or a science. Both Hayek and Foucault dismiss this claim as a fiction. Hayek dismisses it on the basis that it represents an inflated sense of self-importance on the part of the social scientist, resulting from a distortion of Enlightenment rationality. Foucault dismisses it on the basis that it construes 'knowledge' as somehow separate from the political and institutional relationships in which different ways of knowing are validated and invalidated. In both cases, Enlightenment faith in the objectivity of 'Reason' and the truth of 'science' is subjected to critical scrutiny and the Enlightenment project – rational adjudication on and coordination of human affairs in the name of progress – is seen as the expression of relations of power rather than as the highest goal of human civilisation.

Post-Enlightenment problematics

In theoretical terms, the anti-Enlightenment philosophies of neo-liberalism and poststructuralism represent contemporary limit points of a reconfiguration of social theory in which the idea of a historical telos in human societies and the search for an underlying causal mechanism of their change or progress are abandoned. The shift in perspective has resulted in a focus on the relationships between discontinuous social forces in, rather than on the continuous succession of, human societies. In particular, a great deal of contemporary social theory is characterised by a 'reflexive' standpoint towards the analysis of social change. By 'reflexivity', here, we are referring to two, related, theoretical logics. On the one hand, recalling Marxist critical theory, reflexivity refers to an *immanent* critique of social processes. Such a critique contends that the processes that sustain or realise a specific organisation of social life contain within them the logics of its transformation. In other words, social organisation is inherently unstable and precarious, subject to multiple dynamics that push and pull institutions, discourses and traditions in many directions simultaneously. On the other hand, reflexivity refers to the acknowledgement that social experience and social perception are, at least partially, constituted in discourse. Recalling Foucault's thesis on power–knowledge, the meaning or significance of social phenomena is not 'given' directly to experience but is inflected by the *perspective* through which the world is viewed. The theories of political economy, political ecology and postmodernism that we outlined in Part Three do not all have the same relationship to these theoretical logics but the debates within and between them are strongly influenced by the 'immanentist' and 'perspectivist' dimensions of theoretical reflexivity.

Political economy

As we noted in Chapter 5, three issues in particular are highlighted in contemporary theories of the political economy of welfare. First, they draw attention to the relationship between national and international economic organisation. Welfare states display a dual characteristic. On the one hand, they are designed to offer at least some form of minimal protection against the vagaries of the market to citizens of the national economy. On the other hand, they also act as a form of social organisation designed to assist the national economy in the face of international competition. They look both inwards and outwards, oriented towards the social maintenance of the citizenry and the market success of the economy. Changes in the organisation of one of these characteristics has immediate impacts on the organisation of the other. During the first half of the twentieth century the industrial and extractive sectors of the economy – steel, coal, ship-building, chemicals, automobile manufacture, light engineering – provided the basis for economic development. Keynesian Welfare States were predicated on continued growth and competitiveness in these economic sectors and the work patterns and methods of profit accumulation that these implied. In other words, the welfare state and the industrial system amounted to an interlocking, mutually supportive socio-economic structure. Entire communities, ways of life, identities and social norms were rooted in this socio-economic structure. Under pressures of globalisation, it is not only the market economy which changes but the structure itself and its interlocking mechanisms – including patterns of socialisation, norms and types of employment, community networks and the identities of their members. The changed circumstances imply that welfare systems designed for an industrial manufacturing economy are unable to sustain either new forms of socio-economic organisation or manage the increasing complexity of political divisions.

Second, the myriad changes wrought by globalisation connect closely with shifts in the organisation and distribution of employment-related benefits. The British Keynesian Welfare State and its institutions, for example, was underpinned by policies for full employment and industrial growth, a policy framework based on easing the transition between work and non-work – whether the latter is a result of unemployment, sickness, age or education. The social insurance system has been geared towards a norm of secure, permanent employment for the majority of household heads. It is part of a benefits structure that supports family, rather than individual incomes, and presupposes a 'link-worker' (usually a woman) to service the needs of workers and dependants in the household.

However, postwar social and economic change has served to undermine such assumptions and norms. For example, although women's employment is not a postwar phenomenon, during the postwar period considerable numbers of men have been displaced from the workforce whilst women have entered the labour market in large numbers, tending to be concentrated in part-time, insecure and often low-paid work. At the same time as state welfare provision is being increasingly residualised, greater responsibility for caring and welfare functions is accruing to women in workplaces, their homes and communities.

There are two immediate consequences arising from this shift in employment patterns. First, as more women enter the labour market, the link-worker role comes under increasing strain. Women are less available to undertake the roles of nurturing, supporting and organising household needs, undermining assumptions about traditional family forms and the support services they provide, motivating a search for policy frameworks to reconcile the family–employment nexus throughout Western Europe (Hantrais and Letablier, 1996). Second, part-time and low-paid work has both in-work and out-of-work consequences. Part-time workers are easier to sack and often excluded from pay scales, career structures and training programmes; 'flexible' workers are likely to receive less income in work and less income out of work and are often disqualified from receiving benefits altogether. Low pay also means low or no insurance contributions towards retirement and less income in retirement. The diminished amounts being paid in taxation and insurance contributions result in less revenue for benefits and services at a time when there is more demand for these. In these respects new employment patterns have both social and fiscal welfare consequences.

The changes in work patterns and their impacts on family structures draw attention to the final issue raised by the post-political economy perspectives, namely the extent to which contemporary societies are characterised by fragmentation, social fracture and polarisation. Economic globalisation and the parallel dynamics of socio-economic reorganisation intensify existing social divisions and bring to the foreground previously obscured or neglected forms of exclusion and discrimination. Patterns of production and work have an impact on family structures and households but the latter are also strongly influenced by changing cultural and political mores. The growth of sweated and migrant labour, the intensified racial stratification of class relations and the patriarchal regulation of minority ethnic women's labour identified by Lash and Urry (1994) comprise institutional clusters in which family, state and economy intersect in the organisation of racism.

Whilst the contemporary world appears very different from its prewar predecessor, this does not necessarily indicate a transition to a new form of socio-economic organisation. Whether or not the identified changes represent a 'post' condition – either industrial or Fordist – is a matter of dispute concerning, amongst other things, the adequacy of the underlying model of change. Although lacking a clear monocausal mechanism of change and a final end-state to historical development, contemporary political economy retains a familiar evolutionary typology found in social theory. As Kumar (1995: 13), referring to theories of postindustrialism, points out: 'current changes are seen according to a model derived from (assumed) past changes, and future developments are projected following the logic of the model. So just as industrial society replaced agrarian society, the information society is replacing industrial society, more or less in the same evolutionary way.'

In contrast, Kumar argues, *continuity*, not change, is what characterises contemporary societies. The techniques and technologies of production may have been modified but capitalist societies remain organised around the same principles and objectives as always (Kumar, 1995: 24–5, 32–4). In short, the conception of a radical break in social development is greatly overestimated, its evolutionary underpinnings overstating the degree, and the mechanisms, of change.

The neo-Marxisms of Lash and Urry (1987) and Jessop (1994a, *passim*) are intended to overcome this problem by emphasising either the flows of capital or the double dynamic of capitalist development rather than the functional determination by capital of state structures and policies. None the less, through these concepts both the disorganised capitalism thesis and the post-Fordist paradigm attempt to theorise the transition from a capitalism of the nation-state to a capitalism of the global order which has consequences for welfare politics. These consequences, however, are not accepted by all commentators.

For example, the argument that social-structural change generates greater and more complex social divisions, has been criticised on the grounds that it underplays the historical continuity of both social frag-mentation and class divisions in modern societies. Much of this dispute depends on what particular definition or model of 'class' is adopted to examine what dimensions of stratification and political action. Critics of the class-in-decline/fragmentation-in-the-ascendancy thesis point to a conflation of class-based and non-class-based inequalities. This conflation, it is argued, ignores the persistence of the bourgeoisie's control of eco-nomic wealth in capitalist societies, the capacity of wealth owners to influ-ence political processes and the transmission of privilege from one generation to another (Hout et al., 1996: 52). Increasing differences between classes in relation to the distribution of wealth and power are said to attest to the continuing salience of class categories. Hout et al., for example, argue that:

> The complexities of political strategies and tactics make the distinction between class as a causal agent and class or inequality as an object of discussion absol-utely critical. Merely because an issue is not directly couched in terms of class or traditional left–right politics does not mean that class is irrelevant to under-standing it . . . What if some 'new' social issues have become the object of politi-cal struggles and public debate in part because they resonate with people's

traditional left–right political heuristics . . .? Could it be that controversies over affirmative action or the extension of rights to new categories of citizen (such as the disabled) gain their ideological strength from being about 'old' (class) issues, such as equality or social democracy? . . . To say that class matters less now than it used to requires that one exaggerate its importance in the past and understate its importance at present. (1996: 55)

The underestimation of social fragmentation is visible in Offe's comments on the political implications for welfare state development of social divisions and the undermining of social solidarity entailed by these divisions. Such divisions were highlighted by Titmuss (1958) many years ago when he investigated the 'social divisions of welfare' – the ways that social welfare systems reflect and contribute to social inequality. Both the fragmentation of workers and the stratifications in tax and benefit provisions have been evident throughout the postwar period.

Contemporary theories of political economy also underestimate important social processes around gender and ethnicity. The Regulation Approach to post-Fordism, for example, has argued that the state performs a coordination function to maintain the dominant 'strategic line' of accumulation by allocating responsibilities, specifying roles and monitoring actions (Jessop, 1994a: 271–4). The allocation, specification and monitoring are functionally linked to the economy as paradigmatic instances of the 'guidance' and 'integration' of consumption and accumulation within specific nation-states (Boyer, 1990: xiii; Lipietz, 1994: 340). This conception of roles, responsibilities and actions, however, does not account for their gendered and racialised character. Why it is that economies and welfare organisations should be dependent on or reproduce a gendered division of paid work and domestic labour is a question that lies outside the theoretical framework of the Regulation Approach. Similarly, in emphasising the 'newness' of contemporary processes of globalisation, postindustrialist, post-Fordist and disorganised capitalism perspectives also underemphasise the role of imperialism and its relationship to racialised social structures and institutions. The contemporary 'global' economy is not only a transformation of an earlier 'national' economy: it is also an economy that travels through the networks and institutions of the imperialist world system that was forged throughout the nineteenth and early twentieth centuries. The transformation of the Keynesian Welfare State into a Schumpeterian Workfare State or the transition from organised to disorganised welfare does not simply have different effects for different ethnic and gender groups; the logics of transformation are themselves rooted in the gendered and racialised networks of the imperial system.

Identifying a transition to a 'post' condition is fraught equally with methodological problems. For example, Esping-Andersen's model of welfare régimes groups countries into one of three types – liberal, corporatist-statist or universal – on the basis of data about income maintenance schemes, eligibility criteria and extent of population coverage. The 'decommodification' index that determines the positions of countries in régime clusters is derived from the ratio of means-testing to universalism in their income-maintenance programmes: the less the reliance on means-testing the greater the degree of decommodification. The focus on income-maintenance policies has been criticised as an overly restrictive conception of what comprises welfare policy. Feminists (Orloff, 1993; Sainsbury, 1994) have been sceptical of this approach for a number of reasons. First, to determine the position of women in any régime type requires establishing whether women's entitlement to benefit is granted on an individual basis or whether it is attached to marriage status. Women's role in the family has many implications for understanding the relationship between commodification and decommodification. For example, the countries which score highest on the decommodification index, those with the greatest degree of universalism, have a large labour market participation rate for women, meaning that women's labours are commodified to a large extent in decommodified systems. Yet in conservative countries in the corporatist model their labour is more likely to be decommodified, perhaps because of the priority attached to the traditional gendered division of labour in these countries. Thus, it has been suggested that attitudes to gender and the family need to be built into models of welfare régimes (see Hill, 1996: 44–5).

Examining outcomes rather than policies also yields a different régime classification. Decommodification can be achieved by a variety of policy instruments; whereas Australia scores low on this measure when assessed on income-maintenance systems, it has been pointed out that Australia has concentrated on achieving some measure of pre-tax, pre-transfer income equality, mainly by maintaining wage levels. The point here is that taking into account other policy priorities and measures results in yet further régime clusters (Hill, 1996: 46–7). The wealth of research comparing aspects of welfare state provision has been approached from qualitative as well as quantitative perspectives, charting the historical development of welfare states in terms of the institutional, political and ideological characteristics of particular countries, and providing further different classifications.

We have emphasised the difficulties of using comparative social policy approaches to theorising the emergence of postindustrial societies, because the problems of measurement and comparison are germane to all of the political economy perspectives that we outlined in Chapter 5. In order for such theories to maintain their validity it is necessary that the units of comparison are roughly equivalent. Yet it is a moot point whether the Germany, Italy, United States, Sweden and Britain of the later nineteenth century really comprised equivalent political, economic and social units. Italy did not become a nation-state in the manner of Britain and France, for example, until unification under the King of Savoy between 1860 and 1870. Germany unified under Prussian dominance in the 1870s following the Franco-Prussian War. The Civil War of 1861–5 marked the unification of America as the 'United States'. In the European context it is only after the signing of the Versailles Treaty in 1920 that a map of European nation-states passably recognisable by contemporary standards came into existence (Hobsbawm, 1995b: 88–9; 1995c: 144–50). Thus, when discussing the emergence and transformation of 'welfare states' in historical terms it is difficult to avoid comparing chalk with cheese.

Political ecology

Theories of political ecology draw attention to the relationships between development, environment and welfare and, eschewing a strict theoretical focus on 'capitalism' or 'the state', examine the logics of exploitation that connect environmental degradation to the uneven distribution of rights, freedoms and obligations in global socio-economic development. In social policy and sociology there is very little literature on the relationships between social welfare and environmental change and almost none at all that deals with the connections between social welfare *systems* and environmental exploitation. The environment is rapidly becoming an issue for social welfare because, increasingly, it is an arena of struggles over distributive and allocative strategies around resources: clean air and water, common space, productive soils, and so on. The theories of political ecology that we outlined in Chapter 6 indicate that these are struggles over welfare in the widest sense of that term. They involve confrontations over control of and access to resources, over meanings and definitions of what is 'valuable' in environments, over how environmental exploitation is and should be organised and over identities, rights and statuses in the development process or, in other words, over what it means to be a 'citizen' of planet earth (O'Brien and Penna, 1997).

In social welfare terms, however, we need to ask not simply *what* rights and freedoms, obligations and duties are contested and distributed but *how* are they contested and distributed: both who has what rights and undertakes what duties and what are the processes by which this distribution is achieved? As Beck points out, the most common response to the problem of environmental degradation is to argue that 'we' are all responsible and that 'we' all have a duty and obligation to protect, repair and respect the environment. The consequence of this, however, is that, since everyone is responsible, no one is liable for actual environmental destruction. Theories of political ecology do not necessarily advance much beyond this position, either. Gorz blames the 'megamachine' of capitalism, Shiva accuses 'Western' 'monocultures of the mind' and Beck charges the 'risk society' with having embedded within it a logic of hazard production that drives forward economic development and growth.

One effect of this generalised liability is that, as Beck notes, the environmentalist critique of modern industrial organisation draws on the very scientific specialisms and knowledges that it charges with complicity in damaging the environment (see also Yearley, 1990). Part of the reason for this is that these discourses have become one of the few ways, in the public domain, of challenging the power of bureaucratic and commercial institutions in their increasing encroachment on to and control over environmental resources. In this area, the scientisation and rationalisation of the 'environment' – and 'sustainability' or 'sustainable development' – means that the rules of engagement in the debate, the forms that critique and dissent can take, are at least partially predefined by the political-economic control of the environmental agenda.

Theories of political ecology are confronted also with the problem of disentangling the social welfare aspects of the critique from the moral philosophical aspects. As we saw in Chapter 6, concepts of ecological citizenship provide some useful ways of understanding the political dimensions of local struggles over environmental change. At the same time they do not provide solid grounds on which to construct theories of rights and responsibilities: in what, exactly, do environmental 'rights' and 'responsibilities' consist? Who has what rights and what responsibilities and how are these to be encoded so that they can be understood and realised by people? Similarly, if rights are to be awarded to non-human species, how will these non-human species be able to realise them? What court of appeal will hear a claim of discrimination or maltreatment from a heifer cow or a cockroach? Does a virus or bacterium have rights or responsibilities? These questions emerge in political ecologies of welfare because they are strongly normative: the critique of actually existing political ecologies (the critique of the ways that the connections between social and environmental processes are currently organised) rests on the proposition that things *must* be changed in order to offset catastrophe. However, *what* has to change and *how* change should be undertaken are not easily derivable from the theories of political ecology. The most developed positions rest on non-environmental politics – notably feminism, anarchism and socialism – such that theories of political ecology end up in the service of political projects that, in themselves, are not necessarily environmentally friendly.

Since there is no basic or 'paradigm' perspective in political ecology, only an array of competing theories and viewpoints, almost any set of commitments and policies can be termed 'environmental'. Increasing the production and consumption of electricity (because it is an 'environmentally sound' form of energy), building new roads (because it reduces congestion on existing roads), encouraging the development of out-of-town hypermarkets and shopping centres (because they reduce traffic in and erosion of town centres) have all been called 'good' for the environment. That there are environmental problems of some kind is disputed by hardly anyone at all. Precisely what these problems are and whether and how people should respond to them is disputed by just about everyone. Theories of political ecology point to the necessity of developing 'total' solutions – in that every element of human activity and organisation is charged with contributing to environmental change – but at the same time they point also to the divergent and contested projects through which people and groups propose radically different solutions addressing different sets of problems.

Postmodernism

Is the fragmentation in environmental disputes a contingent outcome of people's divergent projects, or does the fragmentation indicate something more fundamental about social and political processes in the modern world? In other words, is there a 'solution', not only to environmental degradation, but also to the numerous divisions and conflicts around possible solutions, or is the fragmentation inevitable and incurable? This question goes beyond the theoretical scope of political ecology. In fact, in some version or other, it lies at the heart of debates about postmodernism. Phrased as a 'problem' requiring 'solutions', fragmentation and divergence appears as a 'cause' of inaction and ineffectiveness in 'responding to' environmental change. However, in theoretical terms, it is not necessary to posit fragmentation as a 'problem' in this way at all. It can be argued that the differences of perspective and the divergences in social and political projects expose acts of resistance to dominant scientific and bureaucratic strategies of centralising knowledge about and control over more and more aspects of people's lives. In spite of the tendency of environmental campaigners to adopt scientific and bureaucratic discourses in their struggles over ecological destruction, environmental disputes continue to pit local knowledges and anti-scientific discourses against them.

Disputes around environmental change can be said to indicate the plurality of voices through which social and political struggles are conducted. Moreover, they indicate that contestation and conflict are endemic to social and political organisation. The formation of an 'environmental' agenda is a process of struggle, as is the formation of a 'disability' agenda, a 'feminist' agenda or a 'development' agenda, and so on. There is not one single environment over which people struggle, any more than there is one single line of historical development through which cultures and societies 'modernise'. Different environmental and historical relations are organised through struggle and dispute and, in the process of struggle different identities, statuses, meanings and perspectives are centralised and marginalised, excluded and included. In postmodern theory there is no solution to this differentiation process: it is not a 'problem' that requires the invention of a unifying ideology under which everyone will reach agreement about 'what is to be done'. Postmodern theory suggests that the analytic categories through which social life has been investigated and theorised do not name portions of the 'real world', the understanding of which will (eventually) guarantee its repair or reform. Rather, they represent unstable, tenuous, political classifications resulting from the investment of certain ways of 'knowing' the world in hierarchical institutions and intellectual networks.

For some, this type of argument is just too much. By politicising even the concepts in which social science has investigated history, culture and politics postmodern theory has gone 'too far', engaging in a series of denials around central logics in mainstream sociology. Amongst these denials, for example, Walby includes 'a denial of significant structuring of power' (1992: 30) and a denial of the 'coherence of classic analytical concepts such as "woman", "class" and "race"' (1992: 31). Others reject postmodernism's apparent dissolution of the emancipatory ideal and accuse postmodernism of a gesture politics that functions as an apologetics for the status quo (Norris, 1990). The impossibility of deriving a future utopia from postmodern theory has led to accusations of 'conservatism', at best, and of nihilism and apathy, at worst (Habermas, 1985; Ebert, 1995). If there is no underlying unity to the social world, if social life is inherently fractured and contestatory, if there are several axes of domination and if even the concepts and logics through which the world is understood in social theory are complicit with power relations, how can an emancipatory political programme be realised? How, even, is it possible to know if things are changing for the better or worse?

A related issue is the postmodern endorsement of multiple 'voices'. This endorsement is attractive in so far as it gives recognition to groups who, historically, have been ignored, excluded or silenced. However, there is a theoretical as well as a moral dimension to the endorsement, one that is not so straightforwardly attractive. The theoretical dimension can be addressed in two parts: first, the problem of 'voice recognition' or of knowing *who* is speaking; and, second, the issue of what is 'voiced', or of understanding the consequences of *what* is spoken. The first problem arises because postmodern theory proposes that identities are unstable: that, rather than 'having' identities people 'practise' them, such that 'identity', in postmodern theory, is an active process rather than a state or condition. But the activity of identity is much more complex in postmodern theory than in, say, symbolic interactionism (where identities are negotiated between people using common symbols), in that it is inescapably political. To realise an 'identity' is to position oneself in specific social, cultural and political locations and not others, in specific relationships, and not others, through a specific configuration of symbolic and social resources. 'Identity' is simultaneously a practice of self-inclusion and other-exclusion. But since postmodern theory proposes that identities are fractured and unstable, then it follows that so also are the 'voices' that contest and dispute the utopian and emancipatory projects of modern social and political philosophy. In this sense, there are no theoretical grounds for deciding which voices are speaking in which locations: whether 'voice' is attached to identity, or not.

The validation of multiple voices simultaneously confronts the problem of what those voices are saying or, in other words, the problem of interpretation. A great deal of postmodern analysis focuses on textual material – deconstructing the narrative forms through which textual meanings are organised. In extending the analytical agenda beyond written or visual texts, however, postmodern theory encounters non-narrative ways of organising meanings. In other words, the social worlds in which multiple voices express claims, realise identities and dispute meanings are subject to processes of physical, economic and military exploitation which may persist in spite of the multi-faceted character of modern identities. Theoretically, the question arises as to whether it is necessary – or helpful – to theorise the social world through located identities in order to grasp the influence of military or economic institutions on social change and social experience. To put this point in reverse, is it not more feasible to theorise the multiplicity of located identities through, for example, the militaristic, economic and political domination of everyday life by highly organised vested interests controlling powerful institutions?

A final criticism that can be applied to postmodern perspectives concerns the extent to which they are often dependent on the logics and conceptual categories that are the target of their radical critique. Although postmodernism contests the traditions and canons of mainstream social theory, it almost invariably uses selected 'classic' concepts in its critique of modern society. Notable amongst these is the concept of 'identity' itself, which has a long sociological pedigree, but we would also point to the notion that a theory of social change, exploitation or exclusion can be derived through an analysis of cultural categories – symbols, signs, texts, meanings, and so on. There are some ambiguities in the relationships between the 'cultural' and the 'social' in postmodern perspectives that seem unresolvable using the theoretical logics of postmodernism's radical perspectivism.

Concluding remarks

'Social welfare' is a label for a complex and unstable mixture of relationships, experiences, processes and structures. The means by and conditions through which individual and collective welfare are achieved or undermined are the focus of intense political action and social struggle. From conditions of employment to the regulation of family life, from the availability of shelter to rights over the environment and its resources, from the classification of social membership or personal need to the management of industrial and municipal waste, social welfare is embedded in a wide range of political, economic and cultural relationships. Thus, to reflect on the acquisition or maintenance of welfare is to reflect on the operations of economies, the procedures of political rule, the categories of cultural definition and classification, and the interactions between social and environmental change. To theorise welfare is to theorise public and private, institutional and communal networks of action and struggle.

These concerns have been central to the development of Western philosophical and theoretical thought. From the philosophies of the Enlightenment – with their attempts to situate human societies within grand, meta-theoretical understandings of the relationships between individuals, communities, state power, political representation, economic development and nation-building – to the post-Enlightenment, reflexive paradigms outlined in Part Three, the organisation of these relationships has been the basis of social theory. Such concerns endure in part because human societies are characterised by both continuity and change: each generation lives through rapidly changing economic and cultural processes, yet at the same time, each generation experiences social division and inequality. Social welfare policies and systems are embedded in visions of the 'good society'; each proposal for, or understanding of, social welfare, is inextricably linked with a wider analysis of social life. In Enlightenment thought, the perfectibility of the individual and the progress of the social whole were bound together as both political and philosophical commitments. The purpose of theorising society was to theorise the potential for a progressive expansion in the welfare of both individual human beings and the social totalities of which they were members. For many, the Enlightenment offered a vision of a world of human affairs in which predictability and control could be effected to a degree previously unimaginable. Important currents in contemporary social theory undermine this faith in predictability and control, pointing instead to the limited capacity of individuals and nations to direct and order the complex, local and global networks and relationships governing modern life.

The 'new world order' creates particular problems for the development of social policies. As Townsend (1995) has argued, welfare policy can no longer limit itself only to the national arena but must address the connections between the local and the global. As we have seen, addressing such connections, necessitates an encounter with political, economic and cultural forces and recognising the structural changes to which they give rise.

We end our assessment of theoretical perspectives in welfare analysis by reaffirming a proposition that we made in the Introduction: there is not and cannot be a single, total or complete theory of welfare. Some theories provide insights into political economy, some into political ecology, some into cultural expressions of identity, inclusion and exclusion. Theories offer prospects and limitations for understanding social welfare and encourage critical perspectives on the world. They do not store up the 'true' answers to the world's problems but, instead, enable different questions to be posed about the world and the problems and potentials it contains.

References

Adam, B. (1994) 'Running Out of Time: Global Crisis and Human Engagement', in T. Benton and M. Redclift (eds), *Social Theory and the Global Environment*. London: Routledge. pp. 92–112.

Adler, M. (1978 [1904–27]) 'Selections on "The Theory and Method of Marxism"', in T.B. Bottomore and P. Goode (eds), *Austro-Marxism*. Oxford: Oxford University Press.

Ahmad, B. (1993) *Black Perspectives in Social Work*. Birmingham: Venture Press.

Allen, J. (1992) 'Post-Industrialism and Post-Fordism', in S. Hall, D. Held and T. McGrew (eds), *Modernity and Its Futures*. Cambridge: Polity/Open University Press.

Althusser, L. (1969 [1965]) *For Marx*. London: Allen Lane.

Althusser, L. and Balibar, É. (1971) *Reading 'Capital'*. London: New Left Books.

Amos, V. and Parmar, P. (1984) 'Challenging Imperial Feminism', *Feminist Review*, 17: 3–19.

Arblaster, A. (1984) *The Rise and Decline of Western Liberalism*. Oxford: Blackwell.

Armstrong, D. (1983) *Political Anatomy of the Body: Medical Knowledge in Britain in the Twentieth Century*. Cambridge: Cambridge University Press.

Aronowitz, S. (1995) 'Against the Liberal State: ACT-UP and the Emergence of Postmodern Politics', in L. Nicholson and S. Seidman (eds), *Social Postmodernism: Beyond Identity Politics*. Cambridge: Cambridge University Press.

Ashford, D.E. (1986) *The Emergence of the Welfare States*. Oxford: Blackwell.

Ashley, D. (1994) 'Postmodernism and Antifoundationalism', in D.R. Dickens and A. Fontana (eds), *Postmodernism and Social Inquiry*. London: UCL Press.

Bagguley, P. (1991) 'Post-Fordism and Enterprise Culture: Flexibility, Autonomy and Changes in Economic Organisation', in R. Keat and N. Abercrombie (eds), *Enterprise Culture*. London: Routledge.

Bahro, R. (1986) *Building the Green Movement*. London: Heretic Books.

Ball, T. and Dagger, R. (eds) (1991) *Ideals and Ideologies: A Reader*. New York: Harper Collins.

Bank Information Centre (1991) *Funding Ecological and Social Destruction: The World Bank and the IMF*. Washington, DC: (World) Bank Information Centre.

de Beauvoir, S. (1964 [1949]) *The Second Sex*. New York: Bantam.

Beck, U. (1992a) *Risk Society: Towards a New Modernity*. London: Sage.

Beck, U. (1992b) 'From Industrial to Risk Society: Questions of Survival, Social Structure and Ecological Enlightenment', *Theory, Culture & Society*, 9 (1): 97–123.

Beck, U. (1995) *Ecological Politics in an Age of Risk*. Cambridge: Polity.

Bell, C. and Newby, H. (eds) (1974) *The Sociology of Community*. London: Frank Cass & Co. Ltd.

Bell, D. (1962) *The End of Ideology: On the Exhaustion of Political Ideas in the Fifties*. New York: Free Press.

Bell, D. (1973) *The Coming of Post-Industrial Society*. New York: Basic Books.

Bell, D. (1980) 'The Social Framework of the Information Society', in T. Forester (ed.), *The Microelectronics Revolution*. Oxford: Blackwell.

Benjamin, W. (1973 [1940]) *Illuminations*. London: Fontana.

Berlin, I. (1968) *Four Essays on Liberty*. Oxford: Oxford University Press.

Berlin, I. (1990) *The Crooked Timber of Humanity: Chapters in the History of Ideas*. London: John Murray.

Bernstein, R. (1983) *Beyond Objectivism and Relativism*. Oxford: Blackwell.

Beveridge, W.H. (1936) *Planning Under Socialism and Other Essays*. London: Longman.

Beveridge, W.H. (1942) *Social Insurance and Allied Services*. Cmnd 6404. London: HMSO.

Bhabha, H.K. (1994) *The Location of Culture*. London: Routledge.

Bhattacharyya, G. (1994) ' "Who Fancies Pakis?" Pamela Bordes and the Problems of Exoticism in Multiracial Britain', in S. Ledger, J. McDonagh and J. Spencer (eds), *Political Gender. Texts and Contexts*. Hemel Hempstead: Harvester Wheatsheaf.

Bookchin, M. (1982) *The Ecology of Freedom*. Palo Alto, CA: Cheshire Books.

Bosanquet, B. (ed.) (1968 [1895]) *Aspects of the Social Problem*. London: Macmillan.

Bosanquet, N. (1983) *After the New Right*. Aldershot: Dartmouth.

Boulding, K.E. (1966) 'The Economics of the Coming Spaceship Earth', in H. Jarrett (ed.), *Environmental Quality in a Growing Economy*. New York: Johns Hopkins University Press.

Boyer, R. (1990) *The Regulation School: A Critical Introduction*. New York: Columbia University Press.

Brah, A. (1992a) 'Women of South Asian Origin in Britain: Issues and Concerns', in P. Braham, A. Rattansi and P. Skellington (eds), *Racism and Antiracism: Inequalities, Opportunities and Policies*. London: Sage/Open University.

Brah, A. (1992b) 'Difference, Diversity and Differentiation', in J. Donald and A. Rattansi (eds), *'Race', Culture, Difference*. London: Sage/Open University.

Bramstead, E.K. and Melhuish, K.J. (eds) (1978) *Western Liberalism: A History in Documents from Locke to Croce*. New York: Longman.

British Medical Association (1994) *Environmental and Occupational Risks of Health Care*. London: BMA.

Brown, C. (1992) ' "Same Difference": the Persistance of Racial Disadvantage in the British Employment Market', in P. Braham, A. Rattansi and P. Skellington (eds), *Racism and Antiracism: Inequalities, Opportunities and Policies*. London: Sage/Open University.

Bryson, L. (1992) *Welfare and the State: Who Benefits?* Basingstoke: Macmillan.

Buchanan, J.M. (1978) *The Economics of Politics*. London: IEA Readings 18.

Bulmer, M. (1987) *The Social Basis of Community Care*. London: Unwin and Hyman.

Burningham, K. and O'Brien, M. (1994) 'Global Environmental Values and Local Contexts of Action', *Sociology*, 28 (4): 913–32.

Burrows, R. and Loader, B. (1994) 'Towards a Post-Fordist Welfare State? The Restructuring of Britain, Social Policy and the Future of Welfare', in R. Burrows and B. Loader (eds), *Towards a Post-Fordist Welfare State?* London: Routledge.

Butler, J. (1993) *Bodies that Matter: On the Discursive Limits of 'Sex'*. London: Routledge.

Butler, J. (1994) 'Contingent Foundations: Feminism and the Question of the Postmodern', in L. Nicholson and S. Seidman (eds), *Social Postmodernism: Beyond Identity Politics*. Cambridge: Cambridge University Press.

Byrne, D. (1987) 'Rich and Poor: the Growing Divide', in A. Walker and C. Walker (eds), *The Growing Divide: A Social Audit*. London: CPAG.

Cable, S. and Benson, M. (1993) 'Acting locally: environmental injustice and the emergence of grass roots environmental organisations', *Social Problems*, 40 (4): 464–77.

Cahill, M. (1994) *The New Social Policy*. Oxford: Blackwell.

Cain, M. (1993) 'Foucault, feminism and feeling: what Foucault can and cannot contribute to feminist epistemology', in C. Ramazanoglu (ed.), *Up Against Foucault. Explorations of Some Tensions Between Foucault and Feminism*. London: Routledge.

Carabine, J. (1992) ' "Constructing Women": Women's Sexuality and Social Policy', *Critical Social Policy*. No. 34 (Summer): 23–39.

Carby, H. (1982) 'White Woman Listen. Black Feminism and the Boundaries of Sisterhood', in Centre for Contemporary Cultural Studies, *The Empire Strikes Back*. London: Hutchinson.

Cochrane, A. (1994) 'Restructuring the Local Welfare State', in R. Burrows and B. Loader (eds), *Towards a Post-Fordist Welfare State?* London: Routledge.

Cochrane, A. and Clarke, J. (eds) (1993) *Comparing Welfare States. Britain in International Context*. London: Sage.

Cohen, S. (1985) *Visions of Social Control*. Cambridge: Polity.

Collins, H. (1991) 'Treatment and Disposal of Clinical and Laboratory Waste', *Medical and Laboratory Science*, 48 (4): 324–31.

Condorcet, Marquis de (1955 [1795]) *Sketch for a Historical Picture of the Progress of the Human Mind* (translated by June Barraclough). London: Weidenfeld & Nicolson.

Copjec, J. (1991) 'The Unvermogender Other: Hysteria and Democracy in America', *New Formations*, 14: 27–41.

Corrigan, P. and Leonard, P. (1978) *Social Work Practice Under Capitalism. A Marxist Approach.* London and Basingstoke: Macmillan.

Crook, S., Pakulski, J. and Waters, M. (1992) *Postmodernization: Change in Advanced Society.* London: Sage.

Dalrymple, J. and Burke, B. (1995) *Anti-Oppressive Practice. Social Care and the Law.* Buckingham: Open University Press.

Davies, J. (ed.) with Berger, B. and Carlson, A. (1993) *The Family: Is It Just Another Lifestyle Choice?* London: IEA.

Davis, K. (1993) 'The crafting of good clients', in J. Swain, V. Finkelstein, S. French and M. Oliver (eds), *Disabling Barriers – Enabling Environments*. London: Sage/Open University.

Dean, M. (1991) *The Constitution of Poverty: Toward a Genealogy of Liberal Governance*. London: Routledge.

DeLue, S.M. (1989) *Political Obligations in a Liberal State*. Albany, NY: SUNY Press.

Denney, D. (1995) 'Hall', in V. George and R. Page (eds), *Modern Thinkers On Welfare*. London: Prentice Hall/Harvester Wheatsheaf.

Dennis, N. and Erdos, G. (1993) *Families Without Fatherhood*, 2nd edn. Choice in Welfare Series No. 12. London: IEA.

Department of Employment (1986) *Building Businesses . . . Not Barriers*. Cmnd 9794. London: HMSO.

Department of Employment (1987) *Trade Unions and Their Members*. Cmnd 95. London: HMSO.

Department of Employment (1988) *Employment for the 1990s*. Cmnd 540. London: HMSO.

Department of Health and Social Security (1985a) *Reform of Social Security*, Volume 1. Cmnd 9517. London: HMSO.

Department of Health and Social Security (1985b) *Reform of Social Security*, Volume 2. Cmnd 9518. London: HMSO.

Department of Health and Social Security (1985c) *Reform of Social Security*. Cmnd 9691. London: HMSO.

Dicken, P. (1992) *Global Shift. The Internationalization of Economic Activity*, 2nd edn. London: Paul Chapman Publishing.

Dickens, D.R. and Fontana, A. (1994) 'Postmodernism in the Social Sciences', in D.R. Dickens and A. Fontana (eds), *Postmodernism and Social Inquiry*. London, UCL Press.

Dickens, J. (1993) 'Assessment and the Control of Social Work: An Analysis of Reasons for the Non-Use of the Child Assessment Order', *Journal of Social Welfare and Family Law*, 2: 88–100.

Dominelli, L. (1988) *Anti-Racist Social Work*. London: BASW/Macmillan.

Donzelot, J. (1980) *The Policing of Families: Welfare versus the State*. London: Hutchinson.

Drachkovitch, M. M. (ed.) (1966) *The Revolutionary Internationals, 1864–1943*. London: Oxford University Press.

Dunant, S. (ed.) (1994) *The War of the Words: The Political Correctness Debate*. London: Virago.

Durkheim, E. (1984 [1893]) *The Division of Labour in Society*. London: Macmillan.

Ebert, T.L. (1995) 'The Knowable Good: Post-al Politics, Ethics, and Red Feminism', *Rethinking Marxism*, 8 (2): 39–59.

Elam, M. (1994) 'Puzzling out the Post-Fordist Debate: Technology, Markets and Institutions', in A. Amin (ed.), *Post-Fordism: A Reader*. Oxford: Blackwell.

Esping-Andersen, G. (1990) *The Three Worlds of Welfare Capitalism*. Cambridge/Oxford: Polity/Blackwell.

Esping-Andersen, G. (1991) 'Postindustrial Cleavage Structures: A Comparison of Evolving Patterns of Social Stratification in Germany, Sweden and the United States', in F. Fox Piven (ed.), *Labour Parties in Postindustrial Societies*. Cambridge: Polity.

Fanon, F. (1969 [1961]) *The Wretched of the Earth*. Harmondsworth: Penguin.

Fanon, F. (1986 [1952]) *Black Skin, White Masks*. London: Pluto.

Finch, J. and Groves, D. (1983) *A Labour of Love: Women, Work and Caring*. London: Routledge & Kegan Paul.

Foley, D. (1991) 'Commodity', in T. Bottomore (ed.), *A Dictionary of Marxist Thought*. Oxford/Cambridge, MA: Blackwell.

Foster, W. Z. (1968) *History of the Three Internationals*. New York: Greenwood Press.

Foucault, M. (1977) *Discipline and Punish*. Harmondsworth: Penguin.

Foucault, M. (ed.) (1978) *I, Pierre Rivière … A Case of Parricide in the 19th Century*. Harmondsworth: Penguin.

Foucault, M. (1981) *The History of Sexuality*. Volume 1: *An Introduction*. Harmondsworth: Penguin.

Foucault, M. (1982) *Madness and Civilization: A History of Insanity in the Age of Reason*. London: Tavistock.

Fraser, N. (1989) *Unruly Practices: Power, Discourse and Gender in Contemporary Social Theory*. Cambridge: Polity.

Fraser, N. (1994) 'Rethinking the Public Sphere: A Contribution to the Critique of Actually Existing Democracy', in H.A. Giroux and P.L. McLaren (eds), *Between Borders: Pedagogy and the Politics of Cultural Oppression*. London: Routledge.

Fraser, N. (1995) 'Politics, Culture and the Public Sphere: Toward a Postmodern Conception', in L. Nicholson and S. Seidman (eds), *Social Postmodernism: Beyond Identity Politics*. Cambridge: Cambridge University Press.

Friedan, B. (1982 [1963]) *The Feminine Mystique*. Harmondsworth: Penguin.

Friedman, M. (1962) *Capitalism and Freedom*. Chicago: University of Chicago Press.

Friedman, M. and Friedman, R. (1980) *Free To Choose*. London: Secker & Warburg.

Gadgil, M. and Guha, R. (1994) 'Ecological Conflicts and the Environmental Movement in India', in D. Ghai (ed.), *Environment and Development: Sustaining People and Nature*. Oxford/The Hague: Blackwell/Institute of Social Studies.

Galton, F. (1889) *Natural Inheritance*. London: Macmillan.

Galton, F. (1907) *Inquiry into the Human Faculty and its Development*. London: J.M. Dent.

Gamble, A. (1985) *Britain in Decline*, 2nd edn. London: Macmillan.

Gamble, A. (1988) *The Free Economy and the Strong State*. London: Macmillan.

Garland, D. (1985) *Punishment and Welfare: A History of Penal Strategies*. Aldershot: Gower.

Garland, D. and Young, P. (eds) (1983) *The Power to Punish*. London: Heinemann.

Gatens, M. (1992) 'Power, Bodies and Difference', in M. Barrett and A. Phillipps (eds), *Destabilising Theory: Contemporary Feminist Debates*. Cambridge: Polity.

Geertz , C. (1975) *The Interpretation of Cultures*. New York: Basic Books.

Gershuny, J.I. and Miles, I. (1983) *The New Service Economy: the Transformation of Employment in Industrial Societies*. London: Francis Pinter.

Giddens, A. (1971) *Capitalism and Modern Social Theory*. Cambridge: Cambridge University Press.

Giddens, A. (1990) *The Consequences of Modernity*. Cambridge: Polity.

Giddens, A. (1991) *Modernity and Self Identity: Self and Society in the Late Modern Age*. Cambridge: Polity.

Giddens, A. (1994) *Beyond Left and Right: The Future of Radical Politics*. Cambridge: Polity.

Ginsburg, N. (1979) *Class, Capital and Social Policy*. London and Basingstoke: Macmillan.

Ginsburg, N. (1992a) 'Racism and Housing: Concepts and Reality', in P. Braham, A. Rattansi and R. Skellington (eds), *Racism and Antiracism: Inequalities, Opportunities and Policies*. London: Sage/Open University.

Ginsburg, N. (1992b) *Divisions of Welfare*. London: Sage.

Goodwin, N. (1995) 'Explaining Geographical Variations in the Contracting out of NHS Hospital Ancillary Services: A Contextual Approach', *Environment and Planning A*, 27: 1397–418.

Gorz, A. (1980) *Ecology as Politics*. Boston: South End Press.

Gorz, A. (1982) *Farewell to the Working Class: An Essay on Post-Industrial Socialism*. London: Pluto Press.

Gorz, A. (1989) *Critique of Economic Reason*. London: Verso.

Gorz, A. (1994) *Capitalism, Socialism, Ecology*. London: Verso.

Gough, I. (1979) *The Political Economy of the Welfare State*. London and Basingstoke: Macmillan.

Graham, H. (1987) 'Women's Poverty and Caring', in C. Glendinning and J. Millar (eds), *Women and Poverty in Britain*. Hemel Hempstead: Harvester Wheatsheaf.

Gramsci, A. (1971 [1929–35]) *Selections from the Prison Notebooks* (edited by Q. Hoare and G. Nowell Smith). London: Lawrence & Wishart.

Gray, J. (1989) *Liberalisms: Essays in Political Philosophy*. London: Routledge.

Gray, J. (1996) *Post-Liberalism: Studies in Political Thought*. London: Routledge.

Green, D.G. (1979) *The New Right*. Hemel Hempstead: Harvester Wheatsheaf.

Green, D.G. (1987) *Medicines in the Marketplace*. Health Unit Paper, No 1. London: IEA.

Green, D.G. (1993) *Reinventing Civil Society. The Rediscovery of Welfare Without Politics*. Choice in Welfare Series No. 17. London: IEA.

Green, D.G. (1996) *Community Without Politics. A Market Approach to Welfare Reform*. Choice in Welfare Series No. 27. London: IEA.

Green, T.H. (1941 [1882]) *Lectures on the Principles of Political Obligation*. London: Longmans, Green and Co. Ltd.

Grimshaw, A. (ed.) (1993) *The C.L.R. James Reader*. Oxford: Blackwell.

Habermas, J. (1976) *Legitimation Crisis*. London: Heinemann.

Habermas, J. (1984) *The Theory of Communicative Action*. Volume 1. London: Heinemann.

Habermas, J. (1985) 'Neoconservative Culture Criticism in the United States and West Germany: an Intellectual Movement in Two Political Cultures', in R. Bernstein (ed.), *Habermas and Modernity*. Cambridge: Polity.

Habermas, J. (1988) *The Theory of Communicative Action*. Volume 2. Cambridge: Polity.

Hall, S. (1982) 'Introduction', in S. Hall and M. Jacques (eds), *The Politics of Thatcherism*. London: Lawrence & Wishart.

Hall, S. (1992a) 'New Ethnicities', in J. Donald and A. Rattansi (eds), *'Race', Culture, Difference*. London: Sage/Open University.

Hall, S. (1992b) 'The Question of Cultural Identity', in S. Hall, D. Held and T. McGrew (eds), *Modernity and its Futures*. Cambridge: Polity/Open University.

Hall, S. (1996) 'For Allon White: Metaphors of Transformation', in D. Morley and K-H. Chen (eds), *Stuart Hall: Critical Dialogues in Cultural Studies*. London: Routledge.

Hall, S. and Held, D. (1989) 'Citizens and Citizenship', in S. Hall and M. Jacques (eds), *New Times: The Changing Face of Politics in the 1990s*. London: Lawrence & Wishart.

Hall, S., Crichter, C., Jefferson, T. and Roberts, B. (1978) *Policing the Crisis: Mugging, the State, Law and Order*. London: Macmillan.

Hamilton, P. (1992) 'The Enlightenment and the Birth of Social Science', in S. Hall and B. Gieben (eds), *Formations of Modernity*. Cambridge/Oxford: Polity/Blackwell/Open University.

Hampton, W. (1970) *Democracy and Community*. Oxford: Oxford University Press.

Hannigan, J.A. (1995) *Environmental Sociology: A Social Constructionist Perspective*. London: Routledge.

Hanson, C.G. and Mather, G. (1988) *Striking Out Strikes*. Hobart Paper No. 110. London: IEA.

Hantrais, L. and Letablier, M.T. (1996) *Families and Family Policies in Europe*. London: Longman.

Harman, C. (1988) *The Fire Last Time: 1968 and After*. London: Bookmark.

Harris, J. (1977) *William Beveridge: A Biography*. Oxford: Clarendon Press.

Harris, R. and Seldon, A. (1979) *Over-ruled on Welfare: The Increasing Desire for Choice in Education and Medicine and Its Frustration by 'Representative' Government*. Hobart Paper No. 13. London: IEA.

Harvey, D. (1993) 'Social Justice, Class Relations and the Politics of Difference', in J. Squires (ed.), *Principled Positions: Postmodernism and the Rediscovery of Value*. London: Lawrence & Wishart.

Hasler, F. (1993) 'Developments in the Disabled People's Movement', in J. Swain, V. Finkelstein, S. French and M. Oliver (eds), *Disabling Barriers – Enabling Environments*. London: Sage/Open University.

Haupt, G. (1982) 'Marx and Marxism', in E. J. Hobsbawm (ed.), *The History of Marxism*. Volume 1: *Marxism in Marx's Day*. Brighton: The Harvester Press.

Hay, C. (1996) *Restating Social and Political Change*. Buckingham: Open University Press.

Hayek, F.A. (1944) *The Road to Serfdom*. London: Routledge & Kegan Paul.

Hayek, F.A. (1952) *The Sensory Order: An Inquiry into the Foundations of Theoretical Psychology*. London: Routledge & Kegan Paul.

Hayek, F.A. (1960) *The Constitution of Liberty*. London: Routledge & Kegan Paul.

Hayek, F.A. (1967) *New Studies in Philosophy, Politics and Economics*. London: Routledge & Kegan Paul.

Hayek, F.A. (1979) *The Counter Revolution of Science*. London: Routledge & Kegan Paul.

Hayek, F.A. (1982) *Law, Legislation and Liberty: A New Statement of the Liberal Principles of Justice and Political Economy*. Volume I: *Rules and Social Order*; Volume II: *The Mirage of Social Justice*; Volume III: *The Political Order of a Free People* (collected in one edition). London: Routledge & Kegan Paul.

Hayek, F.A. (1988) 'The Fatal Conceit. The Errors of Socialism', in *The Collected Works of Friedrich August Hayek* (ed. W.W. Bartley III), volume 1. London: Routledge & Kegan Paul.

Hebdige, D. (1996) 'Postmodernism and "The Other Side"', in D. Morley and K-H. Chen (eds), *Stuart Hall: Critical Dialogues in Cultural Studies*. London: Routledge.

Heilbroner, R. (1986) *The Worldly Philosophers*, 6th edn. London: Penguin.

Hewitt, M. (1992) *Welfare, Ideology and Need: Recent Perspectives on the Welfare State*. Hemel Hempstead: Harvester Wheatsheaf.

Hewitt, M. (1996) 'Social Movements and Social Need: Problems with Postmodern Political Theory', in D. Taylor (ed.), *Critical Social Policy*. London: Sage.

Hilferding, R. (1981 [1910]) *Finance Capital*. London and New York: Routledge & Kegan Paul.

Hill, M. (1996) *Social Policy: A Comparative Analysis*. London: Prentice Hall/Harvester Wheatsheaf.

Hills, J. (1988) *Changing Tax*. London: CPAG.

Himmelfarb, G. (1995) *The De-moralisation of Society. From Victorian Virtues to Modern Values*. Choice in Welfare Series No. 22. London: IEA.

Himmelweit, S. (1991a) 'Gender', in T. Bottomore (ed.), *A Dictionary of Marxist Thought*. Oxford: Blackwell.

Himmelweit, S. (1991b) 'Domestic Labour', in T. Bottomore (ed.), *A Dictionary of Marxist Thought*. Oxford: Blackwell.

Hobsbawm, E.J. (ed.) (1982) *The History of Marxism*. Volume 1: *Marxism in Marx's Day*. Brighton: The Harvester Press.

Hobsbawm, E.J. (1995a [1975]) *The Age of Revolution 1789–1848*. London: Weidenfeld & Nicolson.

Hobsbawm, E.J. (1995b [1962]) *The Age of Capital: 1848–75*. London: Weidenfeld & Nicolson.

Hobsbawm, E.J. (1995c [1987]) *The Age of Empire: 1875–1914*. London: Weidenfeld & Nicolson.

Honneth, H. (1992) 'Integrity and Disrespect. Principles of a Conception of Morality Based on the Theory of Recognition', *Political Theory*, 20 (2): 187–201.

hooks, b. (1989) *Talking Back: Thinking Feminist – Thinking Black*. London: Sheba Feminist Publishers.

hooks, b. (1991) *Yearning: Race, Gender and Cultural Politics*. London: Turnaround.

Horkheimer, M. and Adorno, T. (1973 [1947]) *Dialectic of Enlightenment*. New York: Herder & Herder.

Hout, M., Brooks, C. and Manza, J. (1996) 'The Persistence of Classes in Post-industrial Societies', in D.J. Lee and B.S. Turner (eds), *Conflicts about Class. Debating Inequality in Late Industrialism*. London and New York: Longman.

Hughes, R. (1993) *The Culture of Complaint: The Fraying of America*. Milton Keynes: Open University Press.

Illich, I. (1973) *Tools For Conviviality*. London: Calder & Boyars.

Jacobs, M. (1991) *The Green Economy*. London: Pluto.

Jay, M. (1984) *Marxism and Totality: The Adventures of a Concept from Lukács to Habermas*. Berkeley, CA: University of California Press.

Jessop, B. (1994a) 'Post-Fordism and the State', in A. Amin (ed.), *Post-Fordism: A Reader*. Oxford: Blackwell.

Jessop, B. (1994b) 'The Transition to Post-Fordism and the Schumpeterian Workfare

State', in R. Burrows and B. Loader (eds), *Towards a Post-Fordist Welfare State?* London: Routledge.

Jessop, B. (1995) 'Towards a Schumpeterian Workfare Regime in Britain? Reflections on Regulation, Governance, and Welfare State', *Environment and Planning A*, 27: 1613–26.

Jessop, B., Bonnett, K., Bromley, S. and Ling, T. (1988) *Thatcherism. A Tale of Two Nations.* Cambridge/Oxford: Polity/Blackwell.

Jewson, N. and Mason, D. (1992) 'The Theory and Practice of Equal Opportunities Policies: Liberal and Radical Approaches', in P. Braham, A. Rattansi and R. Skellington (eds), *Racism and Antiracism: Inequalities, Opportunities and Policies.* London: Sage/Open University.

Joekes, S. with Heyzer, N., Oniang'O, R. and Salles, V. (1994) 'Gender, Environment and Population', in D. Ghai (ed.), *Environment and Development. Sustaining People and Nature.* Oxford/The Hague: Blackwell/Institute of Social Studies.

Johnson, N. (1990) *Reconstructing the Welfare State.* Hemel Hempstead: Harvester Wheatsheaf.

Jonas, H. (1984) *The Imperative of Responsibility.* Chicago: Chicago University Press.

Kavanagh, D. (1987) *Thatcherism and British Politics.* Oxford: Clarendon Press.

Kettel, B. (1995) 'Gender and Environments: Lessons from WEDNET', in R. Lesser Blumberg, C.A. Rakowski, I. Tinker and M. Monteón (eds), *Engendering Wealth and Well-Being: Empowerment for Social Change.* Oxford: Westview Press.

Keynes, J.M. (1926) 'Liberalism and Labour', in *Essays in Persuasion.* London: Macmillan.

Keynes, J.M. (1927) *The End of Laissez Faire.* London: Macmillan.

Keynes, J.M. (1940) *How to Pay for the War: A Radical Plan for the Chancellor of the Exchequer.* London: Macmillan.

Kidd, B. (1894) *Social Evolution.* London: Longman.

King, M. (1991) 'Child Welfare Within the Law: The Emergence of a Hybrid Discourse', *Journal of Law and Society*, 18 (3): 303–22.

Korsch, K. (1970 [1923]) *Marxism and Philosophy.* London: New Left Books.

Kumar, K. (1995) *From Post-Industrial to Post-Modern Society.* Oxford: Blackwell.

Lal, D. (1994) *The Minimum Wage: No Way to Help the Poor.* Occasional Paper 95. London: IEA.

Larsson, S. (1991) 'Swedish Racism: The Democratic Way', *Race and Class* 32 (3): 102–11.

Lash, S. and Urry, J. (1987) *The End of Organized Capitalism.* Cambridge: Polity.

Lash, S. and Urry, J. (1994) *Economies of Signs and Space.* London: Sage.

Leach, M. and Mearns, R. (1992) *Poverty and Environment in Developing Countries – An Overview Study.* Brighton: University of Brighton, Institute of Development Studies.

Lemert, C. (1994) 'Post-structuralism and Sociology', in S. Seidman (ed.), *The Postmodern Turn. New Perspectives on Social Theory.* Cambridge: Cambridge University Press.

Lemert, C. (1995) *Sociology After the Crisis.* Oxford: Westview Press.

Lemert, E.M. (1981) 'Diversion in Juvenile Justice: What Hath Been Wrought?', *Journal of Research in Crime and Delinquency*, 18 (1): 34–46.

Levitas, R. (1986) 'Competition and Compliance: The Utopias of the New Right', in R. Levitas (ed.), *The Ideology of the New Right.* Cambridge: Polity.

Leys, C. (1983) *Politics in Britain.* London: Verso.

Lipietz, M. (1994) 'Post-Fordism and Democracy', in A. Amin (ed.), *Post-Fordism: A Reader.* Oxford: Blackwell.

Locke, J. (1978 [1690]) 'The Second Treatise of Government', in E.K Bramstead and K.J Melhuish (eds), *Western Liberalism: A History in Documents from Locke to Croce.* New York: Longman.

London–Edinburgh Weekend Return Group (1980) *In & Against the State.* London: Pluto Press.

Luhman, N. (1990) *Political Theory and the Welfare State.* New York: Walter De Gruyter.

Lukács, G. (1971 [1923]) *History and Class Consciousness.* London: Merlin.

Lyotard, J.F. (1986) *The Postmodern Condition: A Report on Knowledge.* Manchester: Manchester University Press.

Macarov, D. (1980) *Work and Welfare. The Unholy Alliance.* Sage Library of Social Research Volume 99. London: Sage.

Mama, A. (1989) 'Violence Against Black Women: Gender, Race and State Responses', *Feminist Review*, 32: 30–48.

Mama, A. (1992) 'Black Women and the British State: Race, Class and Gender Analysis for the 1990s', in P. Braham, A. Rattansi and R. Skellington (eds), *Racism and Antiracism: Inequalities, Opportunities and Policies*. London: Sage/Open University.

Mamonova, T. (1984) *Women and Russia: Feminist Writings from the Soviet Union*. Oxford: Blackwell.

Marcuse, H. (1964) *One Dimensional Man: Studies in the Ideologies of Advanced Industrial Society*. London: Routledge & Kegan Paul.

Martell, L. (1994) *Ecology and Society: An Introduction*. Oxford: Polity Press.

Martin, C.J. and McQueen, D.V. (1989) *Readings for a New Public Health*. Edinburgh: Edinburgh University Press.

Marx, K. (1986 [1859]) 'Preface to A Critique of Political Economy', in J. Elster (ed.), *Karl Marx: A Reader*. Cambridge: Cambridge University Press.

Marx, K. and Engels, F. (1991 [1848]) 'The Manifesto of the Communist Party', abridged version of the English edition of 1888, in T. Ball & R. Dagger (eds), *Ideals and Ideologies: A Reader*. New York: Harper Collins.

Maser, C. (1991) 'Adaptable Landscapes are the Key to Sustainable Forests', *Journal of Sustainable Forestry*, 1: 47–59.

Mazzini, G. (1867 [1858]) 'On the Duties of Man', in *The Life and Writings of Joseph Mazzini*, IV (translated by Mrs E.A. Venturi). London: Chapman & Hall.

McCannell, D. and Flower McCannell, J. (1993) 'Violence, Power and Pleasure: A Revisionist Reading of Foucault from a Feminist Perspective', in C. Ramazanoglu (ed.), *Up Against Foucault: Explorations of Some Tensions Between Foucault and Feminism*. London: Routledge.

McClintock, A. (1995) *Imperial Leather. Race, Gender and Sexuality in the Colonial Contest*. London: Routledge.

McKibben, B. (1990) *The End of Nature*. Harmondsworth: Penguin.

McLaren, P.L. (1995) *Critical Pedagogy and Predatory Culture: Oppositional Politics in a Postmodern Era*. London: Routledge.

McLellan, D. (1982) 'The Materialistic Concept of History', in E. J. Hobsbawm (ed.), *The History of Marxism*. Volume 1: *Marxism in Marx's Day*. Brighton: The Harvester Press.

McLellan, D. (1983) 'Politics', in D. McLellan (ed.), *Marx: The First Hundred Years*. Oxford: Fontana.

Mercer, K. (1992) '"1968": Periodizing Politics and Identity', in L. Grossberg, C. Nelson and P.A. Treichler (eds), *Cultural Studies. A Reader*. New York: Routledge.

Miles, R. and Phizacklea, A. (eds) (1979) *Racism and Political Action in Britain*. London: Routledge & Kegan Paul.

Mill, J.S. (1948 [1861]) 'Considerations on Representative Democracy', in *Utilitarianism, Liberty and Representative Government*. London: Everyman's Library.

Minson, J. (1980) 'Strategies for Socialists? Foucault's Conception of Power', *Economy and Society*, 9 (1): 1–43.

Moghadam, V.M. (1995) 'Gender Dynamics of Restructuring in the Semiperiphery', in R. Lesser Blumberg, C.A. Rakowski, I. Tinker and M. Monteón (eds), *Engendering Wealth and Well-Being: Empowerment for Social Change*. Oxford: Westview Press.

Mohanty, C.T. (1992) 'Feminist Encounters: Locating the Politics of Experience', in M. Barrett and A. Phillipps (eds), *Destabilising Theory: Contemporary Feminist Debates*. Cambridge: Polity.

Moos, R. and Brownstein, R. (1977) *Environment and Utopia: A Synthesis*. New York: Plenum Press.

Morgan, D. (1975) *Suffragists and Liberals: The Politics of Woman Suffrage in England*. Oxford: Blackwell.

Morgan, P. (1995) *Farewell to the Family? Public Policy and Family Breakdown in Britain and the USA*. Choice in Welfare Series No. 21. London: IEA.

Morley, D. and Chen, K-H. (eds) (1996) *Stuart Hall: Critical Dialogues in Cultural Studies*. London: Routledge.

Morley, D., Rolide, J. and Williams, G. (1987) *Practising Health for All*. Oxford: Oxford University Press.

Morris, J. (1991) ' "Us" and "Them"? Feminist Research, Community Care and Disability', *Critical Social Policy*, No. 33 (Winter): 22–39.

Morris, J. (1993) 'Gender and Disability', in J. Swain, V. Finkelstein, S. French and M. Oliver (eds), *Disabling Barriers – Enabling Environments*. London: Sage.

Mouffe, C. (1995) 'Feminism, Citizenship and Radical Democratic Politics', in L. Nicholson and S. Seidman (eds), *Social Postmodernism: Beyond Identity Politics*. Cambridge: Cambridge University Press.

Murray, C. (1988) *In Pursuit of Happiness and Good Government*. New York: Simon & Schuster.

Murray, C. (1990) *The Emerging British Underclass*. London: IEA.

Murray, C. (1994) *Underclass: The Crisis Deepens*. London: IEA.

Norris, C. (1990) *What's Wrong With Postmodernism? Critical Theory and the Ends of Philosophy*. Hemel Hempstead: Harvester Wheatsheaf.

O'Brien, M. (1998) 'Being Transient: An Essay on the Migrancy of Culture', *Passages: The Journal of Transnational and Transcultural Studies*. 1 (1): (forthcoming).

O'Brien, M. and Penna, S. (1996) 'Postmodern Theory and Politics: Perspectives on Citizenship and Social Justice', *Innovation: The European Journal of Social Sciences*, 9 (2): 185–203.

O'Brien, M. and Penna, S. (1997) 'European Policy and the Politics of Environmental Governance', *Policy and Politics*, 25 (2): 185–200.

O'Brien, M. and Penna, S. (1998) 'Oppositional Postmodern Theory and Welfare Analysis: Anti-Oppressive Practice in a Postmodern Frame', in J. Carter (ed.) *Postmodernism and the Fragmentation of Welfare*. London: Routledge.

O'Brien, M., Clift, R. and Doig, A. (1996) *Social and Environmental Life Cycle Assessment: Report of a Research Project*. Guildford: University of Surrey.

O'Connor, J. (1974) *The Fiscal Crisis of the State*. London: St James Press.

O'Connor, J. (1984) *Accumulation Crisis*. Oxford: Basil Blackwell.

Offe, C. (1984) *Contradictions of the Welfare State* (ed. J. Keane). London: Hutchinson.

Offe, C (1985) *Disorganized Capitalism*. Cambridge: Polity.

Offe, C. (1991) 'Smooth Consolidation in the West German Welfare State: Structural Change, Fiscal Policies, and Populist Politics', in F. Fox Piven (ed.), *Labour Parties in Postindustrial Societies*. Cambridge: Polity.

Oliver, M. (1990) *The Politics of Disablement*. London: Macmillan.

Orloff, A.S. (1993) 'Gender and the Social Rights of Citizenship: State Policies and Gender Relations in Comparative Research', *American Sociological Review*, 58 (3): 303–28.

Parton, N. (1991) *Governing the Family: Child Care, Child Protection and the State*. London: Macmillan.

Parton, N. (1994) ' "Problematics of Government": (Post) Modernity and Social Work', *British Journal of Social Work*, 24: 9–32.

Parton, N. (1996) 'Social Theory, Social Change and Social Work: An Introduction', in N. Parton (ed.), *Social Theory, Social Change and Social Work*. London: Routledge. pp. 4–18.

Pascall, G. (1986) *Social Policy: A Feminist Analysis*. London: Tavistock.

Pearce, D.W., Markandya, M. and Barbier, E.B. (1989) *Blueprint for a Green Economy*. London: Earthscan.

Pearson, K. (1905) *National Life From the Standpoint of Science*. London: Walter Scott.

Peck, J. and Jones, M. (1995) 'Training and Enterprise Councils: Schumpeterian Workfare State, or What?', *Environment and Planning A*, 27: 1361–96.

Penna, S. and O'Brien, M. (1996) 'Postmodernism and Social Policy: A Small Step Forwards?', *Journal of Social Policy*, 25 (1): 39–61.

Perrings, C. (1987) *Economy and Environment*. Cambridge: Cambridge University Press.

Petrovic, G. (1991) 'Alienation', in T. Bottomore (ed.), *A Dictionary of Marxist Thought*. Oxford: Blackwell.

Phillipp, R. (1993) 'Community Needlestick Accident Data and Trends in Environmental Quality', *Public Health*, 107 (5): 363–9.

Phizacklea, A. and Miles, R. (1980) *Labour and Racism*. London: Routledge & Kegan Paul.

Phoon, W-O. (1993) 'Environmental and Occupational Health: The Asia–Pacific Region', *Environmental Management and Health*, 4 (4): 7–14.

Pierson, C. (1991) *Beyond the Welfare State?* Cambridge: Polity.

Pinch, S. (1994) 'Labour Flexibility and the Changing Welfare State: Is There a Post-Fordist Model?', in R. Burrows and B. Loader (eds), *Towards a Post-Fordist Welfare State?* London: Routledge.

Plant, R. (1991) 'Social Rights and the Reconstruction of Welfare', in G. Andrews (ed.), *Citizenship*. London: Lawrence & Wishart.

Pringle, R. and Watson, S. (1992) ' "Women's Interests" and the Poststructuralist State', in M. Barrett and A. Phillipps (eds), *Destabilising Theory: Contemporary Feminist Debates*. Cambridge: Polity.

Rawls, J. (1971) *A Theory of Justice*. Cambridge MA: Harvard University Press.

Roberts, C., Davies, E. and Jupp, T. (1992) *Language and Discrimination. A Study of Communication in Multi-Ethnic Workplaces*. London: Longman.

Robertson, J. (1989) *Future Wealth: New Economics for the 21st Century*. London: Earthscan.

Robinson, F. and Gregson, N. (1992) ' The "Underclass": A Class Apart?', *Critical Social Policy*, 34: 38–51.

Rodger, J. (1992) 'The Welfare State and Social Closure: Social Division and the "Underclass" ', *Critical Social Policy*, 35: 45–63.

Roediger, D.R. (1994) *Towards the Abolition of Whiteness*. London: Verso.

Rosaldo, R. (1989) *Culture and Truth: The Remaking of Social Analysis*. Boston, MA: Beacon.

Rose, J. (1993) 'Highlights: 1, The Planet's Future', *Environmental Management and Health*, 4 (1): 3–5.

Ross, D.P. and Usher, P.J. (1986) *From the Roots Up: Economics as if Community Mattered*. New York: Bootstrap Press.

Sainsbury, D. (ed.) (1994) *Gendering Welfare States*. London: Sage.

Samuel, B. (1902) *Liberalism: Its Principles and Proposals*. London: Grant Richards.

Sartre, J-P. (1976) *Critique of Dialectical Reason*. London: New Left Books.

Sarup, M. (1993) *An Introductory Guide to Post-Structuralism and Postmodernism*, 2nd edn. London: Harvester Wheatsheaf.

Schierup, M. (1994) 'The Right to be Different. Multiculturalism and the Racialization of Scandinavian Welfare Politics: The Case of Denmark', *Innovation: The European Journal of Social Science* 7 (3): 277–88.

Schoon, N. (1996) 'Significant Shorts', *The Independent*, Monday 15 July, p. 2.

Schultz, I. (1993) 'Women and Waste', *Capitalism, Nature, Socialism* 4 (2): 51–63.

Seager, J. (1993) *Earth Follies: Feminism, Politics and the Environment*. London: Earthscan.

Seidman, S. (1995) 'Deconstructing Queer Theory or the Under-theorization of the Social and the Ethical', in L. Nicholson and S. Seidman (eds), *Social Postmodernism. Beyond Identity Politics*. Cambridge: Cambridge University Press.

Seldon, A. (1979) *Whither the Welfare State?* London: IEA.

Semmel, B. (1960) *Imperialism and Social Reform: English Social-Imperial Thought, 1895–1914*. London: George Allen & Unwin.

Shiva, V. (1989) *Staying Alive: Women, Ecology and Development*. London: Zed Books.

Shiva, V. (1992) 'Recovering the Real Meaning of Sustainability', in D.E Cooper and J.A. Palmer (eds), *The Environment in Question: Ethics and Global Issues*. London: Routledge.

Showstack Sassoon, A. (ed.) (1987) *Women and the State*. London: Hutchinson.

Sibley, D. (1995) *Geographies of Exclusion*. London: Routledge.

Sivanandan, A. (1974) *Race, Class and the State*. London: Institute of Race Relations.

Smith, D.E. (1993) 'What Welfare Theory Hides', in G. Drover and P. Kerans (eds), *New Approaches to Welfare Theory*. Cambridge: Cambridge University Press.

Solé, C. (1995) 'Racial Discrimination against Foreigners in Spain', *New Community: European Journal on Migration and Ethnic Relations*, 21 (1): 103–14.

Spencer, H. (1940 [1884]) *The Man Versus the State*. London: Watt.

Steward, F. (1991) 'Citizens of Planet Earth', in G. Andrews (ed.), *Citizenship*. London: Lawrence & Wishart.

Sullivan, M. (1987) *Sociology and Social Welfare*. London: Allen & Unwin.

Taylor, C. (1989) *Sources of the Self*. Cambridge, MA: Harvard University Press.

Taylor, G. (1993) 'Challenges from the Margins', in J. Clarke (ed.), *A Crisis in Care? Challenges to Social Work*. London: Sage/Open University.

Thompson, E.P. (1963) *The Making of the English Working Class*. Harmondsworth: Penguin.

Thorogood, N. (1995) '"London Dentist in HIV scare": HIV and Dentistry in Popular Discourse', in R. Bunton, S. Nettleton and R. Burrows (eds), *The Sociology of Health Promotion*. London: Routledge.

Titmuss, R.M. (1958) *Essays on the Welfare State*. London: Allen & Unwin.

Titmuss, R.M. (1968) *Commitment to Welfare*. London: Allen & Unwin.

de Tocqueville, Alexis (1946 [1804]) *Democracy in America*. 2 volumes. New York: Schoken Books.

Tokar, B. (1987) *The Green Alternative: Building an Ecological Future*. San Pedro: R. & E. Miles.

Touraine, A. (1974) *The Post-Industrial Society*. London: Wildwood.

Touraine, A. (1995) *Critique of Modernity*. Oxford/Cambridge, MA: Blackwell.

Townsend, P. (1995) *The Rise of International Social Policy*. Brighton: The Policy Press.

Ungerson, C. (1987) *Policy Is Personal: Sex, Gender and Informal Care*. London: Tavistock.

Vattimo, G. (1992) *The Transparent Society*. Cambridge: Polity.

Vos, J. (1995) 'Illegal Migrants in the Netherlands', *New Community: European Journal on Migration and Ethnic Relations*, 21 (1): 115–20.

Waerness, K. (1984) 'Caring as Women's Work in the Welfare State', in H. Holter (ed.), *Patriarchy in a Welfare State*. Oslo: Universitetsforlaget.

Waerness, K. (1987) 'On the Rationality of Caring', in A. Showstack Sassoon (ed.), *Women and the State*. London: Hutchinson.

Wainwright, H. (1994) *Arguments for a New Left: Answering the Free-Market Right*. Oxford: Blackwell.

Walby, S. (1990) *Theorising Patriarchy*. Oxford: Blackwell.

Walby, S. (1992) 'Post-Post-Modernism? Theorizing Social Complexity', in M. Barrett and A. Phillipps (eds), *Destabilizing Theory: Contemporary Feminist Debates*. Cambridge: Polity.

Walzer, M. (1983) *Spheres of Justice: A Defence of Pluralism and Equality*. New York: Basic Books.

Ward, B. (1979) *Progress for a Small Planet*. London: Maurice Temple Smith.

Ward, B. and Dubois, R. (1972) *Only One Earth: The Care and Maintenance of a Small Planet*. London: André Deutsch.

Watson, G. (1957) *The Unservile State: Essays in Liberty and Welfare*. London: George Allen & Unwin.

West, C. (1990) 'The New Cultural Politics of Difference', in R. Ferguson, M. Gever, T.T. Minh-ha and C. West (eds), *Out There: Marginalization and Contemporary Cultures*. New York/Cambridge, MA: New Museum of Contemporary Art/MIT Press.

Wilenski, H. and Lebeaux, C. (1958) *Industrial Society and Social Welfare*. New York: Russel Sage.

Williams, F. (1989) *Social Policy. A Critical Introduction*. Cambridge: Polity.

Williams, R. (1979 [1958]) *Culture and Society: 1780–1950*. Harmondsworth: Penguin.

Williams, R. (1981 [1961]) *The Long Revolution*. Harmondsworth: Penguin.

Willmott, P. (1985) *Community in Social Policy*. Policy Studies Institute Discussion Paper No. 9. London: Policy Studies Institute.

Wilson, E. (1977) *Women and the Welfare State*. London: Tavistock.

Winch, P. (1958) *The Idea of a Social Science*. London: Routledge & Kegan Paul.

Witz, A. (1992) *Professions and Patriarchy*. London: Routledge.

Women and Eastern Europe Group (1979) *Women and Russia. First Feminist Samizdat*. London: Sheba Feminist Publishers.

Wrench, J. (1992) 'New Vocationalism, Old Racism and the Careers Service', in P. Braham, A. Rattansi and R. Skellington (eds), *Racism and Antiracism: Inequalities, Opportunities, Policies*. London: Sage/Open University.

Yearley, S. (1990) *The Green Case*. New York: Praeger.

Yearley, S. (1996) *Sociology, Environmentalism, Globalisation: Reinventing the Globe.* London: Sage.

Yeatman, A. (1994) *Postmodern Revisionings of the Political.* London: Routledge.

Young, K. (1992) 'Approaches to Policy Development in the Field of Equal Opportunities', in P. Braham, A. Rattansi and R. Skellington (eds), *Racism and Antiracism: Inequalities, Opportunities, Policies.* London: Sage/Open University.

Name Index

Subject Index